The Rising Clamor

The Rising Clamor

*The American Press, the Central
Intelligence Agency, and the Cold War*

David P. Hadley

UNIVERSITY PRESS OF KENTUCKY

Copyright © 2019 by The University Press of Kentucky

Scholarly publisher for the Commonwealth,
serving Bellarmine University, Berea College, Centre
College of Kentucky, Eastern Kentucky University,
The Filson Historical Society, Georgetown College,
Kentucky Historical Society, Kentucky State University,
Morehead State University, Murray State University,
Northern Kentucky University, Transylvania University,
University of Kentucky, University of Louisville,
and Western Kentucky University.
All rights reserved.

Editorial and Sales Offices: The University Press of Kentucky
663 South Limestone Street, Lexington, Kentucky 40508-4008
www.kentuckypress.com

Cataloging-in-Publication data is available from the Library of Congress.

ISBN 978-0-8131-7737-3 (hardcover : alk. paper)
ISBN 978-0-8131-7739-7 (epub)
ISBN 978-0-8131-7738-0 (pdf)

This book is printed on acid-free paper meeting
the requirements of the American National Standard
for Permanence in Paper for Printed Library Materials.

Manufactured in the United States of America.

Member of the Association
of University Presses

This work is dedicated to the memory of my father,
David Price Hadley, and my grandparents
H. Scott Thomas Jr. and Jane L. Thomas

Contents

Abbreviations

AEC	Atomic Energy Commission
AFL-CIO	American Federation of Labor and Congress of Industrial Organizations
AFME	American Friends of the Middle East
ANPA	American Newspaper Publishers Association
CAT	Civil Air Transport
CCF	Congress for Cultural Freedom
CFR	Council on Foreign Relations
CIA	Central Intelligence Agency
CIG	Central Intelligence Group
DCI	Director of Central Intelligence
DDCI	Deputy director of Central Intelligence
DIA	Defense Intelligence Agency
DNSA	Digital National Security Archive
FBI	Federal Bureau of Investigation
FOIA	Freedom of Information Act
ICBM	Intercontinental ballistic missile
ITT	International Telephone and Telegraph Company
MPLA	People's Movement for the Liberation of Angola
NIA	National Intelligence Authority
NKVD	People's Commissariat for Internal Affairs
NSA	National Student Association
NSC	National Security Council
OPC	Office of Policy Coordination
OSO	Office of Special Operations
OSS	Office of Strategic Services
UFC	United Fruit Company
UNITA	National Union for the Total Independence of Angola
VSS	Veterans of Strategic Services

Introduction

American Opinion Said Go

In June 1975 Director of Central Intelligence (DCI) William Colby sat down for an interview with the *Washington Post* reporter George Lardner Jr. Colby and the Central Intelligence Agency were in the midst of an unprecedented crisis: reporting on CIA domestic spying, in direct contravention of the CIA charter, had finally led to sustained congressional investigation of the CIA's activities, something the agency had long sought to avert. The public airing of many of the CIA's activities since its foundation in 1947 led to unprecedented questions about its role and place in American government and society.

Colby tried to explain that the agency had done only what it was expected to do, what the American people had wanted it to do. Colby argued that "in 1947 we set intelligence to be in the old tradition of something you . . . didn't talk about. . . . Intelligence people were supposed to take care of that, not bother the policy levels with complicated questions of what should be done and what shouldn't be done. Just, well, go do it. That was the climate at that time." The CIA, Colby observed, was "sensitive to American opinion. When American opinion says go, we go. When American opinion [says stop] it stops. In the 1950's the word was 'go.' In . . . 1975 the word is . . . 'stop.'"[1]

The press helped shape expectations about what the CIA was supposed to do. Thus, the press was able to influence the Central Intelligence Agency from its foundation in often unacknowledged ways. Though the Central Intelligence Agency did not initially draw considerable attention, its creation was public. Intelligence reporting developed alongside the agency. Journalists' decisions on which intelligence-related stories to investigate and report, and which to ignore, helped determine which activities the CIA could conduct. The press was a forum for shaping U.S. expectations regarding what an intelligence agency was supposed to accomplish.

What Colby's explanation of the CIA's earlier, aggressive covert action failed to account for, however, was that members of the CIA had played a significant role in making sure the American people would say go. Press coverage of the agency was influenced by interactions between members of the press and CIA officers. Cognizant of the press's importance, those intelligence officers who proved more skilled in using the press in the early years of the agency supported not just the CIA but also their specific vision of what the CIA could and should be. Intelligence officers also recognized the opportunities the press offered for a variety of covert actions.

Some press-CIA interactions were straightforward intelligence operations, such as using journalistic credentials as part of cover identities. The CIA directly paid some reporters and publications to try to influence foreign opinion through manipulation of the press. Some press-CIA interactions were more transactional and ambiguous. CIA officers and members of the press often traded information, and the CIA sought to portray itself as a useful, active part of the U.S. government. Reporters who developed good contacts with CIA officers gained a competitive edge; some also genuinely believed in what the CIA was doing and felt it was their duty to support it. Especially at the upper levels of the CIA and various press organizations, personal ties provided the CIA a platform to attempt to ensure that coverage of the CIA was favorable and ignored activities the CIA wished to keep secret.

As challenges to the CIA emerged in the press in the 1960s and 1970s, so too did questions about the often friendly interaction between the press and the agency over the previous three decades. The implications of the relationship were disturbing. While the amount of attention paid to the press by the American public was limited, those who were attentive to the press were generally more elite and helped determine the national agenda.[2] Stories that began in small publications with few readers could and did catch national attention.

The audience that concerned the CIA the most was Congress. Congressional oversight of the agency before the mid-1970s was informal and dependent on highly personal relationships. The agency fell under the purview of the House and Senate Armed Services Committees, where powerful chairmen such as Richard Russell of Georgia shielded the agency from investigation.[3] The press was a potential alternative path for information to flow to

Capitol Hill; in Congress, readership of the *New York Times* was nearly universal. The press often was a more reliable source on the CIA's activities for the legislature than the CIA itself.[4] Though the size of readership and actual public opinion were consequential, more important was the interplay among the press, the CIA, and Congress, which ensured that the CIA perceived that the press needed cultivation. The potential for manipulation and abuse of the press by the CIA led to serious questions about the legitimacy of the free press.

The CIA and the Press

The first serious major suggestion of a relationship between the CIA and the press appeared in the *Columbia Journalism Review* in October 1974. In an article titled "The CIA's Use of the Press: A 'Mighty Wurlitzer,'" Stuart Loory revealed that the CIA had infiltrated domestic news organizations and had contracts with some thirty journalists overseas to plant false or misleading stories in foreign news outlets. The agency also had extensive and covert access to the internal files of several large news organizations. The term *Mighty Wurlitzer* referred to Wurlitzer theater organs and implied that the CIA could manipulate public opinion as an organist could play a Wurlitzer. A CIA officer, Frank G. Wisner, coined the term and used it to refer to a network of "charitable foundations, labor unions, book publishers, the student movement" and the press that would promote noncommunist movements in Western Europe. Though intended for foreign use, Loory wrote, stories planted by the Wurlitzer abroad could rebound into American newspapers.[5] Victor Marchetti and John D. Marks, two former intelligence officers who published a critique of the CIA the same year Loory's article was published, offered an explanation about why the CIA would want such connections with the press. They explained, "A good part of the CIA's power position is dependent upon its careful mythologizing and glorification of the exploits of the clandestine profession."[6] Supporting some stories and promoting others were useful in that process of "mythologizing and glorification."

In 1976 the release of the final report of the U.S. Senate Select Committee to Study Governmental Operations with Respect to Intelligence Activities, known popularly as the Church Committee, after its chairman, Frank Church, confirmed some of these stories. The report found that the CIA had sought to make use of private institutions, including the press. Some fifty reporters were found to have been employed by the CIA in official, though secret, relationships. The report declined to publish any specific names.[7]

Carl Bernstein expanded on the Church report in October 1977 with an article entitled "The CIA and the Media." Bernstein claimed that the number of press members who had carried out activities for the CIA and were considered assets by the agency was actually something like four hundred. Bernstein interviewed the prominent columnist Joseph Alsop, who admitted that both he and his brother, Stewart, had cooperated with the agency. Publishers such as Arthur Hays Sulzberger of the *New York Times* and Henry Luce of Time-Life were among those whom Bernstein identified as having cooperated.[8]

The continued lack of specific details proved an effective breeding ground for some outlandish claims regarding the CIA and the press. Deborah Davis, for example, in a 1979 biography of the *Washington Post*'s owner and publisher, Katharine Graham, wrote that Graham was part of a CIA program called Mockingbird, purportedly a concerted CIA effort to control and manipulate the U.S. press.[9] Davis provided no information on her sources. The Church Committee, and subsequent investigations, did not reveal any such operation as Davis described. A Project Mockingbird is mentioned in the "Family Jewels" report that described illegal CIA activities from 1959 to 1972, which was revealed during the Church Committee investigation. That Mockingbird, however, referred to the illegal wiretapping of two reporters who were suspected of receiving and disseminating classified information.[10] Mockingbird, as described by Davis, has remained a stubbornly persistent theory.

The CIA has lost much of its mystery from the era of Loory, Bernstein, and Davis. An active literature of the CIA's history over the years has emerged.[11] Especially since the Cold War ended, greater attention has been paid to the CIA's cultural activities, as the agency funded publications, supported student groups, organized artistic exhibitions, and more, in an effort to win the battle of ideas.[12] As the work on the CIA's ties with cultural groups has grown, so too has the nuanced detail of the often contentious relationships between the agency and private actors possessed of their own agendas. These kinds of cultural connections are also useful to examine in light of the increased study of propaganda operations the U.S. government conducted over the course of the Cold War, most but not all of which included the CIA.[13]

The CIA embarked on information programs abroad because it recognized the imperative of gaining mass support in an ideological struggle. The effect of public opinion on foreign policy, its ability to actually have an influence, has been a persistent and at times divisive question since before World War II.[14] Reviewing the recent historiography of studies of public opinion and foreign relations, Douglas C. Foyle notes that the media are important in how the "public's frames are established and sustained" because once a frame of mind has been established, it is difficult to alter.[15] The press, in the words of Douglass Cater, is a gatekeeper, controlling "the flow of information within and beyond the Washington community."[16] When concerned with the Third World, the press can establish ethnocentric frameworks for a population largely unfamiliar with the places in question.[17] The press can be especially important when examining bureaucracies that are often ignored or overlooked. The desire of bureaucrats to avoid drawing the negative attention of elected officials influences their thinking. The press, then, can be both an indicator and a driver of bureaucratic actions.[18] The relevance of this phenomenon to the CIA will be seen in the consistent, strenuous desire of the CIA to avoid congressional oversight of its activities.

Given the importance of the press to American politics and policy and the known history of the CIA's use of cultural activities, it is not difficult to see the potential dangers to democratic society if the press were controlled or otherwise subverted by a covert arm of the government. Thus, the CIA's ties with the U.S. press, the ability of that press to materially affect policy, and the extent to which the press acted as constrainer or facilitator to the CIA and U.S Cold War policy more broadly need to be understood to more fully grasp the effect of the Cold War on American democratic cultural institutions such as the press.

This work explores the different kinds of press-CIA relationships that existed in the agency's early years, the various uses to which those relationships were put by both the press and the CIA, and what actual coverage of the CIA was produced by the U.S. domestic press from the postwar intelligence debate that began in 1945 to the end of the congressional investigations of the CIA in 1976.

Press-CIA Relationships: Different Types, Different Uses, and Their Effects

The press cannot be said to have ever produced a unified response to the CIA; there was no singular press-CIA "relationship." Rather, there were as many press-CIA relationships as there were reporters who, at some point, spoke with a member of the CIA. It is probably impossible to document reliably every connection the CIA had with the press, and this work should not be taken as an exhaustive account of the CIA's various press activities. It is possible, however, to draw conclusions about the different kinds of relationships that existed between the two and the implications these kinds of relationships had on press coverage of the CIA.

The most obvious relationships were, of course, the official, paid arrangements between the CIA and reporters that were confirmed by the Church Committee, the final report of which noted that the CIA had official relationships with approximately fifty reporters. Most of those paid relationships were, apparently, with stringers. As contract workers paid by the story, stringers were important in foreign reporting. A stringer based in a foreign city could provide stories quickly to a publication that lacked a nearby foreign correspondent, and stringers were a natural avenue for the CIA. These types of relationships are the hardest to draw firm conclusions on because of the lack of reliable sources. From what information is available, however, it is possible to determine that such relationships were not restricted to stringers. There were attempts by the CIA to hire non-stringers employed at major U.S. publications, but they do not appear to have been as common as those efforts with stringers.

Unofficial relationships overshadowed official ones. Unofficial relationships can be divided into two semi-distinct categories. The first were those relationships, like those with the Alsops, in which reporters actively cooperated with the CIA to promote agency interests out of a combination of social ties, a sense of patriotism, and a desire for access. Cooperation in unofficial activity encompassed a variety of forms that went beyond what might be considered standard journalistic practice. For example, they would work to suppress stories, plan ways to defend the agency in print, and develop stories that would paint the agency in a positive light.

The second type of unofficial relationship was one in which reporters sought or received information from the CIA as they would any governmental entity. Reporters seeking to use the CIA mainly as a source of information wanted accuracy, and the CIA was understood to be a legitimate place to look for such accurate information—much like the White House, the various executive departments, and Congress. Such relationships did not necessarily preclude criticism of the CIA as an institution or reporting on the CIA's activities. CIA station chiefs were often sources of information for reporters in a foreign capital, but so were embassy officials.

The line between these two unofficial relationships was fluid. Different reporters had different standards regarding what kind of contact with the CIA was acceptable. Major newspapers like the *New York Times* and the *Washington Post,* for example, arranged for off-the-record meetings between CIA officials and their senior staffs. The practice of off-the-record meetings with governmental officials was and is not unusual, but what such meetings produced could vary wildly; the line between usual and special practice is what can be difficult to determine. As the historian Richard Aldrich notes, press-CIA relationships could at times be schizophrenic, as the parties veered between acting as "collaborators and competitors."[19]

Personal connections were important for unofficial relationships, especially in those cases in which the relationship went beyond normal procedure. Vitally important in the early years of the agency were those connections rooted in the so-called Eastern Establishment. Men such as DCI Allen Dulles, *Foreign Affairs* editor Hamilton Fish Armstrong, and Joseph and Stewart Alsop had gone to Ivy League universities, participated in elite clubs, and shared a relatively common, stable view of the world.[20] Others, such as the *Times* reporter James Reston and the *Washington Post*'s owner, Philip Graham, adopted the ethos of the Establishment even if they had not been born to it. Still others, outside the Establishment, shared common ties of combat and service from World War II. As will be seen, many of the reporters covering the CIA had served at some time or another in the military or had experience reporting from war zones. This study focuses most on those relationships between figures in the higher echelons of the press and the CIA. This focus reflects the importance of elite relationships in shaping overall coverage. The DCI and the publisher of the *New York Times* had a greater ability to influence media coverage than the average CIA officer and reporter. Early on, the CIA knew the best way to get a desired result was to go to management rather than individual reporters.

Finally, there were institutions and reporters that cannot be said to have had any real relationship with the CIA in terms of contact with CIA officials. Many national and foreign reporters at major publications had no interaction with the CIA throughout their careers, even if some of their colleagues did. Employees of some of the agency's most consistent critics, such as the *Nation,* did not have the same kind of unofficial contact that other reporters at more mainstream publications enjoyed.

Though different reporters and institutions moved between these different types of relationships at different times, examples of these broad categories of relationships can be found throughout the 1945–1976 period. Even as many reporters grew to criticize the CIA in the late 1960s and 1970s, they were still willing to speak to CIA officers for information and listen to requests for discretion.

The CIA sought to use these various relationships in three different ways, depending on to whom in the press it was speaking. First, there were uses of the press in covert operations, either to gather information or covertly spread propaganda abroad. These were mainly but not exclusively conducted by reporters paid by the CIA. As that is the most difficult category of relationship to gain significant information on, so too is this use of the press the murkiest in detail. The CIA has maintained that its efforts to plant stories were directed only at foreign audiences; while acknowledging that some of those stories could have been picked up by U.S. papers, the CIA argues there was no effort to manipulate U.S. opinion.

Whether or not blatantly doctored stories made their way to the American people, it is clear that the CIA often sought to promote itself or defend its reputation through connections with the press. When reporters were willing to actively cooperate, some directors leaked information to ensure a favorable response. Allen Dulles, in particular, sought to use his personal connections to celebrate his agency's achievements while maintaining plausible deniability. Rather than leak information about the CIA's exploits, other CIA officials leaked information about world situations to demonstrate the competence of the CIA in intelligence gathering and analysis. This proved useful in fostering reporters favorable to the CIA even if those reporters did not see themselves as actively working with the CIA.

Another use to which the CIA sought to put its relationships with the press was the suppression of stories about the CIA. A significant number of cases can be found that demonstrate the general pattern of the CIA's efforts in cases of suppression. The CIA appealed to national security and reporters' patriotism to prevent undesirable information about its activities from being released. If that failed, offers of access were made in exchange for journalistic restraint. Often, in the agency's early days, the CIA had to make no explicit request.

An examination of the relationships between the CIA and the press, however, should not be conducted in a vacuum. By focusing solely on cases in which the CIA intervened in some way, the power and influence of those relationships can be overstated. Rather, these relationships must be understood in the broader context of press coverage of the CIA. An examination of the actual press record from 1945 to 1976 reveals important shifts in the CIA's coverage by the press: early problems, Cold War success, uneasy relations after the failure of the Bay of Pigs invasion, and, eventually, widespread press hostility toward the agency.

By a considered survey of major newspapers and periodicals, it is possible to reach reliable conclusions about trends in coverage of the CIA and to see at what points the CIA sought to make an effect. In terms of newspapers, I have for this project examined the *New York Times, Washington Post, Chicago Tribune,* and, to a lesser extent, *Los Angeles Times.* The *New York Times* can truly be said to live up to its claim as the "paper of record." It was, and remains, a cornerstone of U.S. journalism, and it was especially of interest to the CIA owing to its unrivaled overseas resources.[21] Though for much of the period between 1945 and 1976 the *Post* was not comparable to the *New York Times,* it grew in prominence over the period; its Washington-based viewpoint is also useful to consider in light of its close ties to officialdom. Finally, the *Tribune* and the *Los Angeles Times* are representative of non–East Coast, often proudly nonliberal publications that reflected views outside New York City and Washington, D.C.

In terms of periodicals, the generally "middlebrow" sensibilities of *Time, Life, Atlantic Monthly, Harper's Magazine, Saturday Evening Post,* and *U.S. News and World Report* are valuable for their portrayal of mainstream, Cold War consensus opinion and the eventual dissolution of that consensus. Finally, though possessing a smaller readership than their more mainstream peers, *Foreign Affairs, Reporter, New Republic, Nation, Progressive,* and *National Review* all sought to speak to an elite or partisan audience; they proved an important battleground in discussions over the CIA.

While I note isolated television programs and television press personnel when relevant, I have not included in this work a sustained examination of television programs. Television news was an increasingly important presence in the United States, and its rise was a major contextual factor in the media environment of the period under examination. It was, however, a different kind of system from print media. Television news was still developing as the CIA was founded and was rarely at the forefront of journalistic investigation for much of this period. Further work will be necessary, however, for a useful consideration of television news across the period under consideration.[22]

Using this review of the output of relevant publications, declassified CIA records, and the professional and personal papers of figures in the CIA and the press, I advance four principal arguments about the relationships between the CIA and the press.

First, the press is an important part of the history of the CIA. The evolution of the agency was affected by the discussion that was carried out in the press about its proper structure and activities. The discretion and cooperation of the press were valuable to the CIA as it established a place for itself in the bureaucratic hierarchy of the U.S. government. As members of the press grew increasingly less cooperative with the CIA's agenda during the 1960s and 1970s, the agency was forced to adapt in the face of intense public and congressional attention.

Second, as I noted above, the press's response to the CIA was not unified. The CIA and "the press" in fact developed varied relationships. Even up to 1975 and the congressional investigation of its activities, the CIA maintained some positive relationships with the press. The problem for the CIA was that, while those positive relationships had generally served its needs before the 1960s, it was unable to counter effectively the proliferation of reporting critical of the CIA and revelatory of its activities that followed. Third, and related to the second point, even when the CIA enjoyed its most positive press relationships, during the 1950s, there were countertrends hostile to the agency.

Finally, press-CIA relationships were important in determining what information U.S. citizens received about their government's activities, and the CIA did make efforts to shape U.S. opinions about the agency and its activities. The Davis/Mockingbird theory, that the CIA operated a deliberate and systematic program of widespread manipulation of the U.S. media, does not appear to be grounded in reality, but that should not disguise the active role the CIA played in influencing the domestic press's output. With the exception of the few CIA-paid reporters, though, members of the press retained their independence. Even the most cooperative relationships with reporters tended to be the product of negotiation and mutual interest. The friendly environment for the CIA in its earlier years was the result of the Cold War consensus and the view of the Soviet threat, shared by people on both sides of the press-CIA divide, rather than a system of direct CIA control.

This work is organized in seven chronological chapters. The first chapter begins with the debate over postwar intelligence that began in 1945 and continues to the appointment of Allen Dulles as DCI in 1953. The initial idea of Chief William Donovan of the Office of Strategic Services (OSS) for a strong, centralized, civilian agency capable of conducting its own intelligence activities was initially defeated. When the CIA was founded in 1947, it did not achieve Donovan's vision. Criticism of early intelligence arrangements, press discretion on the operational failures of covert activities, and consistent campaigning by Donovan, Dulles, and others, however, fostered support for Donovan's kind of active and aggressive agency originally envisioned in 1945.

The second and third chapters examine the critical years of Allen Dulles's directorship. During this time, the CIA successfully overthrew two foreign governments, those in Iran and Guatemala. Dulles used his connections with the press to publicize the operational successes of the CIA, establish a positive reputation for his agency, and rebut criticism of perceived CIA intelligence failures. The CIA, however, continued to face challenges stemming from the expectation that it would anticipate all world events. Dulles's tenure culminated in disaster, as his decreasing concern for the CIA's public profile and his recklessness led to an ill-conceived attempt to overthrow Fidel Castro in the Bay of Pigs invasion.

Chapter 4 examines the CIA under a succession of directors from 1961 to 1967 as the agency struggled to move past the Bay of Pigs and establish a different, more formal, and more effective system of working with the press to protect itself. Though Dulles's immediate successor, John McCone, was successful in this goal in the short term, these efforts were not ultimately sustainable. The publication of a five-part *New York Times* series in April 1966 on the CIA was a turning point in the evolution of a more aggressive mainstream press. The following year, the agency's decades-long foray into supporting private organizations to fight the Cold War on a cultural front was exposed when a disaffected former National Student Association (NSA) member revealed the CIA's ties with the NSA.

Chapter 5 examines the challenging atmosphere the CIA faced during Richard Nixon's presidency, as the administration's activities in Vietnam and Laos were increasingly called into question. The Watergate scandal ultimately proved disastrous for the CIA, as distrust in the political order and questions about the CIA's domestic activities led to increased investigation of the agency. When in December 1974 Seymour Hersh revealed that the CIA conducted an illegal domestic surveillance program, the agency could no longer avoid intensive investigation.

Finally, chapters 6 and 7 examine the press and the CIA's "Year of Intelligence," as a presidential commission and two congressional committees investigated the CIA. The future of the agency was debated and fought over in the press. Though the agency emerged intact from a combative eighteen months of investigation, its relationships with the press were dramatically redefined.

The story of the CIA and the press is a microcosm of the larger story of the U.S. Cold War consensus. When there was a sense of common cause, the CIA's relationships with the press tended to be helpful to the agency, even though critics remained. That positivity was fragile and often more contested than the agency's leaders expected. When the CIA was formed in the aftermath of World War II, its members believed they had to fight for its existence and to establish its place, and that the press could be a valuable tool in that effort. They would learn later that the press could also be significant, and at times, the sole challenge to their agency.

1

The Postwar Intelligence Debate and the CIA

In January 1953 the *Washington Post* published an unusual editorial. In response to the announcement that DCI Walter Bedell Smith was leaving the CIA to become undersecretary of state for the incoming Eisenhower administration, the author of the editorial took the opportunity to argue that the CIA was in need of reform.[1] The CIA, the editorial noted, had embarked on dangerous activities, such as covert propaganda and secret operations, which were "incompatible with a democracy."[2]

The editorial warned that the CIA was "apt to play hob with our foreign policy—indeed, to create trouble and even land us in war."[3] The author cited several worrisome stories that had emerged in the five years since the CIA had been founded. The CIA had illegally detained a Japanese citizen for eight months, had been caught tapping the phone of President José Figueres of Costa Rica, had armed guerrillas in Burma, and had tried to overthrow the democratically elected government of Guatemala. The CIA had even funded a neo-Nazi organization in Germany. With these facts public, the editorial noted, "God only knows" what the CIA had been up to that had not emerged in the press.[4]

Tucked away as it was on page 20 of a midsize newspaper, this editorial would have garnered limited attention. The *Post* in 1953 had a limited readership and geographic range compared to the *New York Times*. As recently as 1948 it had a circulation of only 180,000. Under the management of its new owner, Philip Graham, readership had increased, but not dramatically.[5]

The article, however, was an early criticism of the CIA's operational record. The CIA certainly took notice, and, when it found that the Soviets had commented on the article, the agency sent a message to Graham to note that his paper's criticism was aligned with Soviet interests. Though much of the CIA memorandum in which the editorial was discussed remains classified, the intent of the CIA in communicating with Graham can be inferred; it did not want to see more such editorials.[6] Criticism of the CIA did not reappear in the *Post*'s editorial pages in the immediate future.

While not the center of attention, the CIA was not absent from the public eye in its early years. Commentators had criticized the agency's creation out of fear of its potential to violate civil liberties. Others condemned the agency as an ineffective tool in the Cold War because of poor management, dilettantism, communist infiltration, or some combination of the three. The *Post*'s editorial was unusual, in that it actually discussed covert actions themselves. Despite occasional criticism, the general attitude of the U.S. press during the early Cold War was one of cooperation with the government and, at times, with U.S. intelligence services. These habits of cooperation proved significant to the growing U.S. intelligence establishment.

From 1946 and the creation of the first peacetime U.S. central intelligence organization, the Central Intelligence Group, to the eventual appointment of Allen Dulles as director of Central Intelligence in 1953, the issue of creating and refining a U.S. intelligence system was present though not prominent in U.S. newspapers and magazines. A key issue in discussions of intelligence was whether the focus of a covert intelligence agency ought to be limited to intelligence gathering or include more expansive covert warfare against communist powers. The latter dynamic was already winning out by 1953, when Dulles was made DCI and ensured the CIA would be conducting covert warfare.[7]

Press coverage alone was not causative in this shift toward operations, but it was an important contextual factor. Prominent reporters grew to favor an aggressive agency and refrained from reporting on the outcome of such aggression. As the CIA was under press scrutiny from the beginning of its existence, the press had a greater opportunity to affect the CIA than it had with older, established military intelligence agencies. Relationships between intelligence officers and members of the press began even before the CIA existed and helped shape the environment in which the CIA operated.

The Media Landscape before the Cold War

The experience of World War II was vital to shaping the generally cooperative nature of press relationships with the government in general and the CIA in particular in the immediate postwar era; the necessities of total war led to an understanding on the part of the press about cooperating with necessary secrets. Many foreign correspondents in the years after World War II had seen firsthand the toll the war had taken. James Reston, for example, a *New York Times* columnist and eventually chief of the *Times*'s Washington Bureau, had lived through the Blitz in London and later traveled to the Soviet Union as part of a junket with the *Times*'s owner and publisher, Arthur Hays Sulzberger. Before they became prominent columnists, Stewart Alsop and Thomas Braden had been members of the CIA's predecessor, the Office of Strategic Services. Both had parachuted into occupied France.

Journalists working during the war operated under a system of press censorship. There were formal controls, but the system heavily depended on the discretion and loyalty of the press. Discretion was especially important among domestic reporters, who were guided by a system of voluntary censorship. The chief of the Office of Censorship, Byron Price, a former reporter himself, was aided by the fact that journalists were just as invested in U.S. victory as the average citizen.[8]

Of the 2,700 daily newspapers, 11,000 weekly newspapers, and 7,000 journals that the Office of Censorship identified during the war, there were no domestic cases of deliberate efforts by the print media to buck the censorship code. Though there were violations, these generally were accidental in nature.[9] Several journalists, including the widely read Washington columnist Drew Pearson, knew some details of the Manhattan Project, but none revealed the existence of that secret initiative before the use of the bomb against Hiroshima.[10]

The war provided vivid examples to reporters of the need to accept censorship to prevent death and destruction from enemy action. When arguing for caution in the *Times*'s approach to stories, for example, Sulzberger reminded managing editor Turner Catledge of a story published in Britain that had resulted in the deaths of several relief workers. The story had contained a picture of an undetonated bomb being removed from ruins in London. This picture, according to Sulzberger, revealed enough about British procedures for the Germans to decide to hinder removal efforts and kill aid workers by booby-trapping bombs that would appear to be duds, only to explode when removed.[11]

Given their centrality to shaping the media landscape, it is worthwhile to examine some of the major publications and their leadership in detail. For example, Sulzberger's thoughts on the subject of what to publish and what to avoid were particularly important given his position. The *New York Times*'s daily circulation was in the hundreds of thousands. It was one of the most prestigious papers in the United States, with a proven capability and experience in reporting foreign affairs. Even if a person did not read the newspaper itself, the stories the *Times* broke became national news.

Sulzberger had come to own the *Times* almost accidentally. He had in 1917 married Iphigene Ochs, daughter of the *Times*'s publisher at the time, Adolf Ochs. Taking a job with the *Times* shortly after his marriage, Sulzberger learned the newspaper business from his father-in-law. Ochs was by nature a cautious and conservative publisher, at times criticized for taking objectivity and neutral reporting so seriously that the finished product was too dull to read. Though he would seek to provide a more interesting product, Sulzberger sought to emulate the care and caution of Ochs.

Educated at Columbia University, Sulzberger was also well versed in the world of the American political elite. Throughout his life he maintained friendly relationships with such Establishment figures as Allen Dulles and Hamilton Fish Armstrong. He was something of a late entrant to this overwhelmingly Protestant group, having been born to a prestigious Jewish family in New York. While never seeking to distance himself from his Jewish heritage, Sulzberger strongly believed in the assimilation of ethnic minorities in American society.

Echoes of Sulzberger's background and philosophy can be seen in another newspaper owner and publisher, Eugene Meyer. Like Sulzberger, Meyer was an assimilated Jewish American. Meyer purchased the *Washington Post* in 1933, two years before Sulzberger began his long tenure as the *Times*'s publisher. Meyer had gone to Yale, and he subscribed to its ethos of public service on the part of the elite and able.[12] The *Post,* like the *Times,* cooperated with censorship during World War II.

Not everyone agreed with the principles of caution and patriotic cooperation with the government. The Washington Bureau of the *Times,* led by the so-called Dean of the Washington Newsmen, Arthur Krock, enjoyed and fiercely fought to defend a substantial degree of autonomy from the New York office. Originally from Kentucky, Krock was a Democrat vehemently opposed to the New Deal.[13] He was frustrated on several occasions with the stories Sulzberger would prevent from running, such as a report that the U.S. Navy captured a German raider in late 1941 and a detailed report on the attack at Pearl Harbor.[14]

Krock was constrained by his publisher; there were no such issues at the *Chicago Tribune*. Its owner and publisher, Robert McCormick, was committed to freedom of the press and to total opposition to the New Deal. The grandson of the Chicagoan Joseph Medill, who purchased the *Tribune* in the 1880s, McCormick took over as publisher upon his return home from military service in World War I. McCormick had spent a great deal of his childhood in England, and he had attended both Groton and Yale. He wholeheartedly rejected, however, the Anglophilia and internationalism of many of his classmates, seeing only decay in the Old World while being totally convinced of "America's moral and political superiority."[15]

McCormick's deeply conservative and decidedly isolationist worldview led him to be one of the foremost critics of Franklin Roosevelt. McCormick believed Roosevelt's administration heralded a disaster for democracy in the United States, and he mightily resisted what he saw as undue government intervention in private business and U.S. engagement in the crisis engulfing Europe. McCormick spent a significant portion of the 1930s opposing New Deal regulations concerning newspapers as chair of the Freedom of the Press Committee of the American Newspaper Publishers Association (ANPA).

Knowing he was a controversial figure, and facing the escalating crisis in the Atlantic in the summer of 1941, McCormick offered to resign from the committee so that it could defend the freedom of the press without the distraction of attacks on him. The reply to his offer, however, delivered the unwelcome news that the ANPA had decided to close the committee entirely because of "present national conditions."[16] An unhappy McCormick did not follow the lead of his eastern fellow publishers in his approach to publishing during the months leading to war. He continued to fiercely criticize the government, dictating to his editorial writers which topics they should address, how the writers should address them, and, at times, phrases for them to use.[17]

While generally cooperative with the wartime censorship program, the *Chicago Tribune* famously circumvented that censorship to publish a potentially damaging revelation of U.S. intelligence abilities. The source was the *Tribune*'s reporter Stanley Johnston, who had been reporting from the USS *Lexington* until that ship sank because of damage inflicted during the Battle of the Coral Sea. On a transport to San Diego, Johnston struck up a friendship with a naval officer who informed him that Japanese ships were headed toward Midway. Following the Japanese defeat at Midway, Johnston reported that the United States had known about Japanese fleet movements in advance of the battle, which could have suggested to alert readers that the United States had broken Japanese codes.[18]

The U.S. government brought the *Tribune* before a grand jury on suspicion of violating the Espionage Act. McCormick, Johnston, and the *Tribune* escaped charges solely because the navy feared that the evidence necessary to penalize the newspaper would only further expose U.S. Signals Intelligence.

As the United States transitioned to peace in 1946, the experiences of the war might not have seemed immediately relevant. The differences between the Sulzberger and the McCormick approaches to relations with the government and to demands for secrecy and discretion would, however, become highly relevant to their coverage of intelligence matters in the early Cold War. A reputation for discretion and engagement with the Eastern Establishment left Sulzberger and his paper with strong contacts in the world of intelligence. While the *Tribune* had its connections with government, it seems to have lacked the ties to the intelligence world that the *Times* and the *Post* enjoyed.

There would be plenty of opportunities to put these different approaches into practice because after World War II, the press began to pay greater attention to foreign U.S. activities. Reporting on foreign affairs had, by obvious necessity, increased during World War II. After the war, journalism as a profession sought to improve and codify journalistic practices.[19] Papers built up their foreign reporting staffs, and their needs were also met by contract reporters in foreign locations. These stringers were, as mentioned previously, those most likely to be in direct, paid relationships with the CIA. In addition, the wire services, such as the Associated Press, the United Press, and Reuters, would prove to be an important source of international news. Occasionally, members of the wire services would be identified as cooperating with the CIA, such as a UP member in Rome in the 1950s. Stuart Loory later discovered that Reuters, as a foreign wire service, was especially apt to be used by the CIA.[20]

Besides the newspapers, Henry Luce of Time-Life notably sought to fill this demand for international news. Luce dominated the news journal field; an estimated one of every five Americans read at least one of his publications in a given week.[21] Luce's strategy of accessibility in writing and synthesis of reporting and opinion was adopted by competitors, even ideological opponents like McCormick and former vice president Henry Wallace.[22] Luce cooperated with the government, and *Time* was generally an ally of the CIA in terms of both positive coverage for the agency and not reporting on the agency's covert activities. Luce's attitude differed from that of *U.S. News &*

World Report's David Lawrence. A Princeton alumnus and a friend of future DCI Allen Dulles, Lawrence personally supported the CIA's activities. He laid down a "strict prohibition," however, on any of his staff or reporters doing work with or for the CIA.[23]

The newspapers, while not enjoying the kind of national omnipresence established by Luce, could create in a major market a comfortable level of readership and income. Markets like New York, Chicago, and Washington sustained multiple major newspapers, such as the *Chicago Daily News, New York Herald Tribune,* and *Washington Evening Star,* in addition to the *Tribune, Times,* and *Post,* respectively. Until Eugene Meyer bought the *Washington Times-Herald* from McCormick in 1954, the *Post* was one of the dwarves of the Washington market. The newspaper market was changing, however, as rising costs of production and the suburbanization of the U.S. population, which placed many Americans outside a major market, forced numerous newspapers to adapt to remain solvent.[24]

In addition to juggernauts like Luce and steady metropolitan newspapers, smaller periodicals sought to communicate their world vision for the postwar era. Prominent among these were the *New Republic* and the *Nation,* which by 1947 had a circulation of 90,000 and 45,000, respectively.[25] The magazines were thus engaged in a constant struggle to survive. By 1948 the *New Republic* had a running yearly deficit of $225,000; the *Nation* was better off, its yearly deficit only $60,000.[26] The ability of these periodicals to do substantive foreign reporting was limited.

The Intelligence Landscape after the War

Major intelligence issues appeared in the press in 1945, when the question arose of what to do with the wartime intelligence agency, the Office of Strategic Services, after the war. Created on Roosevelt's order in 1942, the OSS was led by William Donovan, who began formulating plans to establish a postwar future for his agency as early as 1943. That September he had drawn up a proposal for the OSS to be integrated as a standing part of the U.S. military establishment, coequal with the army and navy. Though the proposal received no response, Donovan again in 1944 proposed that the OSS be transformed into a central service that would coordinate all U.S. intelligence activity, conduct its own espionage and subversive warfare, and report directly to the president.[27]

That plan was leaked to Walter Trohan of the *Chicago Tribune,* who in February 1945 published a story condemning Donovan's design. It is unclear who leaked Donovan's plan; Trohan would later claim it had been Roosevelt himself, who was lukewarm on the plan. Donovan thought it was FBI Director J. Edgar Hoover.[28] The intelligence historian Christopher Andrew, in addition to seeing both Hoover and Roosevelt as possible candidates, observes it could easily have been any number of people involved with military intelligence who felt threatened by the proposal.[29]

After the leak and subsequent negative attention, Donovan's proposal was unlikely to be acted on. Making matters worse for the OSS was a report of its effectiveness commissioned by Roosevelt and given to Harry S. Truman in April 1945. It was extremely negative and claimed that the OSS had made profound miscalculations. Its offices worldwide, according to the report, had become centers of parties and debauchery. The report concluded that the OSS "may easily prove to have been the most expensive and wasteful agency of the government."[30] In August the OSS was dissolved; its Research and Analysis branch was transferred to the State Department, and its Secret Intelligence and Counter-Espionage branches were assigned to the War Department.

Donovan, lacking allies in government, continued his lobbying efforts after the official dissolution of his agency. The OSS was gone, but he remained committed to the kind of central, powerful organization he had recommended to Franklin Roosevelt. Especially important to Donovan's efforts were *Life* and the *Saturday Evening Post.*[31] His subordinates were eager to help, many taking part in the Veterans of Strategic Services (VSS). Part of what made these VSS members happy to help was their sense of the OSS as a special, elite place. The OSS had made intelligence a glamorous activity; Allen Dulles, an OSS officer himself, explained that intelligence work tended to keep former members involved because "once one gets a taste for it, it's hard to drop."[32] For Dulles and other VSS members, the task of convincing the public to support the ideal of the OSS meant both communicating to a large audience the sense of the romanticism and glamour that invigorated them, and convincing that audience of the need for a strong intelligence service to protect national security.

Dulles reached out to the *Saturday Evening Post* to relate that, as head of OSS activities in Central Europe during the war, he masterminded Operation Sunrise, in which U.S. intelligence cooperated with disaffected Nazis to bring about the surrender of German forces in Italy.[33] Dulles's effort resulted in a two-part series that, in addition to painting the OSS in a positive light, was very complimentary toward Dulles. Dulles was described as a "judgmatical [sic] man of genuine charm" who had made substantial contributions to Allied victory.[34]

Donovan continued to support the publication of OSS-related articles; Thomas Braden, for example, later revealed that he and Stewart Alsop wrote several promotional articles at Donovan's behest. Alsop and Braden openly collaborated to write a book about the OSS, written with Donovan's assent.[35] In *Sub Rosa,* Alsop and Braden highlighted OSS successes in espionage and in aid provided to resistance movements.[36]

A significant supporter of the OSS and its legacy was Arthur Krock. Writing in July 1945, he responded to the criticism that the OSS was filled with Ivy League types by arguing that the OSS simply sought the best men wherever it could find them, and that it was overall "a remarkably balanced and representative group."[37] In addition to celebrating the OSS's accomplishments, Krock advocated for Donovan's intelligence plan, as good intelligence was especially important in the age of the atomic bomb. Despite fears about its misuse, Krock was sure Donovan's arrangement would avoid any possibility of becoming a Gestapo-like organization.[38]

Krock's support for the OSS may seem surprising, as he was generally suspicious of government and tended to be deeply unhappy with its expansion. That by supporting the OSS Krock was able to criticize Harry S. Truman's policies probably helped, as Krock continued to be angry at the New Deal turn in the Democratic Party. Probably more important, however, were Krock's social connections with OSS officers. He knew Donovan and Dulles, and Donovan wrote to thank Krock for his aid.[39]

As the historian Larry Valero notes, it can be difficult to determine whether favorable coverage resulted from the influence of Donovan or from personal opinions on intelligence.[40] In the case of Braden and Alsop, Donovan clearly took a significant role. With Krock, however, there is no evidence that Donovan prompted Krock's support; given their acquaintance, it is certainly possible that they discussed the OSS's situation in a general way. It is ultimately, however, only a minor distinction whether Donovan specifically asked Krock to write, or Krock on his own took the opportunity to support a friend and poke a foe in the eye. Either way, it demonstrates how social and ideological cohesion aided Donovan's goals.

The *Chicago Tribune,* meanwhile, articulated criticism of the OSS. The *Tribune* tended to portray the OSS as staffed by dilettantes avoiding real service. The *Tribune's* journalist Chesly Manly, for example, referred to the OSS veterans as "'professionals' who had bombproofed wartime jobs."[41] In May 1946 the *Tribune* published an article by Edgar Bundy, a captain in the 14th Air Force in China, who wrote that the greatest danger for both the air force and the OSS in China was a hangover. Members of the OSS, Bundy claimed, gorged themselves on luxury food and drink while the Chinese people starved.[42]

The *New York Times's* military editor Hanson Baldwin stood between the *Tribune's* strident criticism and the friendliness of the *Saturday Evening Post.* An Annapolis graduate and retired naval officer, Baldwin had won a Pulitzer for his reporting from the Pacific Theater. He became one of the chief figures in writing about the new national security establishment built after World War II, including intelligence. American intelligence, Baldwin warned, lagged significantly behind that of its foreign counterparts. Rather than agree with Donovan's proposal, Baldwin supported the creation of the National Intelligence Authority (NIA) and the Central Intelligence Group (CIG) in January 1946.[43]

Though often viewed as only a stopgap between the dissolution of the OSS and the creation of the CIA, the NIA/CIG framework can be seen as an attempt by Truman to build an intelligence apparatus distinct from the OSS. The NIA consisted of the secretaries of state, war, and the navy and the chief of staff to the president. Also at meetings would be the director of Central Intelligence, a nonvoting member of the NIA who would oversee the CIG. The CIG focused on research and analysis rather than secret intelligence gathering and covert action. The CIG would collect and process intelligence provided by the intelligence services of the various agencies attached to the NIA.[44] The architect of this arrangement was the first DCI, Sidney Souers. Truman reportedly celebrated Souers's swearing-in ceremony by presenting guests with black cloaks, black hats, and wooden daggers and by affixing a fake black mustache to Souers's face.[45]

This new intelligence organization was quite different from the central, powerful organization Donovan had proposed. The CIG was a facilitator between existing agencies, rather than a new and powerful bureaucracy in its own right. Even in this early period, though, leaders in Congress and the intelligence community were concerned that too many people were involved in the oversight and funding process. The CIG sought to establish for itself an independent budget and avoid widespread congressional knowledge of its activities.[46]

Donovan's supporters viewed the CIG as a first step, but one that required further work. Stewart and his brother, Joseph Alsop, now nationally syndicated columnists, hailed the agency as the "first national independent foreign intelligence system." They continued to argue against a division of the functions of the OSS, however, hoping these functions would provide a basis for a more active CIG.[47] The Alsops' position, while supportive, indicated a continued desire for the NIA/CIG framework to take an OSS-like form. Others supported the CIG as its own effective body. Krock wrote in 1946 that Truman was the best-informed chief executive in history because of the efforts of the CIG and the president's daily briefing.[48] According to George M. Elsey, assistant to White House Counsel Clark Clifford, Krock's celebratory column was the result of the efforts of Clifford and Hoyt Vandenberg, the second DCI, drumming up support for the new agency.[49] Some picked up this supportive thread, such as Baldwin and the *Washington Post*'s editorial page.[50]

Even as many were commenting on the particulars of American intelligence, though, the circumstances of postwar intelligence began to change. Donovan had made his proposal for an expansive, active intelligence organization at a time when many Americans hoped the war's end would remove the necessity of such an organization. Such hopes were dashed as tensions with the Soviet Union only continued to worsen through 1946 and 1947. U.S. policy makers increasingly sought ways to respond to the perceived threat of the Soviet Union. Preparations for confronting the Soviets demanded the reform of the U.S. national security bureaucracy, accomplished through the National Security Act of 1947, introduced to Congress in March that year. Section 102 of the act created the CIA.

The Creation of the CIA

The creation of the CIA was a minor part of the National Security Act. The section of the act establishing the agency was only two and a half pages long and consisted of six clauses. One clause set the date when the creation of the agency would go into effect and dissolved the CIG. Four of the clauses dealt with the position and powers of the DCI as leader of the new agency and the intelligence community as a whole. The sole clause relating to the CIA's duties established that the CIA would advise the National Security Council (NSC), take on intelligence activities of the whole intelligence community as directed by the NSC, and be responsible for correlating, evaluating, and disseminating intelligence. The agency would have "no police, subpena [*sic*], law-enforcement powers, or internal-security functions." Finally, the CIA would "perform other such functions and duties related to the existing national security as the National Security Council may from time to time direct."[51] This last clause provided the legal basis for all the CIA's propaganda, political warfare, and paramilitary actions.

Of all the many parts of the National Security Act, the CIA did not command the most attention, but it was not ignored. Hanson Baldwin repeatedly returned to the intelligence question as part of the larger national security debate. He stressed two main themes: the need for a strong intelligence service to serve as the country's first line of defense, and the need to staff that service with professionals who viewed intelligence as their first career. Given that many in the military, such as then-DCI Vandenberg, viewed intelligence work as a temporary stop in their larger military careers, Baldwin argued instead for an intelligence bureaucracy, staffed by trained civil servants.[52]

Baldwin's support of the CIA and his stress on the need for civilian officials suggest he had been dissatisfied with the overwhelmingly military nature of the previous framework. The secretary of state was the only representative of a civilian agency on the NIA. The first two DCIs had tenures of less than a year. Admiral Roscoe Hillenkoetter was appointed to be the third DCI in April 1947. The *Washington Post*'s editorial page joined Baldwin's criticism: editorialists argued that a civilian could both better address the wider concerns with which intelligence needed to grapple and better protect the American democratic system.[53] The *Post*'s editorial writers, and Baldwin, were thus disappointed when the National Security Act did not bar an active military officer from serving as DCI.

The criticism from Baldwin and the *Post*'s editorial page was focused on how to ensure the CIA would be an effective agency, not whether the CIA should exist in the first place. The *Chicago Tribune* came at the debate from a different position and rejected the proposed CIA entirely. According to the *Tribune,* the agency was too expensive and too much a threat to American democracy to be permitted. One editorial, for example, criticized the creation of a CIA with "a $12,000 a year director" as a waste of resources, in service to an "extraconstitutional supergovernment."[54] Another *Tribune* editorialist argued in "The Budding American Gestapo" that the CIA would be a "new weapon in the hands of the military junta headed by Gen. Marshall which is rapidly taking over control of the country."[55]

This hostility to the CIA extended beyond the editorial page and into the *Tribune*'s objective reporting. Walter Trohan, for example, wrote a news article on the CIA in which he barely gave any attention to the advocates of the agency. Instead, he focused almost solely on the agency's critics.[56] Other *Tribune* reporters followed suit, writing ostensibly noneditorial stories that served mainly as a platform for critics of the government.[57]

These criticisms were very much in line with McCormick's views. He believed no perfidy was beyond Truman. For example, he directed one of his editorialists to prepare an article alleging that the Marshall Plan, "a conspiracy to bankrupt America," was created because of blackmail on the part of the governments of France, the United Kingdom, and Holland. This blackmail stemmed from the fact that their foreign offices apparently had evidence of their plot with Franklin Roosevelt to bring about war. "Using this blackmail," McCormick wrote, "those countries are demanding the impoverishment of America for their socialism."[58]

Such theories were not unusual from McCormick. His biographer Richard Smith comments that McCormick "was drawn to conspiracy theories like a small boy to a burning building."[59] The extreme outlandishness of this charge, though, demonstrates the commitment of the *Tribune* to an anti–Truman administration line. The CIA was a secondary question; the main opposition to its creation from the *Chicago Tribune* was part of its wider rejection of the proposed changes to the federal government in the National Security Act.

Public engagement with this debate was limited. There was popular support for the idea of an American intelligence agency; the few Gallup polls conducted on the issue saw up to 77 percent approval for such an agency.[60] Public engagement with the important questions of intelligence, such as what an intelligence agency could be reasonably expected to accomplish, is impossible to tell.

The creation of the CIA, met as it was with little fanfare and little attention, did not end the debate about what proper form U.S. intelligence ought to take. Hillenkoetter remained DCI, and the agency did not either immediately adopt a Donovan-style approach or recruit OSS veterans. The CIA did not have its own independent budget. Instead, it received funds from the Departments of State and Defense. The CIA's ability to conduct its basic task of intelligence gathering was uncertain: the National Security Act did not provide an explicit mandate for covert operations.[61] This lack of a mandate was skirted by the "other such functions" clause of Section 102, but it was a disturbing ambiguity.

This ambiguity initially meant that propaganda and political warfare operations were conducted not by the CIA, but by the obliquely named Office of Policy Coordination (OPC). The brainchild of George Kennan, the OPC had originally been called the Office of Special Projects, but that name, it was apparently felt, gave too much of the office's purpose away. The OPC was led by an OSS veteran, Frank Wisner, who embraced the prospect of aggressive warfare against the communist powers. The OPC occupied a curious space in the national security bureaucracy; it received its funding from the CIA but was overseen jointly by the CIA and Kennan's Policy Planning staff. Effectively, Wisner operated outside the control of the CIA.

This arrangement did not end until Hillenkoetter left the CIA in 1950. His successor, Walter Smith, asserted the CIA's authority over the OPC and folded it, along with the CIA's covert intelligence gathering branch, the Office of Special Operations (OSO), into the Directorate of Plans. Smith favored emphasizing CIA collection and analysis over covert action, but he proved unable to prevent the continued growth and aggressiveness of Plans. He was hindered by his choice of Plans' first leader. Seeking an intelligence veteran, Smith chose Allen Dulles for the task. Dulles, however, shared Wisner's great enthusiasm for covert warfare.

With the exception of changes in the DCIs, these organizational changes to the CIA drew little comment. It was because of the limited attention paid to the agency, however, that those journalists who did spend any time on intelligence issues could exercise influence out of proportion to their numbers. The media scholar Delmer Dunn, explaining the interaction of Congress and the press, describes a process of symbiosis in which congressmen use the press to introduce new ideas to the public, while the press can help make such ideas more familiar and more readily seized on when new solutions are called for. It is by this process, Dunn explains, that "ideas that may at first seem radical become familiar and less imposing."[62] This principle can be seen at work outside Congress, as the interaction between members of the press and the burgeoning intelligence community helped develop an idea about what a U.S. intelligence establishment should look like. As those few who wrote on intelligence grew closer to having the same conception of what an intelligence establishment should do, they were able to influence the parameters of its evolution.

The Intersections of Intelligence, the Press, and Social Life

There were a variety of places and opportunities for members of the press to interact with the early intelligence community. The Metropolitan, Yale, and Harvard clubs, for example, operated as they had long before the OSS or CIA existed, to ensure opportunities for the right kind of people to meet. Meetings in civic groups, at think tanks, and informally over lunch were often the order of the day. Two venues stand out as particularly important to shaping the early reporting on the CIA: the Council on Foreign Relations (CFR) and the Alsops' Washington social circle.

Since its founding in 1921, the CFR had been a center of American foreign policy thinking. Its bimonthly journal, *Foreign Affairs,* published a variety of distinguished authors addressing foreign policy issues. For example, it published George Kennan's famous article "The Sources of Soviet Conduct," a key document in the early Cold War. The CFR would also help establish the cutouts through which the CIA diverted aid to its many allied private organizations.[63]

The CFR had strong connections to the *New York Times.* Arthur Hays Sulzberger began an association with the CFR in 1938. Hanson Baldwin joined the same year. By 1940 both men were regularly corresponding with Hamilton Fish Armstrong, editor of *Foreign Affairs.*[64] Soon after World War II, Baldwin organized a group within the CFR devoted to the study of national security and military affairs. Sulzberger became a member, along with prominent policy makers such as Robert Lovett and John McCloy. Also present was William Harding Jackson, eventually a deputy DCI. Their meetings were off the record and held in confidence. The group met with Dulles, himself a longtime member of the council, who supported the project and was the guest for their first meeting. Baldwin and another CFR member, Langbourne Williams, also met privately with Dulles in early 1947. By April 1947 the group became an official subgroup of the CFR.[65]

Baldwin was also part of an informal group based in New York that discussed military affairs, which included George Kennan, Maxwell Taylor, and

Dwight D. Eisenhower. Baldwin drew on these meetings, and those at the CFR, to write a book on U.S. defense issues, *The Price of Power,* to communicate his Cold War defense concerns to the public.[66] This book demonstrates how the CFR could influence the coverage of policy questions, including intelligence.

Baldwin released *Price of Power* in February 1948, having written it during the debate over the National Security Act of 1947.[67] He devoted a chapter to intelligence. Returning to a recurrent theme, he argued that intelligence was vital to modern warfare to prevent a surprise attack. Because the stakes of conflict included the United States' position in the world, and possibly its very existence, intelligence could not afford to be limited. Intelligence required, Baldwin argued, "all means and methods; [intelligence] is amoral and cynical."[68]

By 1947 Baldwin had moved to a generally negative view on U.S. intelligence arrangements at that time. He was skeptical of the newly formed CIA, arguing that it was internally fractured and enmeshed in Washington bureaucracy. This condition interfered with its vital coordination mission. Baldwin also argued that the CIA needed to carry out its own collection activities in addition to its coordination role, essentially casting off the legacy of the CIG framework.[69] Finally, Baldwin again argued that the CIA needed to establish "a cadre of long-term, stable, efficient and high-calibre intelligence officers."[70]

Baldwin's views had changed from his earlier approval of the NIA/CIG framework to something more akin to Donovan's vision while working with many OSS veterans at the CFR. Dulles and Jackson, especially, advocated a much stronger and more active intelligence agency, though their arguments may simply have served to channel an already present frustration Baldwin felt with the undervalued U.S. intelligence system and its transient leadership. Baldwin valued Dulles's opinion, and he sent Dulles a draft of his chapter on intelligence for Dulles's opinion and advice. Dulles provided a lengthy comment from which Baldwin repeated passages verbatim in *Price of Power,* crediting them to an anonymous veteran intelligence officer.[71] It is reasonable to conclude, on the basis of their communications, that Dulles had some influence in the evolution of Baldwin's views on the U.S. intelligence system.

Taking advice from Dulles did not mean that Baldwin lost his independence; he continued to express concern over control of the Central Intelligence Agency even as Dulles became its director in 1953. By 1970, when the intelligence scholar Harry Howe Ransom wrote on the U.S. intelligence establishment, he cited Baldwin and the *New York Times* as "leaders among those advocating a closer congressional surveillance of the government's foreign intelligence operations."[72] Baldwin's caution, though, did not in his mind exclude arrangements for an active and effective intelligence organization. What exactly those arrangements should be drew heavily from his experience at the CFR, which provided a forum in which certain beliefs, opinions, and assumptions could be inculcated.

Unlike Baldwin, the Alsops were not members of the CFR. Joseph Alsop refused the CFR's membership offer, explaining that he and his brother turned down the offers of "rather numerous organizations," as they wanted to avoid any tie that might inhibit their reporting.[73] The Alsops did not need the access provided by the council, as they were a social scene unto themselves. There was significant overlap in the two worlds; guest lists for the Alsops' parties included Kennan, Dulles, Lovett, and McCloy. Other major policy makers, such as James Forrestal and Paul Nitze, were also Alsop party attendees. From the CIA came the likes of Richard Bissell, Richards Helms, Frank Wisner, Tracy Barnes, and Thomas Braden. Eugene Meyer's son-in-law and successor at the *Washington Post,* Philip Graham, was a regular attendee until the psychological problems that eventually drove him to suicide interfered with his engagement in social events. His successor at the *Post* was his wife, Katharine, who was also a frequent guest of the Alsops. Thanks largely to Joseph Alsop's efforts, their social events were no less refined than those of the council. They also added the benefit of greater informality, and, in the case of the Sunday night dinners that Joseph Alsop came to call "Sunday night drunks," considerable alcohol.[74]

The Alsops drew heavily from these parties for their columns, taking the opportunity to get ideas, impressions, and contacts. Joseph Alsop occasionally took the opportunity to express to his distinguished guests his philosophy about proper relationships between government officials and members of the press. In a 1945 letter, for example, Alsop urged Secretary of State James Byrnes to let more members of the press into his confidence; it was his lack of such activity, Alsop felt, that led to the unpopularity of Byrnes's policies as secretary of state. Alsop wrote that Byrnes should realize that it was not the case that what "cannot be said at a press conference cannot be said at all." The press conference was a place for press releases. There was, Alsop noted, "a distinction . . . between those newspapermen who are, so to speak, only of press conference caliber, and those whose background, training, and reliability fits them for a fuller disclosure of the facts." Byrnes should, according to Alsop, set up a small group of reporters of the second category, to whom he could explain himself and from whom he could garner support.[75]

Joseph and Stewart Alsop both also contributed to the *Saturday Evening Post* and used this connection to put their intelligence friends into contact with a friendly publication. Having previously recommended his cousin Kermit Roosevelt to the OSS, after the war Joseph recommended Roosevelt to the *Post*'s editor Martin Sommers for a story on intelligence.[76] Alsop recommended a story on the intelligence arrangements under Vandenberg.[77] Braden was floated as a possible author. Sommers assured Alsop that "if he has the Vandenberg stuff we surely want to see it as soon as possible."[78] By the time the article came together, however, Vandenberg was already out and Hillenkoetter was coming in. The development of the CIA outpaced Joseph Alsop's first efforts to get a CIA story. Both Alsops, though, remained consistently on the lookout for the opportunity to relate stories that advocated for U.S. intelligence to the public.

Forums such as the Council on Foreign Relations and the Alsops' dinner parties helped shape the early discourse on the CIA. Especially given that writers paying attention to intelligence issues in these early years were few and far between, the opportunity for men like Allen Dulles, Thomas Braden, and Richard Helms to convince writers such as Hanson Baldwin and Joseph Alsop to accept their vision of intelligence was especially significant. These forums helped form a friendly environment as the CIA began to act in earnest.

The CIA under Roscoe Hillenkoetter

In 1963 Harry Truman wrote that he never intended the CIA to have a covert-action role; rather, he intended it to focus on collection and analysis.[79] This claim was disingenuous. While its operations were modest in comparison to its future activities, the CIA engaged in covert action soon after its official foundation on 18 September 1947. In the spring of 1948 the CIA funneled extensive money into the Italian national parliamentary elections. U.S. policy makers feared the influence that the Communist Party could wield in Italy, and so they supported the Christian Democrats.

With authorization in December 1947 by NSC 4/A, the CIA transferred to the Christian Democrats $10 million; the funds had been seized from the Axis during World War II.[80] Though it is difficult to determine how important the funds were to the outcome of the election, the operation would have an important place in the CIA's history.[81] As the historian Zachary Karabell put it, through the Italian election "the CIA was transformed from a bureau of intelligence and analysis into an architect of covert action."[82]

The CIA also engaged in various partisan warfare activities. In some cases, this meant supporting friendly governments in their efforts to thwart the threats of communist insurgents, such as when they provided support to the Filipino government against the Huk rebellion. The OPC attempted to conduct subversive operations behind the Iron Curtain. Wisner continued these missions despite a distinct lack of success. In Eastern Europe, it was eventually revealed, the OPC/CIA missions had in some cases succeeded only in providing millions of dollars to Eastern Bloc intelligence agencies that had created fictional partisan groups.[83]

These activities were for the most part successfully kept out of the press. *Time* reported that the CIA had been involved in the Italian elections, but only in the sense that it uncovered communist intentions that then allowed the United States to take the proper public policy position to win over Italian voters. A brief report on CIA activity in Romania had no ramifications.[84] Reviewing the CIA's amateurish efforts in its early years, Bradley Smith observes that seeing widespread CIA control of the press is unrealistic. Rather, "A far more plausible explanation is that . . . the press were quiet because at that time the great sweep of American public opinion not only supported an intelligence build-up, but also tacitly agreed that it should occur behind a screen of secrecy."[85] While Smith is undoubtedly correct that the public would probably have supported intelligence activities because of the Cold War, it is likely that he overestimates the amount of attention given to intelligence matters at all.

Additionally, beyond immediate Cold War concerns, the CIA was aided by the press code of World War II. Arthur Sulzberger, writing to Turner Catledge following an internal debate on censorship in Korea, explained his approach most clearly. Sulzberger continued to insist that the *Times* had to exercise caution to avoid being responsible for any advantage gained by an enemy. Thus, while Sulzberger explained he would "be very slow in putting a 'secret' label on any document . . . I think I'd be a lot slower in taking it off during times like these."[86] This attitude led to a cautious reporting policy.

There were also logistical challenges to getting information on covert activities in the countries in which the CIA operated. While there were some foreign correspondents in the countries that Frank Wisner sent OPC groups into, their movements were closely controlled by communist governments. In some foreign markets, even major papers like the *Times* had to rely on stringers. Though a paper such as the *Tribune* probably would have reported on massive CIA failures if it had information on them, practical considerations limited the CIA's exposure.

Other publications that probably would have reported on the CIA's activities if they were aware of them were the *New Republic* and, especially, the *Nation*. A political cartoon in the *New Republic* at the time of the Italian election portrayed Truman in a stall marked "Italian election" with cash bulging out of his pockets.[87] The cartoon accompanied a larger article castigating Truman, but the piece did not mention anything directly relating to the election. The *New Republic* remained largely silent about the CIA, and it did not comment regularly on the agency until the 1950s. It was constrained by its poor financial position and the uncertain liberal politics at the time.

The *New Republic* and the *Nation,* meanwhile, began in 1948 to flirt with the idea of a merger to shore up their financial positions and focus their combined efforts on a single influential leftist weekly. Intermittent talks of a merger lasted until 1953. That year Larry Siegel, from the *New Republic,* warned a *Nation* editor that the *New Republic*'s publisher, Michael Straight, "was bent on putting *The Nation* out of business." Part of the reason seems to have been that, while wanting a single leftist voice, Straight feared the consequences of a merger. Siegel reported that "Michael was afraid of teaming up with *The Nation* for fear that this would make him a livelier target for congressional investigators."[88] Unlike many of those investigated by Congress during the Red Scare, Straight had actually been a spy for the People's Commissariat for Internal Affairs (NKVD); he was approached while studying at Cambridge in 1937 because of his family connections to the Roosevelts. Straight refused to continue to work for the NKVD in 1942, and his connection with the agency was not revealed for some time.[89]

Freda Kirchwey and the staff of the *Nation* were willing to go through a prolonged back-and-forth with Straight because of their hope that a merger could help solve their financial problems. It would also clarify their mission, which at times was somewhat murky. Kirchwey was ultimately unable to transform the *Nation* into the kind of platform she wanted, and the publication would not have a significant effect on the CIA during the agency's early years.

In addition to the patriotic ignorance of some major papers and the incapacity of the CIA's greatest potential critics, Hillenkoetter consciously sought to cultivate friendly relationships with the press. For example, he provided Hanson Baldwin figures on military strength in Europe.[90] He also communicated on several occasions with Joseph Alsop. He seems to have taken an approach similar to that which Alsop advised Byrnes to take—that is, to cultivate trusted reporters to try to get his narrative of the CIA out.

Alsop may very well have used the same pitch with Hillenkoetter that he did with Byrnes. In reporting to Martin Sommers on contact with Hillenkoetter, Alsop explained that he had first approached Hillenkoetter with a proposal that the *Saturday Evening Post* might be of some use to national security. Alsop observed that the CIA had a great deal of information on communist activities in Eastern Europe, but it could not disseminate that information without revealing its role in obtaining it. Alsop proposed to Hillenkoetter, and then to Sommers, that "a reliable Post reporter could be fully briefed by the [CIA] here. . . . He could then go abroad to complete his inquires and get what they call cover; and that he could write from abroad, thus seemingly presenting his pieces as entirely foreign in origin." This kind of activity, he argued, would benefit the nation and the *Saturday Evening Post*. Alsop informed Sommers, "Admiral H agreed this was an entirely practical and unobkectionable [*sic*] system, and promised to cooperate with any reporters you might select and vouch for."[91] This kind of arrangement, unpaid and apparently instigated by Alsop and not the CIA, is a clear example of an informal relationship well outside the bounds of normal journalistic practice.

Sommers was reserved but interested; he did not want to jump into anything with the CIA without considering the consequences. It is difficult to determine if this proposed arrangement came to fruition. Regardless of that specific plan, however, CIA-related material continued to find its way to Alsop. "Hillie," as Joseph Alsop was calling him by 1949, sent along a report on Yugoslavia that could be of use. Also floated was the possibility of using CIA material to write an article on the death of Andrei Zhdanov, the chairman of the Supreme Soviet of the Russian Soviet Republic. Stewart Alsop, too, was able to get "up-to-the-minute dope" about such things as the Soviet atomic bomb.[92]

The silence of the mainstream, the incapacity of the left, and the cooperation of elite reporters like the Alsops aided the advocates of covert action. Those advocates were insulated from covert action's failures by the lack of specific stories. The consequences of an aggressive, expansive intelligence organization remained theoretical. Those who emphasized collection and analysis were hampered, meanwhile, because the CIA was not entirely out of public view. Though covert action was not reported, critics of the CIA expected the agency to be perfect in its predictions of the world situation.

There were thus two types of stories in which the CIA tended to appear. The first involved cases in which some misfortune for the United States had occurred, which led to questions about why the CIA had not provided warning of such setbacks. The second, often following shortly after the first type, addressed ongoing questions of the CIA's shape, purpose, and role, and how to ensure that in the future no event would catch the United States off guard. The demand for perfection in analysis and prediction significantly hampered the prospects for an agency focused on analysis over action.

A crisis in Bogota in April 1948 demonstrates the pattern of negative CIA press attention. Riots had broken out in Bogota following the assassination of the popular leftist leader Jorge Gaitán on 9 April. Gaitán's death led to an outbreak of violence referred to as the *Bogotazo,* in which thousands were killed. Most American media sources focused on the fact that the riots had disrupted the Ninth Pan-American Conference, where George Marshall was negotiating to strengthen U.S. ties with Latin America. In the immediate aftermath, the CIA was called to explain why it had not warned of potential instability in Colombia. The popular view was that, if the CIA was supposed to be the first line of defense through intelligence, it should have predicted something like the *Bogotazo.*[93]

The outcry over Bogota shifted fairly quickly to the State Department after Hillenkoetter was called to Congress; there he explained that the CIA had warned of tension in Bogota, but its warnings needed the authorization of the U.S. ambassador to Colombia to be dispatched. Thus, the real fault, Hillenkoetter implied, lay with the State Department. As the State Department was already in the early stages of a congressional investigation for supposed communist activities, both relatively friendly CIA outlets like *Time* and CIA critics like the *Chicago Tribune* focused their criticism on the State Department.[94] In the course of investigations into the State Department and the dismissal of several department members for alleged communist sympathies, however, several CIA employees were also caught up in charges of disloyalty and dismissed.[95]

Though the CIA avoided the lion's share of criticism, the imbroglio did present a view of the agency as weak and ineffectual, unable to act effectively in the Washington bureaucracy. In the aftermath, one congressman proposed the creation of a joint intelligence committee, which would have led to the kind of congressional oversight the CIA wished to avoid; that proposal ultimately went nowhere.[96] This weakness was an opportunity for proponents of CIA reform. In the fall of 1948, two reports, one from Ferdinand Eberstadt and another from the joint effort of Dulles, William Harding Jackson, and Mathias Correa, highlighted CIA weakness and advocated changes to make the agency more effective. Baldwin had been a part of the Eberstadt committee and was referred to by the CIA as one of the "most inquisitive members" of the group.[97] The Dulles-Jackson-Correa committee proved more important over the long term. Its report was critical of the agency's coordination abilities and concluded that the intelligence community was not led by the CIA or, apparently, anyone. Dulles, who was most responsible for the review of the CIA's operations, advised that collection of intelligence, both open and covert, and the conduct of secret operations, be carried out within the same division of the CIA.[98]

The report's recommendations were foreshadowed when Baldwin publicly returned to the topic of intelligence in a five-part series in the summer of 1948. He began with the pronouncement that intelligence "was one of the weakest links in our national security." Mentioning the review under way by Dulles as a good sign, Baldwin blamed the bulk of the CIA's problems on the lack of cooperation by the other members of the intelligence community, especially the FBI. Baldwin, however, cast doubt on the CIA's excuse that it had warned the State Department about the possibility of a problem in Bogota.[99] Baldwin proffered the same solution as he had in *Price of Power*, that the CIA needed to develop a civilian intelligence bureaucracy.[100] Though Baldwin never directly mentioned the Veterans of Strategic Services, his consistent argument that what the CIA really needed was an experienced intelligence bureaucracy left supporters of intelligence with only the VSS as a real avenue to which to turn.

In his final article in the series, Baldwin articulated a new development in his thinking on intelligence activities. He emphasized that the CIA could, and in his opinion should, be the chief conductor of "secret operations" in the Cold War in addition to being the authority on "secret intelligence." He argued that the CIA would be especially valuable at running "black" radio stations that would broadcast propaganda into the Soviet Bloc. While arguing for this stronger, active role, however, Baldwin also warned that an effective watchdog would be needed to keep the CIA in check. After his series was completed, Baldwin would return to the topic to highlight the problems he saw with intelligence arrangements and support Dulles's reform efforts.[101]

As someone with his own intelligence-related sources, Stewart Alsop readily discerned who was giving information to Baldwin; it was "obviously Allen Dulles." Stewart Alsop, by the summer of 1948, had begun editorial work for the *Saturday Evening Post;* he was responsible for contributing story ideas every week. Inspired by Baldwin's series, he recommended that the *Saturday Event Post* follow the *Times*'s lead and prepare a story on the CIA. "People are always interested in intelligence," Alsop noted. They should seek first Dulles, or, failing him, Baldwin, to write the article.[102] Martin Sommers was not sold on the idea, as he found Baldwin's series "some of the dullest he had ever done."[103]

Baldwin had, by 1948, moved into the camp of those who supported a more aggressive CIA. Many of that camp were, like Baldwin, associated with Dulles. This camp saw the agency's current activities as a failure to live up to its full potential as a Cold War weapon. Those who had sought to apply a different standard to the CIA, one that sought a more restrained role for intelligence, had been undermined by the apparent weakness of the CIA's evaluative capacities and its inability to establish a strong position for itself in the federal bureaucracy.

These currents of discussion led to one immediate change in the CIA. In May 1949 Congress passed an intelligence bill to strengthen the CIA, providing the agency with its own budget.[104] Hillenkoetter remained DCI, despite a flurry of rumors in the *Washington Post* that he was retiring.[105] Hillenkoetter apparently did make known later, however, that he wanted to resign as DCI and return to a naval command. Though he had a line of communication with Hillenkoetter, Joseph Alsop was glad of the change because he remained convinced the agency could and should be more active. He wrote to Sommers that "the intention now [that Hillenkoetter will be out] is to step up the whole CIA effort, with special emphasis on what [the future *National Review* editor James] Burnham called political-subversive warfare. Thus CIA will become a vital important cold war instrument."[106] He advocated again for an intelligence story.

Sommers, however, was frustrated with the CIA and Hillenkoetter. While there was some back-and-forth, Sommers felt that "we have never been able to get any kind of clearance on material which would put meat on the bones of an article. . . . We do not recommend any writer going ahead on this one unless he is firmly promised a reasonable amount of cooperation."[107] Before plans could advance further, however, a new crisis broke out in June 1950: the Korean War.

The Korean War was a severe shock to the American leadership and public, exponentially worse than the *Bogotazo*. Questions about whether the CIA should have provided better warning emerged quickly after the North Koreans crossed the 38th parallel. Drew Pearson wrote that the CIA had reported immediately before war broke out that the world was at its most peaceful state in some time. Baldwin, though more charitable than Pearson, listed intelligence as one of a host of U.S. errors in Korea. The *Chicago Tribune* reported that there had been an *Izvestia* article essentially announcing that the invasion would take place that had been entirely ignored by the CIA. Calls arose for a congressional investigation of the CIA.[108] As he had after the *Bogotazo,* Hillenkoetter tried to defend the CIA by appealing to institutional restrictions. Hillenkoetter incorrectly claimed that the CIA was charged only with collating intelligence, not analyzing it.

The CIA was not blamed across the entire press. For example, a *Time* article explained that no troop buildup could be detected because the border had apparently been so permanently prepared for war. This explanation was a poor defense, though, because it meant the CIA was being outpaced in a dangerous world situation.[109] Hillenkoetter's and *Time*'s excuses implicitly admitted to Congress and the U.S. public that the CIA had no capability to spy within the Soviet Union or China. Shortly after the invasion, Hillenkoetter left office as DCI. Having wanted to resign anyway, no doubt Hillenkoetter was at least partly glad when he finally left the agency.

The CIA under Smith

Walter Bedell Smith replaced Hillenkoetter as DCI in October 1950. Smith was a very different kind of leader from Hillenkoetter. His experience as Eisenhower's chief of staff during World War II led him to appreciate solid organization and the benefits of occasionally letting loose his explosive temper on those who displeased him. Smith, in addition to having been

Eisenhower's chief of staff, was also a former ambassador to Moscow. Unlike Hillenkoetter, he had built up a reputation with the press, and he had been positively portrayed by many of the East Coast mainstream press institutions. He had even published part of his account of his time in Moscow in the *New York Times*.[110] The *New York Times, Los Angeles Times,* and *Washington Post* greeted Smith's appointment with enthusiasm.[111] The *Chicago Tribune,* which had long blamed Smith for negligence at Pearl Harbor, simply did not comment.[112]

Smith also brought into the CIA some of the veterans of the OSS, such as William Jackson and, most notably, Allen Dulles. Dulles served first as deputy director for plans, and later as Smith's deputy director. Dulles would eventually replace Smith as DCI and play a vital role in shaping the agency into the kind of aggressive, active organization he had long desired. Despite his connections with the press, Smith took a limited view on working with the press while he was DCI.[113] He succeeded in preventing the CIA from being dragged further into the public spotlight. After the Chinese attacked across the Yalu River into Korea, the main press attention was on issues with MacArthur's G-2 rather than the CIA, as MacArthur had reportedly excluded the agency from his area of command.

Stewart Alsop was heartened by the news coming from the CIA after Smith took over. In November Alsop observed enthusiastically that "the Smith-Jackson regime in the CIA is pretty rapidly giving the country what we have never had before, a professional intelligence service." Alsop thought the national estimates system being set up under Sherman Kent demonstrated that Smith had the right ideas.[114] Kent, a historian and a veteran of the OSS, came into the agency first as a deputy and then as leader of the Office of National Estimates. Part of a broader system of improving intelligence analysis and dissemination, Kent's office put out the National Intelligence Estimates, which collated information gathered by both overt and covert means. The estimates made the CIA's intelligence accessible and comprehensible to policy makers while incorporating dissenting views, and they helped strengthen the CIA's contribution to providing a useful, strategic intelligence outlook. Stewart Alsop urged Sommers once again to focus an article on the CIA.

Previous failed efforts at a story still frustrated Sommers. He felt nothing could be done without considerable cooperation from intelligence officials, and he complained, "Cooperation was promised again and again, only to evaporate." He was willing to investigate the possibility, especially in light of the fact that the *Post*'s editor Ben Hibbs had met Smith and thought that Smith might be open to cooperation. Sommers agreed to have the Alsops sound out Smith but made no commitments.[115] Stewart Alsop agreed to go ahead only if they could get "a certain amount of inside dope, semi-secret stuff." They would approach both Smith and Jackson.[116]

For whatever reason, though, Ben Hibbs seems to have misread Smith, or Smith changed his mind. Joseph Alsop's proposal of cooperation with Jackson was shot down, and discussions with Smith never reopened. Joseph Alsop had made the argument for cooperation with Jackson at one of his dinner parties. As he had with Byrnes, he wrote to Jackson to explain in more detail his rationale for leaking. He defended again the idea that "responsible newspapermen" could be relied on to be discreet while providing an outlet for "hard fact, concrete fact" that would influence public opinion. Alsop assured Jackson that cooperation would not mean a standing relationship. Jackson responded that, while he respected Alsop's opinion, he felt he could not, in his present position, make a decision about which classified information might be entrusted to a reporter.[117] Rather than a CIA effort to influence public opinion, under Smith's leadership it was people outside the CIA who most wanted to shape public opinion of the agency.

While not establishing a relationship with the Alsops or the *Saturday Evening Post,* Smith's CIA did keep an eye on what was being written about it. For example, several CIA staff memoranda from the summer of 1951 indicate some CIA officers were concerned with a forthcoming article by Drew Pearson in his syndicated column that offered a negative evaluation of the CIA. A CIA officer met with Pearson over lunch and managed to get him to soften his criticism.[118] Some members of the contentious *Chicago Tribune* were even more cooperative. An unnamed reporter from the *Tribune* asked a CIA officer if the CIA would mind of he wrote a story that included the full name of the OPC; the CIA requested this not be done, and the *Tribune* complied.[119]

The most dangerous possibility for the CIA was being blamed for failing in Korea, but the agency was helped by press attitudes toward Douglas MacArthur, who had alienated many in the press with his imperious nature. Joseph Alsop had, in 1948, tried to get Sommers to allow him to write an anti-MacArthur story, only for Sommers to inform him that Baldwin was preparing a similar story that was based on years of building up evidence.[120]

MacArthur's actions in Korea once the war broke out did nothing to endear him further to the press. In his role as commander of United Nations forces in Korea, MacArthur refused to initiate a press censorship system like the one that had been developed during World War II. Censorship depended on the judgment of individual officers and was, supposedly, reliant on good judgment from reporters. The press, however, did not greet this apparently liberal policy warmly because in the absence of a formal system, censorship became arbitrary. MacArthur's one rule was that "unwarranted criticism" would not be permitted, but it was not clear what counted as unwarranted criticism.[121] The situation was so frustrating for reporters that by early 1951 correspondents were calling for a censorship code, preferably the one that had been in effect during World War II.[122]

The focus on MacArthur helped the CIA. Despite positive developments from Smith's tenure, however, several reports emerged concerning the CIA's activities. The *New York Times* reporter James Reston alleged that millions had been spent on activities behind the Iron Curtain that included subversion, and that the CIA had spent a considerable amount of money in the 1948 Italian election. The CIA also became embroiled in an early McCarthyite investigation.[123] Eventually, some of the smaller stories ended up collated in the editorial "Choice and Chance" in January 1953 that was mentioned at the beginning of this chapter. Though barely causing notice in 1953, reporting on the actual activities of the CIA, not just on its structure, would soon be more widespread.

The CIA, and intelligence issues more broadly, never truly dominated public discussion during the Truman administration. Intelligence reporting in periodicals such as the *Saturday Evening Post* and *Life* was limited. Newspaper coverage of intelligence matters was considerably more regular, but not a single story involving the CIA appeared on the front page of the *New York Times, Washington Post, Chicago Tribune,* or *Los Angeles Times* during that time.

While modest, though, press coverage of the CIA ought to be considered as part of the general environment in which the U.S. intelligence system evolved. The public lens under which the CIA was created constrained some of its options for development. There were advocates for a limited system, either because of fear of abuses of power, as seen in the *Chicago Tribune,* or from a genuine belief in the need to give precedence to intelligence gathering over operations, as was the case with Walter Smith. The intense Cold War environment countered fears of abuse. Advocates of intelligence gathering were stymied by the tendency of the press to criticize when any event harmful to U.S. interests occurred. Burdened by the unrealistic expectation of predicting everything, the CIA needed positive action to demonstrate its worth.

Positive action was exactly what men like Allen Dulles and Frank Wisner had in mind. Veterans of the OSS, who had believed in Donovan's model for intelligence, had continued work that advocated for their intelligence model even while initial decisions over intelligence did not go their way. They also did not face real pushback on covert action because, with a few isolated exceptions, the press was generally willing to ignore the CIA's operations, including disasters in Eastern Europe.

This period also demonstrates the origins of some of the types of relationships between the press and the CIA. Reporters like Baldwin and the Alsops came to contact and cooperate with intelligence officers and veterans. Institutions such as the *Saturday Evening Post,* which would be useful in the future to the CIA, had their first contacts with the intelligence system. The *New York Times* continued a cautious stance on reporting U.S. Cold War activities that carried over from the days of the Second World War. The *Washington Post* adopted a standard similar to the *New York Times*'s.

The CIA's structure and its relationships with the press were still in their early stages between the CIA's creation in 1947 and Allen Dulles's appointment as DCI in 1953. The tilt toward the CIA as an aggressive, expansive, professional service, however, was aided both by early, personal relationships with the press and by the willingness of the press to keep quiet about the CIA's activities in the world.

2

Allen Dulles and Covert Intervention

Though it had improved since Hillenkoetter's departure, by the summer of 1954, the CIA's public position remained challenging.[1] Joseph McCarthy threatened that the CIA would be investigated. That May the CIA was blamed for failing to predict the fall of the French fortress at Dien Bien Phu. Senator Mike Mansfield (Democrat of Montana) proposed a bill to establish a Joint Committee on Intelligence, which would function much like the Atomic Energy Commission and empower congressional oversight of the agency, something the CIA sought assiduously to avoid. Though Mansfield's proposal was defeated, in early June, Hanson Baldwin returned to commenting on intelligence with an article that supported Mansfield's efforts and called for greater congressional oversight of the CIA.[2]

Baldwin argued that oversight of the CIA was needed because of its publicly mixed record and its high budget, which Baldwin estimated to be $1 billion. He saw the Mansfield proposal as a way to bring much-needed oversight to the CIA while avoiding a disastrous McCarthyite hearing. Baldwin also criticized Allen Dulles for opposing the bill. While acknowledging the need for secrecy, Baldwin warned that "secrecy, unless somehow scrutinized, can breed inefficiency or danger to a democracy."[3]

Dulles wrote to Baldwin to reject the assertion that he and the CIA had opposed Mansfield's proposal. Dulles also defended himself from accusations that the CIA had not predicted the fall of Dien Bien Phu. Dulles informed Baldwin, "While there was no formal estimate when Dien Bien Phu would fall, our current appraisals as to that situation, viewed now from hindsight, were reasonably accurate."[4]

His position on the Mansfield proposal and the CIA's predictions on Dien Bien Phu aside, Dulles informed Baldwin that the "most serious and frankly damaging misstatement in your article relates to our annual budget." Dulles said the estimate was incorrect, though he acknowledged that the CIA's decision not to publicize its budget meant such misinformation was inevitable. Dulles added: "It is only because I respect your judgment and enjoy and profit by your writings that I have felt justified in commenting on your article in this detail. Naturally, it is purely personal, as I do not wish to get into public print on the subject."[5] Despite Dulles's assertion that his comments were for Baldwin's personal consumption only, his effort to persuade Baldwin that Baldwin's reporting on the CIA was flawed had clear implications for the coverage of the agency.

Baldwin stressed to Dulles his desire to be fair and accurate, but he also reiterated that he "had some worries about the growing police power of the FBI and . . . other secret agencies of the government like the CIA." While believing in the importance of such agencies, Baldwin wanted oversight in the system. Baldwin also asked permission to use Dulles's statements in an article.[6] Dulles explained to Baldwin that he wanted Baldwin to redress the issue of the budget, but not Dien Bien Phu.

Dulles's correspondence reveals his priorities where the public image of the CIA was concerned, as he seems to have realized that blame was inevitable for events such as the fall of Dien Bien Phu. The CIA had faced similar charges after the crisis in Bogota and the North Korean attack. Concerns over the budget, though, could lead to actual, practical action to curtail the agency. Dulles suggested that Baldwin cite a "responsible government source" and explain that "the actual amount of the expenditure was only a fraction" of what Baldwin had written. An article released by the *Times* several weeks later on the CIA scaled back the highest estimate of the agency's budget to half of Baldwin's original.[7]

It was only a modest achievement for Dulles; the Mansfield proposal had already been temporarily defeated, so Baldwin's support on that question was inconsequential for the moment. Mansfield, however, would be seen as a persistent threat to the CIA's independence.[8] The episode revealed Dulles's approach to the press: solicitous, friendly, and drawing on personal connections. This approach achieved significant early success. In the initial years of his tenure as DCI, Dulles enjoyed one of the friendliest media environments the CIA ever experienced.

The CIA under Allen Dulles

Allen Dulles was appointed to be the director of Central Intelligence in February 1953. Dulles was the logical choice for the position; he enjoyed a reputation, which he had to some extent crafted himself, as one of the great spymasters of World War II for his work for the OSS in Switzerland. Beyond this reputation, Allen Dulles, like his brother, John Foster Dulles, had been expected from a young age to play a major role in determining the United States' role in the world.

Allen Dulles was born in April 1893 in upstate New York, near Watertown, in the Adirondack Mountains. Both Allen and John followed the example of their maternal grandfather, former Secretary of State John Foster.[9] Both the Dulles brothers attended Princeton University; Allen Dulles would maintain strong ties with the university for the rest of his life. He enrolled in 1910; among his classmates were the future policy makers James Forrestal and Ferdinand Eberstadt.[10] At Princeton, Allen established a reputation as a more charming, entertaining man than his dour older brother. His social graces proved useful in his professional life, as he often made use of private connections for professional purposes.

Dulles had an eclectic early career, but all his various activities spoke to his interest in the world outside the United States. After graduating in 1914, he traveled internationally, teaching in India and visiting China. He joined the Foreign Service shortly before the United States entered World War I, and he served in Bern, Switzerland, during the remainder of the war. After the war, he left the Foreign Service, obtained a law degree, and in 1926 joined the law firm Sullivan and Cromwell, which focused on international law. Dulles also joined the Council on Foreign Relations (CFR), becoming one of its directors in 1927.

Dulles's combination of the personal and the professional can best be seen in his relationship to his fellow Princeton alumnus and CFR member Hamilton Fish Armstrong, the long-serving editor of the CFR-published *Foreign Affairs*. The two first met when Dulles returned home in 1915. Armstrong was a friend and frequent collaborator. In 1954, early in his tenure as director, Dulles provided Armstrong with a list of some of his "own people in Iran" in order to allow Armstrong to prepare an article for *Foreign Affairs*. When a 1958 article in the *National Review* contained information that might have been leaked from a "Council" meeting, presumably referring to the CFR, Armstrong offered to assist in discovering the leak.[11] Armstrong became one of the Princeton Consultants, a group of experts from government and universities who met annually to serve as a think tank for the CIA. Armstrong was involved at least as early as 1954. Armstrong was held in high regard as a consultant, and Abbott Smith, the CIA contact with the group, asked him to advise on the membership of each meeting.[12]

Intelligence was a natural route for Dulles to take, enmeshed as he was in international law and CFR affairs, once the United States entered World War II. Shortly after the attack on Pearl Harbor, Dulles joined the OSS and was dispatched to Switzerland. There he would spend the rest of the war conducting intelligence activities against the Nazis. Most famous was Operation Sunrise, discussed in the last chapter. Sunrise was one of the stories Dulles used to bolster his own reputation and that of the OSS.

Dulles returned to full-time intelligence work in 1951, when Walter Smith asked him to join the CIA. Smith sought to place Frank Wisner's OPC firmly under CIA control, and he appointed Dulles to be the chief of the CIA's Directorate of Plans, which Smith had formed to govern the OPC and the secret intelligence-gathering OSO. While not as reckless as Wisner, Dulles shared Wisner's enthusiasm for covert action against the Soviets. He was dubbed the "Great White Case Officer" of the CIA.[13]

By the time Dulles was appointed DCI in 1953, the CIA had decisively tilted its focus toward covert action against the Soviet Union. The National Security Council had already approved NSC-68, which called for a more intense Cold War effort, and NSC 10/5, which expanded the operations of previously established covert-action organizations and called for an intensification of covert activities. These decisions privileged the CIA's covert-action arm. In 1952 the OPC employed 2,812 personnel, operated forty-seven overseas bases, and had a budget of $82 million; this was 60 percent of the CIA's personnel and 74 percent of its budget.[14] The new president did not check this growth in 1953; Eisenhower was also enthusiastic for covert operations.[15] Dulles embraced his new role. Even after the Korean War ended, he continued to promote aggressive covert action.

Dulles was also concerned with how he and his agency were viewed by the press. Soon after Dulles became DCI, Joseph McCarthy began to pose a serious threat. The Wisconsin senator had begun to criticize the CIA the previous year, after a CIA officer, William Bundy, had donated money to the Alger Hiss defense fund. Dulles refused to fire Bundy and resisted

McCarthy's proposed probes. Press support for the CIA in its feud with McCarthy was limited. The paper most likely to write about the feud was the *Chicago Tribune,* which entirely supported McCarthy. Robert McCormick instructed his editorial page writers that they should "upon every suitable occasion get [the] back of McCarthy."[16]

Dulles had moved to establish a base of CIA support before McCarthy's threats. While still deputy director under Smith, Dulles met with Philip Graham of the *Washington Post* to discuss keeping an open line of communication on stories that might touch on the CIA.[17] After he became DCI, Dulles kept himself available as a resource for reporters like Arthur Krock.[18] As mentioned before, Dulles had a strong relationship with Hanson Baldwin; he also was on good terms with Henry Luce, Arthur Hays Sulzberger, and the syndicated columnist Walter Lippmann.[19]

Dulles's communications with these figures in the press ranged in subject matter. For some, such as Sulzberger and Lippmann, they dealt mainly with personal matters. Dulles would write to others, as he had to Baldwin over the budget, to defend the CIA if he felt a story needed correcting. He sent a gentle note to Marquis Childs, for example, protesting a story that claimed the CIA was compiling internal surveys on the United States; he explained this would be against the CIA's charter and so was not done.[20] With less well-established reporters, Dulles could be more confrontational, such as when he demanded from an editor an explanation for why one of the editor's reporters had called for an investigation of the CIA.[21]

Dulles also met with reporters off the record. While there are only a few definitive accounts of such meetings, they suggest the briefings occurred regularly. As early as April 1953, he gave a background talk at the Overseas Writers' Luncheon. According to the *Times* reporter Walter Waggoner, Dulles began by explaining the differences between the U.S. and British intelligence systems, noting that the U.S. system could never enjoy the anonymity that the British one did. Dulles then explained the origin and function of the CIA and complimented the press on being a valuable source of open information. He assured his audience that the CIA did not use newspapermen to conduct intelligence activities; this point was important enough to Waggoner that he wrote it capitalized as "THEY DO NOT USE NEWSPAPERMEN" in his notes on the talk.[22] This pledge was disingenuous.

Dulles's use of the press was not just the result of self-interest. There is no reason to doubt that Dulles was, ultimately, a true believer in an active role for the United States in the world. Throughout his career, his interests were international in nature. His advocacy in the VSS, his participation in the survey of the CIA, and his work in the CFR all demonstrate Dulles's genuine commitment to an effective intelligence organization. Dulles was extremely useful to the intelligence cause, as he was willing to use his extensive personal connections to further his goal. Dulles was also clearly willing, though, to use those same connections to further his own interests. Throughout his advocacy for Donovan's intelligence ideal, he had also burnished his own reputation with reports of his activities in World War II. It is unlikely that he saw any conflict between the promotion of the CIA and the promotion of his own reputation.

Dulles also supported the CIA's ongoing efforts to influence opinion in foreign nations, including allies, through use of the press and international, liberal organizations. He supported a proposal by Thomas Braden to centralize the agency's efforts to counter Soviet propaganda and furnish a consistent U.S. message. The International Organizations Division coordinated front groups, contacts with labor unions, groups like the Congress for Cultural Freedom, CIA-funded publications such as *Encounter,* and more. Braden became the head of this new division.[23]

Braden's deputy and eventual successor, Cord Meyer Jr., was in many ways emblematic of the new men being brought into the agency. Born in Washington, D.C., in 1920, Meyer went to St. Paul's School in Connecticut and graduated from Yale. Enlisting in the marine corps during World War II, Meyer lost an eye to a Japanese grenade on Guam. After he returned to civilian life, Meyer supported world federalism as a way to avoid violent conflict in the future, and he hoped that the United Nations would emerge as a strong governing world body.[24]

Increasingly disillusioned with world federalism because of the growing Cold War, Meyer initially sought a job in academia. Finding a challenging job market, eventually Meyer sought work in the government, contacting, among others, Allen Dulles, who was happy to find a place for the young man.[25] Meyer would go on to be an effective communicator of the agency's message. In addition to his formal duties with the International Organizations Division, Meyer followed the lead of other CIA officers and developed ongoing contacts with reporters and journalists, such as James Truitt at *Newsweek* and John Fischer at *Harper's Magazine.*[26] Fischer's contact demonstrates especially the mutually beneficial relationships between reporters and

CIA officers. Before a trip to Yugoslavia in 1961, Fischer sought Meyer's assistance with background material. Meyer was happy to oblige; for example, when providing the information to Fischer, he noted, "My associates here are naturally quite interested in your trip and would like very much to see you before you go and after you return."[27] Whether or not Fischer was asked to look for specific things or carry out any tasks before going to Yugoslavia is unclear. Cooperation, though, clearly suited both Fischer's and Meyer's interests. In such a way, Dulles, Meyer, and others like them built support for the agency as it cemented itself in the national security establishment.

The CIA Intervention in Iran

Long an advocate of covert action, Dulles had an opportunity to prove its worth shortly into his tenure, as Eisenhower decided to support British desires in Iran and authorized the CIA to covertly overthrow the nationalist Iranian government of Mohammad Mossadegh of Iran. Kermit Roosevelt of the CIA was dispatched in the summer of 1953 to help organize joint American-British activities against Mossadegh in Operation TPAJAX.

U.S. coverage of the Anglo-Iranian dispute tended to favor the British. Joseph and Stewart Alsop's columns especially reflected the Eisenhower administration's belief that Iran was on the verge of collapse. In March they portrayed Mossadegh as a would-be dictator who caused chaos in his country by attacking a genuinely popular monarch, the shah. The Alsops argued that the "pacification" of Iran was needed to secure order in Middle East.[28] The Alsops' views on the situation in Iran might have been influenced by the fact that Kermit Roosevelt was their cousin. Joseph Alsop had in fact introduced Roosevelt to William Donovan in 1941, thereby beginning Roosevelt's intelligence career.[29]

Events in Iran came to a head in August 1953. The shah fled the country on 16 August, after his attempt to dismiss Mossadegh failed. As many in Tehran protested against the shah, Roosevelt hired agents to enter crowds of the Tudeh (communist) Party and vandalize both statues of the shah and mosques. During street clashes on 19 August, the army remained loyal to the shah and placed Mossadegh in custody. The shah returned to Tehran on 22 August in triumph, and Fazlollah Zahedi was then installed as premier.[30] In the days leading up to the toppling of Mossadegh, Allen Dulles was in Zurich to keep an eye on the situation in Iran from a closer vantage point. While his travels were publicized, the reasons for those travels were not; the *Times* reported on Dulles's trip to Zurich on 10 August as a summer holiday.[31]

The U.S. press generally welcomed the fall of Mossadegh.[32] Reporters did not challenge the assertion that Mossadegh had been tilting toward communism, and initially none deviated from the story that the United States had put international pressure on Mossadegh but had played no direct role in his fall.[33] Joseph Fromm, of *U.S. News and World Report,* remembered years later that when reporters suggested to CIA officials they knew in Tehran that the CIA was involved, the CIA men laughed and dismissed the idea out of hand.[34] Even leftist periodicals did not express suspicion that the United States had intervened in Iran.[35] An article in the *Progressive* titled "The Curious Capers of the CIA," which criticized the CIA's attempts to remain free of public scrutiny, made no mention of potential activities in Iran.[36] References to a CIA role in Iran did not emerge until the fall of 1954, and these were minor and attracted little attention.[37] *Time* magazine, which reported on Iran fairly consistently, did so in ethnocentric terms; as John Foran observes, *Time* and the U.S. government both "drew on and contributed to Orientalist discourses."[38] This coverage helped establish the positive public reception to Mossadegh's fall.

Some prominent journalists were not in the dark about the operation, although they did not report on events in Iran. The Alsops knew what had happened and drew on that knowledge in making recommendations in their articles on how to deal with Gamal Nasser during the Suez crisis.[39] Joseph Alsop informed his editor that John Foster Dulles had wanted to call off the intervention, but Allen Dulles had been more decisive. As a result, "the tanks were in the streets when the telegram ordering the American revolution to halt reached our embassy there." Alsop did not explain the source of his information. Given its pro-CIA, pro–Allen Dulles slant, it is likely that the account came from one of Alsop's contacts in the CIA, though that is conjecture. Regardless of the source, Alsop did not think such stories should be reported. "Obviously, the real story cannot and should not be written."[40]

Henry Luce also had some possible direct knowledge of U.S. involvement, though it is less clear than Joseph Alsop's obvious knowledge. One of his staffers reported to him in September 1953 that there were differences between the new prime minister, Fazlollah Zahedi, and the shah. The shah suffered "from a 'deep complex' that he was called back only because his people love him." In reality, "60–70% of the people of Iran are still Pro-Mossadegh and the Shah's impractical attitude created a difficult and dangerous situation."[41] The source of this information was a member of the American Friends of the Middle East (AFME), which received support from the CIA and acted as a front for agency funding.[42] Luce and his staff also appear to have had some knowledge of the AFME's connections; when some questions arose about possible disreputable contacts AFME had, the Time-Life staff went directly to Allen Dulles for his opinion.[43]

From the CIA's point of view, intervention in Iran had been enormously successful, and it heralded further CIA intervention. When Kermit Roosevelt returned from Iran and briefed Foster and Allen Dulles, he reported that Foster was "alarmingly enthusiastic" about the success of TPAJAX. Roosevelt declined an offer to follow up on his success with a similar operation in Guatemala.[44]

CIA Intervention in Guatemala

The Dulleses contemplated action in Guatemala because of U.S. concerns with the direction of Guatemalan political reforms following the ouster of the dictator Jorge Ubico in 1944. The democratic governments of Juan José Arévalo and Jacobo Arbenz Guzmán disquieted the United States because they tried to rein in U.S.-based companies, primarily the United Fruit Company (UFC), used the services of communists in their government, and applied communist or socialist solutions to Guatemala's social and economic problems. Tensions increased when Arbenz's land-reform program of April 1952 greatly affected the UFC.[45] The company ran an anti-Arbenz media campaign, spearheaded by a veteran press relations specialist, Edward Bernays, beginning in January 1953. Bernays was generally successful in mobilizing reporters, especially from the *New York Times,* against Arbenz.[46]

The public U.S. position was explicitly anti-Arbenz. In March 1954 John Foster Dulles personally attended the Organization of American States conference in Caracas, Venezuela, to urge the adoption of a resolution against the introduction of communism to South America. Though Guatemala was not named specifically in the resolution, it was obviously the target. In May the United States revealed that Arbenz had purchased Czech arms, which it cited as proof that Arbenz's government was communist.

As the public campaign against Guatemala proceeded, the CIA prepared Operation PBSUCCESS. While future critics of the CIA cast the operation as a rogue activity, Eisenhower was clearly aware and deeply involved.[47] The agency would covertly support Colonel Carlos Castillo Armas in his campaign to overthrow Arbenz. Following a victory, Armas's coup would be explained as the will of the Guatemalan people. Castillo Armas had spent his adult life in the Guatemalan army. He attended Guatemala's military academy and later received training at Fort Leavenworth. In 1950 Castillo Armas had first sought to rebel against President Arévalo. Imprisoned after the attempt failed, Castillo Armas escaped prison and became active in expatriate Guatemalan circles opposed to the post-Ubico reforms to Guatemalan society. He was apparently identified as a potential American partner by a public relations specialist hired by United Fruit.[48]

In early June 1954 Castillo Armas publicly launched an invasion of Guatemala from exile to play his role in PBSUCCESS. Castillo Armas had few men under his command, and his invasion quickly faltered. Arbenz's minister to the United Nations called for U.N. intervention and accused the United States of conducting the operation.[49] In an effort to stave off defeat, Eisenhower authorized the limited use of aircraft against Arbenz. Attacking at night, the aircraft seemed much more numerous than they were and indicated a level of opposition that the Guatemalan military was unwilling to face on behalf of Arbenz. He was forced to resign on 27 June, and, after a brief interlude, Castillo Armas gained power.[50]

The operation had been plagued with security breaches, and the general belief outside the United States was that Castillo Armas had been able to succeed only with U.S. help.[51] This was less apparent in mainstream U.S. publications, however.[52] This observation reflected the view widespread among the mainstream press that Arbenz's government was communist-controlled. Typical were assertions such as those of the columnist George Sokolsky, who condemned Guatemala as "the first 'people's republic' to have been established on the American continents."[53] The mainstream press also largely disputed accusations of U.S. complicity when they arose. Jules Dubois, a columnist for the *Chicago Tribune* based in Guatemala during the crisis, reported in May that some of the weapons being shipped to Guatemala included Lend-Lease weapons; Dubois explained that these weapons would be used to argue that the United States had been arming the opposition.[54] About a week after Arbenz resigned, *Life* explained that international communism was "efficiently using the Guatemalan show to strike a blow at the US" by trying to portray the United States as an aggressor.[55]

There were suggestions even at the time, however, that the United States had played a major role. James Reston, writing for the *New York Times*, remarked, "If somebody wants to start a revolution in, say, Guatemala, it is no good talking to Foster [Dulles]. But Allen Dulles, head of the Central Intelligence Agency, is a more active man." An op-ed published by the *Times* on 24 June criticized the lack of media coverage of Guatemala in light of Reston's comments. Reston acknowledged in a private letter later that summer that the *Times* "left out a great deal of what we knew about U.S. intervention in Guatemala."[56] In the *Los Angeles Times,* two reporters in separate stories suggested that the United States had played a covert role.[57]

This skepticism of the official story was not shared by all parts of the *Los Angeles Times,* as it was one of several papers that reported on the recovery of mutilated bodies apparently killed by the Arbenz government.[58] Dubois also wrote after Castillo Armas's victory that in the capital "a long line of persons filed past a row of mutilated bodies . . . to identify persons that the new government says were tortured to death by the leftist secret police."[59] Keith Monroe of *Harper's* was more graphic, describing photos shown to him after the ouster taken by members of Arbenz's government "apparently as a hobby." The pictures "show men under torture. The snapshots are murky, but even the dim images of those bloody, screaming, writhing figures are too clear."[60]

These reports were not accurate; Thomas McCann, the UFC press officer, would later admit that he provided pictures of bodies ostensibly slain by the Arbenz regime but which had died from unrelated incidents or by order of Castillo Armas.[61] It is unclear whether Monroe was aware of the inaccuracy. Dubois is likelier to have been a knowing cooperator owing to his contacts with Castillo Armas and the U.S. embassy in Guatemala.

Dubois was friendly in his public attitude toward the American ambassador to Guatemala, John Peurifoy.[62] He also seems to have had a clear idea of what was happening in Guatemala, at least in terms of U.S. involvement. Dubois knew Castillo Armas personally; Castillo Armas had been a student of his at Fort Leavenworth.[63] In a letter to Francis Corrigan, a longtime U.S. diplomat in Latin America, a reporter recounted meeting with Dubois at a dinner after the ouster of Arbenz. According to this reporter, "Jules was on hand about three days before Castillo attacked, since, he, of course, knew all about it before hand." Dubois also claimed that Peurifoy had told him either the army would take control in Guatemala or "we press a button, and Castillo moves in."[64]

Dubois was shocked that Peurifoy would be so careless, and he was apparently more concerned with keeping things quiet than Peurifoy himself was. The reporter recounting this meeting was assured that a correspondent with his publication had been "on top of the situation. . . . At the same time . . . [he] didn't stick his nose into things and, in general, acted with complete correctness."[65] Correctness, for Dubois, meant ignoring what exactly the United States was doing in Guatemala. Dubois kept his boss, Robert McCormick, informed of events in Guatemala, but there is no record that he informed McCormick of the U.S. government's involvement.[66]

McCormick did, however, hear reports to that effect. One acquaintance let him know that the revolution in Guatemala was probably supported by "the secret funds at the disposal of Bedell Smith and Allen Dulles."[67] Even if McCormick did not believe reports of CIA activity in Guatemala, that no hint or rumor of the CIA's actions appeared in the *Chicago Tribune* reflects a conscious decision on his part. McCormick was not a supporter of the CIA but felt that "it is essential that the Caribbean be an American lake to protect the Atlantic side of the Panama Canal for absolutely free communication in the Caribbean and to extend our military power as far south as possible."[68] McCormick was thus sympathetic to anti-Arbenz action.

The *Tribune* was hardly alone in its support for U.S. intervention in Guatemala. Several *Time* magazine reporters whose stories were rewritten to be more negative toward Arbenz later related that they believed the stories were rewritten because of CIA ties with Henry Luce and Time-Life.[69] Joseph Alsop knew what was happening in Guatemala because of his ties with the U.S. ambassador to Honduras.[70] When Stewart Alsop wrote to Sommers to suggest an article on the Swedish freighter that had taken arms to Guatemala, Sommers replied that such reporting would be "both too early and too late," as it was unclear how events in Guatemala would be resolved. Sommers thought, though, that it was "a pretty good bet that we'll play some dirty tricks via Nicaragua."[71] The CIA's actions in Guatemala remained secret to the U.S. public not because of good operational security, but because of the cooperation of the press. McCormick, the Alsops, and others did not have to be convinced not to report on the CIA's activities.

That lack of persuasive effort needed was not universal. In a now well-known case of CIA interference, Allen Dulles maneuvered the *Times* correspondent Sydney Gruson, whose reporting concerned the CIA, from being present in Guatemala during the coup.[72]

Gruson himself was accused on several occasions of being employed by dictators or communists to influence his reporting. He was sympathetic to Arbenz's land-reform program, but he was also an anticommunist and was eventually expelled from Guatemala for criticizing Arbenz. He urged his editor, Emanuel Freedman, to send someone to Guatemala, as he had heard rumors that some kind of U.S. activity was under way. He was skeptical, but he wrote that "it would be extremely f[r]ustrating and annoying, to say the least if, after all the attention we have paid the situation something were to pop and we had no one on the spot."[73]

While Gruson's sympathy for land reform distinguished him from many of his fellow U.S. reporters, it was his report that the people of Guatemala were "unequivocally" supportive of Arbenz's government that most strongly disturbed the CIA and State Department. Gruson knew that Peurifoy was angry with him over the article.[74] Frank Wisner was also concerned, as reports that Arbenz enjoyed popular support could discredit the cover story that Arbenz had been overthrown by popular Guatemalan action. Wisner questioned Gruson's sources and contrasted Gruson's criticism with writing in the *Washington Post* that was more supportive of U.S. foreign policy. Wisner suggested that "this matter be brought [to the] attention [of the] top hierarchy [of the] *New York Times*."[75]

At a private dinner, Allen Dulles informed Julius Adler, at the time general manager of the *New York Times* and a former Princeton classmate of Dulles's, that Gruson had questionable political connections. Gruson was vulnerable to such suggestions because he was not a native-born American; he was born in Dublin to a Lithuanian family, had immigrated to Canada as a boy, and traveled on a British passport issued by Warsaw. Dulles wrote to Adler on 3 June 1954 to obliquely confirm what he had privately related at their dinner. Dulles informed him of the passport information of "the person we discussed."[76]

Adler informed Sulzberger, who then responded by ordering that Gruson stay in Mexico City. Gruson was frustrated both by the fact that Mexico was obviously unrelated to the story and because he could not get a clear picture of what was happening in Guatemala.[77] Gruson's wife, the journalist Flora Lewis, remained in Guatemala City and worked with the *Times* reporter Paul Kennedy, but they were unable to get a more accurate picture of the situation than Gruson despite their location. When Gruson eventually reached his wife by phone, he was informed that if they spoke any language other than Spanish, they would be immediately disconnected.[78] Lewis, for her part, would eventually provide supportive coverage of Peurifoy, much as Dubois treated the U.S. ambassador.[79]

After the coup, Sulzberger apologized for having detained Gruson in Mexico City. He falsely claimed that he had "received a tip (which proved to be a false one) that Mexico City would be involved in the incident, and consequently I did not wish to leave it uncovered."[80] Sulzberger's apology letter was blind-copied to Allen Dulles, letting him know that Gruson would not learn from Sulzberger the reason he had been prevented from returning to Guatemala.

Sulzberger did, though, further investigate the matter of Gruson's supposedly problematic connections. Dulles responded to his queries cagily and claimed only to have wanted to alert Sulzberger to a potential problem. Dulles denied that he sought to dictate a course of action to Sulzberger, and he insisted, "We merely passed on to you information available to us."[81] By late July, Arthur Sulzberger believed that "there appeared to be very little substance to the objections to Gruson other than that he was known to be a liberal."

Sulzberger asked his cousin Cyrus Sulzberger, a *New York Times* correspondent, to approach Dulles to determine better whether there were any problems with Gruson. Cyrus Sulzberger was a natural choice, as he had been a foreign correspondent since the 1930s and had reported on the Balkans, the Middle East, and the Russian war effort in World War II, and in 1944 he was made the chief foreign correspondent of the *Times*. From his home in Paris, Cyrus Sulzberger established a wide network of connections.[82] He was named as a point of contact in the press by the CIA in the 1960s and would prove willing to brief members of the CIA on his travels; a CIA officer would later claim that the Paris-based Sulzberger accepted tasks handed down from the CIA, though Cyrus Sulzberger denied the charge.[83] These contacts apparently informed Cyrus Sulzberger that it was official antipathy, and not actual communist connections, that led to reports against Gruson. On the basis of his cousin's report, Arthur Sulzberger concluded, "Gruson was merely a good reporter and had antagonized some of our official representatives by publishing stories which they would rather not have seen printed." While regretful, Sulzberger kept the knowledge of what had happened close. The only people who knew the truth at the *Times* where Arthur and Cyrus Sulzberger, Adler, assistant managing editor Turner Catledge, Sulzberger's son-in-law, Orvil Dryfoos, and Sulzberger's secretary.[84]

Arthur Sulzberger's communications with Dulles were not his first brush with the world of intelligence. The former *Times* reporter Wayne Phillips revealed that in the early 1950s a CIA officer approached him with an offer of dual employment that would guarantee him a post in Moscow; Sulzberger apparently had told Phillips the CIA would be contacting him.[85] Sulzberger's actions, however, suggest ambivalence on his part about cooperation with the CIA. Sulzberger reportedly had stressed to Phillips that it was Phillips's choice whether to accept the CIA's offer, and that he preferred Phillips not make an agreement with the CIA. Once Carl Bernstein's allegations emerged in 1977, Sulzberger's son, Arthur "Punch" Sulzberger, *Times* managing editor Abraham "Abe" Rosenthal, and Gruson (then a *Times* vice president) investigated whether there was any accuracy to the allegations as part of their larger effort to determine the extent of CIA influence on the *Times*. Ultimately, they found nothing.[86] It is also suggestive that Dulles had to deceive Sulzberger about Gruson's questionable connections to gain his cooperation.

Frank Wisner remained concerned about Gruson's potential for causing problems after the coup. In the weeks following Arbenz's ouster, Gruson joined many of his colleagues in the press in writing that Arbenz was sympathetic to communists. Wisner believed that this reporting was only a smokescreen and was convinced that Gruson acted against U.S. interests. Wisner's suspicions were especially piqued because Gruson had tried to arrange a deal with Guatemala's foreign minister, Jorge Toriello, to reenter the country after he had been expelled. As Wisner saw it, "When the chips were down, [Gruson] was not only going all out in his reporting the Toriello-Arbenz line—he was going out of his way to support it." Wisner warned that "Gruson remains in my book a man to be watched."[87] Wisner was deeply paranoid, but his interpretation of Gruson's reporting as fundamentally threatening demonstrates recognition of the potential harm an unfriendly reporter might do to agency operations.

Press Coverage of the CIA during the Summer of 1954

Despite the CIA's success, there were countertrends to the general lack of reporting. Some publications were willing to write about the CIA's activities. Some of this kind of reporting consisted of circumspect references.[88] That September, the *Progressive* ran an explicit acknowledgment of the U.S. covert intervention, arguing that since the United States had used "the surgeon's knife of force, to cut out the cancer of Communism," foreign aid to Guatemala was a priority.[89]

Early, explicit accusations that the United States had secretly acted to overthrow Arbenz came mainly from the *Nation,* and, to a lesser degree, from the *New Republic,* though the CIA was still unknown enough that the charges tended to be against the United States in general, rather than the agency in particular. Julio Alvarez del Vayo, writing in the *Nation* during the conflict, condemned both Washington for its embargo on Guatemala and the UFC for its exploitative policies.[90] After the coup, his editor, Freda Kirchwey, was most explicit. She criticized the U.S. government for insisting that Arbenz was a communist and that his government was linked to the Soviet Union. Kirchwey refused to dismiss the charges of interference made by the Guatemalan government. She reported that some stories "credit the State Department and Central Intelligence Agency—both Messrs Dulles—with organizing and carrying through the political operation which dumped the Arbenz regime."[91]

The importance of stories disputing this mainstream narrative in the summer of 1954 is fairly negligible. They merit attention because they demonstrate the beginning of a larger leftist rejection of the CIA that, by the mid-1960s, would move beyond smaller journals to such organizations as the *New York Times* and the *Washington Post.*

Though the *Times* was not yet ready to publicly challenge the CIA in 1954, its senior management demonstrated greater wariness regarding CIA activities later that summer. On 20 July Otto John, the first head of Federal Republic of Germany's investigative Office for the Protection of the Constitution, disappeared. He reappeared a few days later in East Germany, claiming to have defected. The West German government suggested that John had not defected but had been lured over to East Berlin by a friend and then abducted by East German authorities.

Early reporting in the *New York Times* cast doubt on that theory. Tadeusz "Tad" Szulc, a young, Polish-born *Times* reporter who had joined the paper the previous year, wrote a front-page article titled "Bonn Aide's Defection Deliberate, U.S. Officials Who Knew Him Say."[92] Szulc, described by the *Times* reporter Harrison Salisbury as looking "like a secret agent," would go on to have a colorful career at the *Times* and as an independent reporter, during which he had contacts with the CIA. He would prove willing, after gaining an interview with Castro, to brief the CIA on the Cuban leader in 1960.[93]

Szulc was also perfectly willing to dispute the CIA. On the John case, other reporting by the *Times* supported him.[94]

Turner Catledge was very disturbed by the situation in Germany after seeing private reports from the *Times* reporter Meyer Srednick (M. S.) Handler. Catledge warned Sulzberger that, according to Handler, "[Germany] is 'crawling' with security operatives of the State Department, the Office of Central Intelligence and other investigative services of our government." Handler warned that this proliferation had reached absurd extremes, as "there are so many [security operatives], they spend a lot of their time investigating each other." Much less humorous to Catledge was the effect these secret agents could have on reporting. He wrote:

> More recently they seem to feel that it is part of the duty to investigate newspaper people and the sources of their information. . . . [Handler] has been approached by these operatives at various times in their efforts to spy on other newspapermen. He has reacted by refusing, I think quite rightly, to talk to any of these people. Unfortunately, it appears that certain newspapermen whose names he did not give me, have rather readily joined in this sort of business hoping to get, in return, certain sources of inside information. Another, and very alarming phase of it is that, according to Handler, some of these people are operating with "official" newspaper credentials.[95]

As the security services scrambled to protect themselves, bad news continued to emerge. The East Germans announced that they had captured three U.S. agents in East Berlin, presumably using information John had supplied. John then held a press conference explaining he had decided to defect, citing his concern with the number of former Nazis who had been entrusted with positions in the West German government.[96] John eventually returned to West Germany, claiming he had in fact been abducted; however, a West German court did not accept his explanations, and he was found guilty of treason.

The case of Otto John is important because of what the *New York Times* refused to do with the story: namely, to accede to a CIA request to support the notion that John had been abducted. James Reston expressed his concern with the CIA request in a memo sent out on 10 August to the *Times*'s senior management. As Reston saw it, there was a key difference between silence and cooperation. He wrote, "Since we are clearly in a form of warfare with the communist world it has not been difficult to ignore information which, if published, would have been valuable to the enemy."[97]

Reston was not willing to cooperate with the CIA on "speculative articles which may or may not be based on correct premises . . . without attribution." Reston highlighted the Otto John case as an example of this behavior by the CIA, remarking, "The CIA is, of course, very embarrassed by what happened in the John Case."[98] Reston noted that several articles, most notably some from the Alsops, had recently been published supporting the kidnapping narrative the West German government put forth. Reston did not want the *Times* second-guessing its reporters on location on the basis of reports of officials who refused any kind of attribution.[99]

Sulzberger agreed with Reston's concerns. He remarked, "We cannot permit ourselves knowingly to pull chestnuts out of the fire even for our own government or any administrative agency of it, if we know in advance that the chestnuts are no good." Sulzberger also agreed that "there are times when the Government is entitled to ask us not to use a particular story," but that the decision had to be made by the home office.[100]

The *Times*'s managers were especially wary of the CIA's using the press as a cover. A potential problem came up in September 1954, only a month after the decision to avoid CIA entanglement. Harold Milks, the bureau chief of the *New York Times*'s office in India, reported that a CIA officer was attempting to infiltrate the Associated Press office as a photojournalist. Milks warned that if the CIA used the press as a cover, it would "jeopardize the position of every American correspondent now working here, and I hope those in charge in Washington can be made to realize its dangers." Once the CIA officer in question was exposed, Milks warned, "no Indian would then be convinced of our objectivity."[101]

Milks wrote a letter to the U.S. ambassador to India, George V. Allen, complaining about the CIA's efforts to use the press in India. Milks told Allen that the "the practice of sending people into Europe as 'correspondents' has became so general that the [*New York Times*] is readying a series of stories exposing it. How stupid can we get?"[102] Milks's note of a potential series on the practice was probably a bluff; other *Times* documents do not refer to it, and it would have violated the unofficial policy of avoiding direct coverage of the CIA. The threat seems to have been effective, however, as Milks reported no further CIA efforts to use the *New York Times* as a cover in India.

This example serves to demonstrate the difficulty in attempting to view "the press" as a coherent entity, even among major newspapers, with regard to the CIA. Some, such as the Alsops and Jules Dubois, were apparently willing to publish deliberately false or misleading information in order to support the CIA's desired version of events. The *New York Times,* on the other hand, was unwilling, as an organization at least, to cooperate in this manner, and it sought to prevent any collaboration between reporters and the CIA. It was, however, willing to accept the notion that it ought at least to omit mention of the agency's involvement in incidents like Guatemala, given its understanding of the nature of the Cold War as a real kind of war.

After PBSUCCESS, 1954–1957

The anti-CIA strands notwithstanding, good press relations helped the CIA capitalize on its success in Guatemala. In October 1954 the husband-and-wife writing team Richard and Gladys Harkness revealed in the *Saturday Evening Post* that the CIA provided vital intelligence on a Czech arms shipment to Guatemala, helping stir the Guatemalan people against Arbenz.[103] The article was written with the knowledge and support of Allen Dulles.

Richard Harkness was mainly a television commentator for NBC, but he also occasionally wrote for periodicals such as the *Saturday Evening Post* and *U.S. News and World Report.* He and his wife wrote several pieces in the *Post* about the social scene of Washington, D.C., focusing on prominent people.[104] Harkness had been a booster of Dulles since the 1948 campaign trail, sponsoring him for the Gridiron dinner in Washington, D.C., and supporting him and his family on a morning talk show.[105]

It is unclear from their correspondence whether Dulles approached Harkness to write a story on the CIA's activities or vice versa. Regardless of who initiated contact, however, Dulles actively cooperated with the *Saturday Evening Post* on the story. The *Post's* editor Martin Sommers explained in a private letter that Dulles had given "full cooperation, and told his outfit to open most of the files" to the Harknesses.[106] Sommers, long dissatisfied with the access the CIA offered during its earlier unsuccessful efforts to generate a story, was satisfied with Dulles. The long-delayed *Saturday Evening Post* intelligence story thus finally came to fruition.

By early August 1954, a little over a month after Arbenz had been ousted, the Harknesses had written a draft and Dulles was coordinating with the

Post's photographer to set an appointment to take pictures for the article. Robert Fuss, managing editor of the *Saturday Evening Post,* sent drafts to Dulles, because "this was one story we wanted to be absolutely sure of." Harkness wrote to Dulles directly, explaining that the material Dulles had provided would be able to fill three articles. Harkness assured Dulles that they would include in the articles, as Dulles suggested, "a constructive quality by pointing out the Red gains through subversion, and the fact that CIA is the agency to combat those tactics."[107]

Such a constructive quality is evident in the three articles that ran 30 October, 6 November, and 13 November 1954. In addition to the Guatemala story, the Harknesses revealed that the overthrow of Mossadegh was "another CIA-influenced triumph." The third article was the most laudatory of Allen Dulles personally. The Harknesses wrote that Dulles was "a tough-minded, hardheaded, steel spring of a man with an aptitude and zest for matching wits with an unseen foe." The series ended with an appeal: "Whether the squeamish like it or not, the United States must know what goes on in those dark places of the world where our overthrow is being plotted by the communists."[108]

Dulles's cooperation was not revealed when the articles were published. Dulles specifically denied having made any contribution to the articles in a letter to a Princeton acquaintance. He commented that such charges were "based on a misunderstanding. I have no way of controlling the American press that is relatively free to print what it chooses. . . . I make it a practice to neither confirm nor deny press speculations about our organizations."[109] As Sommers later confirmed, however, this statement was false. Dulles certainly did not provide all the information available to the Harknesses, but the Harknesses and the *Saturday Evening Post* did have access to CIA files, or facsimiles thereof.

With this series Dulles was able to take credit for CIA successes while retaining deniability. Guatemala had been an operation that, in conjunction with the one in Iran, convinced many in Washington that the CIA was capable of carrying out successful anticommunist operations abroad without risking much to the United States.[110] The CIA's position seemed more secure than it had been at any time since its founding.

Dulles reinforced his victory by sending to David Lawrence of *U.S. News & World Reports* an exchange he had had with McCarthy during the summer. Dulles had written to McCarthy, asking that he be provided with any information McCarthy might have regarding subversion in the CIA. If McCarthy did have evidence to back up his claims, Dulles observed, he as director should be informed immediately so he could take steps to ensure the security of his agency. The timing of the letter is pertinent; it was sent in early July, when Dulles apparently decided to confront McCarthy directly following the success of Guatemala and his agency's strengthened reputation.[111]

Since the CIA's victories were publicly if unofficially celebrated, it is unsurprising that references to the two overthrows, most especially that in Guatemala, continued to emerge, which hadn't been the case with earlier CIA activities. In 1957, when Castillo Armas was assassinated, an author for the *New Republic* wrote that Castillo Armas had been chosen by the United States to replace Arbenz. Other periodicals behaved similarly, some as early as 1955.[112] This was true in newspapers as well. In 1958, for example, the *New York Times* reporter Russell Baker profiled the agency and explained, "It has been established . . . that the agency was behind Guatemala's 1954 revolution against the Americas' first communist regime."[113] The *Los Angeles Times's* Holmes Alexander, skeptical of U.S. actions in Guatemala at the time of the coup, continued to protest the lack of CIA oversight in its spending and dangerous plots, "which include the overthrow of friendly governments and assassination of their leaders for reasons of double deceit and multiple intrigue."[114]

The interventions would live on as examples of the CIA's influence on U.S. foreign policy. As a small but growing number of writers critical of the CIA emerged in the 1960s, these two examples were frequently cited as emblematic of the CIA's activities and the damage the agency did to the U.S.'s reputation in the world. Though initially useful for the CIA's purposes, the interventions came to represent for many critics the danger of the CIA.

In the immediate aftermath of the interventions in Iran and Guatemala, the CIA was not concerned about the possible long-term consequences. Dulles had good reason to boast, as he did in a letter to an acquaintance in 1955, about the quality of the CIA's relations with the press. Good press relations, Dulles explained, led to the CIA's positive relationship with Congress. He wrote, "There is a great deal that one must keep secret, but without a reasonable friendly public opinion to back congressional support, this Agency would be in trouble indeed. By and large, the press comment throughout the country is on the whole friendly and so far my relations with Congress are on a satisfactory basis."[115]

Walter Smith, Dulles's predecessor, had helped stabilize the agency after a rough period in its early years, but Dulles began the process of positively building the agency's reputation. Dulles used the press to exploit his agency's recent successes for as much political gain as possible, most notably in regard to the Harkness series. Dulles did not want the U.S. actions in Guatemala to be a secret; he just needed that they not be officially exposed.

Even as early as 1954, however, there were countertrends to the general positivity that would cause trouble for the CIA in the years to come. If these trends did not trouble Dulles considerably, they ought to have. There were reporters willing to comment on the CIA. While major papers were not willing to print the details of CIA activities yet, the *New York Times* at least proved uncooperative in playing a part in the CIA's foreign activities. The years 1953 and 1954 saw the greatest successes for the CIA in terms of both its actual operations and its relations with the press, but those successes were more fragile than many agency officials realized at the time.

3

The Increasing Public Profile
of the CIA

While the increasing public profile of the agency under Dulles was initially beneficial, it was not something the CIA could control.[1] This fact would be seen soon after the successful messaging regarding Guatemala, in the reporting over the construction and dedication of the CIA's new headquarters in Langley, Virginia.

When the CIA was founded in 1947, it took up residence in a set of old buildings in the navy's Bureau of Medicine and Science, in Foggy Bottom.[2] By 1955 a vigorous search for a new headquarters location was under way in the regions surrounding Washington, D.C. The search attracted considerable attention, especially in the local news section of the *Washington Post,* because of the efforts of Virginia and Maryland to woo the CIA to their states.[3] The final site of the CIA's headquarters was still unresolved in December, but the size and expense of the proposed building had emerged publicly through congressional hearings. The building's $38 million price tag drew attention. A *Chicago Tribune* reporter charged that the size and extravagance of the building demonstrated the "Pharaonic ambition" of Allen Dulles. A *New York Times* reporter observed that the dispute over the location of the building was the fiercest development issue in Washington since the debate in the 1930s over the location of the Washington airport.[4]

President Eisenhower finally laid the cornerstone of the building in November 1959 at a dedication ceremony to which members of the press were invited. The *Times* reporter Felix Belair wryly observed that the official program for the dedication ceremony "included everything but a map" to the headquarters.[5] Some journalists wrote approvingly that the public building was, they hoped, a sign of a more public, open role for the CIA.[6] Dry humor that a secret intelligence agency would have so public a building, however, was more the order of the day.

Stewart Alsop privately thought the headquarters was a symbol of Dulles's folly. Alsop admired Dulles to some extent, but he believed that the new CIA headquarters was a monument Dulles made to himself. Alsop's sources in the CIA told him that they had urged Dulles to adopt a more discreet headquarters plan, to no avail. Alsop predicted that the new headquarters, which he derisively called "Spooks Hall" and "Little-Spiesville-by-the-Potomac," would prove troublesome. A greater public profile meant that Congress would practice more oversight. This development was dangerous, Alsop believed, because "sooner or later somebody on the Hill is sure to figure out [what] a goldmine of headlines [the agency] will provide."[7]

Stewart Alsop's prediction was well founded. Already in the late 1950s, as fears of Soviet technological advances grew and inevitable setbacks in U.S. foreign policy occurred, the CIA was criticized, along with the rest of the Eisenhower administration, for failing to be as effective as it ought to be. Alsop also correctly saw the danger of Dulles's state of mind as embodied by the ambitious headquarters building. Dulles appeared increasingly unconcerned with CIA publicity and was overconfident in his agency's abilities. Dulles allowed the spectacularly ill-conceived effort to overthrow Fidel Castro in 1961 to go forward. That plan was reminiscent of the operation against Arbenz in Guatemala, yet the agency did not seem to realize the situation in Cuba was profoundly different. The total failure of the effort to oust Castro in an environment of more regular press attention resulted in the greatest public crisis the CIA had yet experienced.

The Evolving Press, 1955–1961

Part of the problem for the CIA was the fact that the press, never a static institution, was gradually but significantly changing in the late 1950s. From 1955 to 1961, the leadership of the *Chicago Tribune* and the *New York Times* changed as a result of either death or retirement. The *Washington Post* began to emerge as a force with which to be reckoned. The *Nation* continued to struggle, which eventually forced a leadership change; the periodical began to recover by the end of the decade. Inchoate strands of conservatism opposed to the established political order found a home in the newly founded *National Review,* which tended to criticize the agency for a lack of aggression toward the communist world. A new generation of reporters and editors, including those who would be instrumental in future reporting on the CIA, began to gain prominence.

The *Tribune* publishing empire established by Robert McCormick went through some of the earliest and most obvious changes. In 1954 McCormick sold the *Washington Times-Herald*, which he had purchased in the late 1940s in an attempt to expand the *Tribune*'s influence. The *Times-Herald* proved unprofitable, so McCormick sold it to the *Washington Post*, over the fierce objections of many conservatives, including his own niece.[8] After McCormick died, on 1 April 1955, management of the *Tribune* passed to a group of trustees. McCormick had served as editorial head, company president, and business manager of the *Tribune*; those three roles were dispersed to three different trustees.[9] His death meant that there was no single, unifying voice at the *Tribune*.

For a time, the *Tribune* continued to reflect McCormick's views, including his hostility to internationalists like Allen Dulles.[10] Though the *Times* and the *Post* generally reported on Allen Dulles's appearances before Congress in a positive light, the *Tribune* tended to portray Dulles as absentminded.[11] The *Chicago Tribune* was changing, though. The newspaper eventually drifted away from McCormick's determined isolationism and began to employ political pundits, who contributed to the debate on the CIA. Though it would continue to criticize the CIA, and advocates of CIA oversight would still be found in its pages during the 1975 investigations into the agency, the editorial line of the *Tribune* came to support the CIA as a weapon against communism in the Cold War.

Julius Adler, the general manager of the *New York Times*, died a few months after McCormick. Adler was a veteran of both world wars who had retired as a major general; he tended to be sympathetic to national security concerns. Hanson Baldwin believed that Adler's death marked a shift in the *Times*. Baldwin had liked working for Adler because, he later explained, Adler was "sympathetic to a sound and very strong defense," a perspective that Baldwin felt was missing in the *Times*'s management following Adler's death.[12]

Adler's replacement was Turner Catledge. A Mississippian who had joined the *Times* in 1929, Catledge worked under Arthur Krock in the Washington Bureau of the *Times*. Like Adler, he was skeptical of Roosevelt and the New Deal. Unlike Adler, Catledge possessed a well-honed skepticism of government and power that seems to have made him unsympathetic to national security arguments against publishing certain stories. He was also not a hard-line anticommunist; he, the editorial page chief John Oakes, and Reston all had worked to persuade Sulzberger against adopting a total anti-communist line with regard to *Times* employees.[13]

Times management changed even more considerably in April 1961, when Arthur Hays Sulzberger retired as publisher and moved away from a day-to-day role. His successor was Orvil Dryfoos, his son-in-law. Dryfoos had begun working for the *Times* in 1943, after he married Arthur Sulzberger's daughter, Marian, and he had been groomed for the publisher's position. He served as an assistant to Sulzberger before being made vice president in 1954 and Times Company president in 1957.[14] Dryfoos was thus present at some of the *Times*'s early decisions regarding the CIA. While in the loop regarding the *Times*'s concern over the CIA's efforts to unduly influence the paper, he was not as connected as Sulzberger to those who worked for the agency; he had not, for example, worked with Dulles on the Council on Foreign Relations. The question of the CIA became very important as Dryfoos transitioned to power because it was during that transition that the Bay of Pigs invasion was attempted. While not formally publisher at the time of the invasion, Dryfoos was empowered to decide whether, and to what extent, the *Times* should report on U.S. covert activities.

The reporter who would present Dryfoos with that conundrum was Tad Szulc. Szulc had joined the *Times* in 1953, and by 1961 he was an established and experienced reporter. Szulc, like Gruson, came from a very different background from that of traditional *Times* reporters. Born in Poland to a Jewish family, Szulc had immigrated to Brazil at a young age, then relocated to the United States. He had angered the government with his reporting on Otto John in 1954. Possibly in retribution, he was denied accreditation by the Pentagon for national security–related reporting; an anonymous government official also passed along information suggesting that Szulc had communist connections. Unlike, and possibly because of, its experience with Gruson, *Times* management did not take the charges seriously.[15]

The effect of these leadership and personnel changes was not immediately apparent in the *Times*, which officially remained attached to the principle articulated in August 1954 that it would keep silent about CIA activities while remaining wary of CIA interference. Hanson Baldwin continued to be the *Times*'s most prolific writer on intelligence issues, and his attitude toward national security reporting remained unchanged. He preferred to give up significant stories if he felt their national security value was more important than their value to the paper.[16]

As Baldwin explained in a lengthy note on proper national security reporting standards in 1962, there were several major stories that he and other *Times* reporters had refrained from publishing out of respect for the national interest. CIA aid in rescuing a prominent Pole from behind the Iron Curtain, the CIA's U-2 spy plane operation, and the CIA's spy satellites were among the stories that Baldwin and his fellow reporters had ignored. The key, Baldwin stressed, was that the judgment about what should or should not be published had to be the decision of reporters and not the government. Baldwin continued writing in the *Times* until 1968, and he increasingly clashed with reporters like Szulc. The *Times* had not so much shifted in a new direction on the CIA as it had become divided between what was to be considered appropriate to report and what was not.

The *New York Times* also increasingly had a real competitor in the *Washington Post*. The sale of the *Washington Times-Herald* had dramatically transformed the situation of the *Washington Post,* which thereafter published as the *Washington Post and Times-Herald* until 1973.[17] The sale made the *Post* the largest paper in the Washington market. Before the sale, the *Post* had a daily circulation of fewer than 200,000; after the sale, circulation was over 380,000. By 1960 the *Post*'s circulation was over 400,000.[18]

More readers meant more ad revenue, which in turn allowed the *Post* to improve its operations. In 1957 the *Post* finally began to send its own foreign correspondents abroad regularly. Murrey Marder was the first *Post* foreign correspondent; he was sent to London. Chalmers Roberts also eventually became a foreign correspondent for the *Post*.[19] This change increased the *Post*'s respectability and prominence, and it also made it a paper that the intelligence community had to take more seriously.

The *Post* tended to be friendlier to the CIA than the *New York Times,* and it maintained that tradition well into 1975. The leadership of the *Post* was an important part of that friendliness. The paper's owner, Eugene Meyer, had ceased taking an active role in the paper when he accepted a position at the World Bank in 1946. Though Meyer was occasionally involved in its affairs, the management of the paper increasingly fell to his son-in-law, Philip Graham, who with his wife, Katharine Graham, was intimately involved in the Washington social scene.[20]

Joseph Alsop's publishing circumstances had also changed. Though they still occasionally collaborated in the late 1950s, the Alsop brothers slowly diverged. In 1957 Joseph Alsop traveled out of the country widely.[21] Stewart Alsop had long been the junior partner in the Alsop brothers' collaboration, and he desired to establish his own individual reputation and earn a greater profit for his work. Stewart took primary responsibility for their "Matter of Fact" column while his brother traveled; their collaboration lasted only a few months after Joseph's return, their final column together being published in March 1958.[22] Stewart moved to the *Saturday Evening Post* as a full-time staff member, responsible for eight stories a year and a weekly list of article suggestions. From this position, he would continue to serve as a conduit for cooperation between the *Saturday Evening Post* and the CIA.

The periodical scene was also changing. The *Nation* was hampered from significant investigative reporting by internal problems. The *Nation* had long struggled with its finances, but the situation continually deteriorated over the 1950s and prompted considerations of staff reductions.[23] Circumstances became so desperate that Kirchwey agreed to a limited partnership that reduced her status and led to her resignation as owner and publisher. Carey McWilliams became the leading force at the *Nation*.[24] The *Nation* would need some time to regroup and recover, but by late 1960 it would be able to produce significant reporting on the CIA.

The *National Review,* meanwhile, began publishing in November 1955.[25] The *National Review*'s founder, William F. Buckley Jr., had briefly been a member of the CIA. He had been stationed in Mexico and served under the notorious E. Howard Hunt.[26] One of the most prominent contributors to the journal, the former communist James Burnham, had worked with the Office of Policy Coordination in the early days of the Cold War. Burnham offered advice on enlisting intellectuals, especially former communists, in the struggle against the Soviet Union.[27]

These changes in the press environment were not sudden or dramatic, and they coexisted with continued stability for mainstream publications like *Time*. The changes were not all negative for the CIA, as the *Chicago Tribune* had been one of its main critics. The *Washington Post,* with which the CIA enjoyed close ties, was now more powerful. Many relationships remained stable; Charles Douglas "C. D." Jackson, for example, between his involvement in *Time* and service in the Eisenhower administration, remained happy to pass along information to people like Cord Meyer; shortly before the Bay of Pigs invasion, for example, Jackson wrote to urge that a businessman from Chicago receive a special debriefing from the CIA because of the man's intelligence and perceptiveness.[28]

Trends such as those in the *New York Times*, however, presaged future problems for the CIA. The management of the major newspapers, and new editors and reporters, altered the dynamic of CIA relationships with the press and the coverage of the CIA in reporting. While the CIA had additional allies, it also faced more hostile voices.

Public Criticism of the CIA, 1955–1961

Aside from the occasional trickle of stories related to Guatemala or coverage of the CIA's new headquarters, from 1955 to April 1961 the CIA most often appeared in the press as a result of congressional attention to the agency or speeches by Allen Dulles that attempted to deflect congressional criticism. The trend of congressional criticism was especially notable in 1958, following the shock of Sputnik the previous fall and fears that the United States was falling behind the Soviet Union in the Cold War.

Before the revived congressional attention, the greatest forum for criticism of the CIA was the second Commission on Organization of the Executive Branch of the Government, led by former president Herbert Hoover. The final report, released in the summer of 1955, criticized the CIA. Dulles thought the commission was dangerous enough that he met with over twenty reporters from print and television news, including William "Bill" Lawrence of the *Times*, Murrey Marder of the *Washington Post*, David Lawrence of *U.S. News and World Report*, James Truitt of *Time*, and representatives from the AP, UP, Scripps-Howard News Service, *Christian Science Monitor*, and the *Wall Street Journal*.[29] Ultimately, little came of the commission's report.

Senator Michael Mansfield was the most active member of Congress in directing attention toward the CIA and calling for reform to agency oversight.[30] The *New York Times* and the *Washington Post* editorial pages consistently supported Mansfield. The various editorials shared the same basic theme: oversight was held to be essential to prevent abuse, guarantee efficiency, and protect the CIA from constant criticism by allowing Congress to actually understand and appreciate its activities.[31] The support for Mansfield's proposed oversight committee, something Allen Dulles fought tenaciously against, demonstrates that even papers that fully supported the goals of the CIA did not necessarily accept the CIA's desired policy positions.

As had happened during Hillenkoetter's tenure, the CIA was also criticized when it was perceived to have failed to warn of major events. For example, Mansfield criticized the CIA following the Suez crisis in 1956 for overlooking the activities of the French, British, and Israelis in the days before their invasion of Egypt. Commentators in the press followed his lead.[32] Similar criticism came with other incidents, such as when Richard Nixon's tour of South America was derailed when a Venezuelan mob attacked his car.[33]

The overthrow of the allied monarchy in Iraq in 1958 was especially jolting. Dulles was called before Congress to explain why the CIA had failed to anticipate the coup. The *National Review* was especially critical and castigated the agency for inefficiency and wasting funds. As part of an internal review, the CIA compiled a list of papers that criticized the agency for failure to warn of the coup in Iraq. It found 466 cases around the country of journalistic and legislative comment critical of the CIA because of the events in Iraq.[34] Such a review demonstrates the CIA's concern that negative press coverage could still harm the organization.

The Suez and Iraq crises were ultimately transitory, however. Anxiety about the Soviet missile and space programs had a greater staying power. The Alsops led the way in vocally criticizing the supposed missile gap between the United States and the Soviet Union. The Alsops criticized Eisenhower's efforts to cut defense spending, and they argued that the U.S. reliance on nuclear superiority was unsustainable owing to rapid Soviet technological advances. Other commentators, such as Drew Pearson, joined them. Allen Dulles attempted to allay these concerns, but to little avail.[35] The successful Soviet launch of Sputnik in October 1957, followed by a second launch in which a dog was apparently sent into space and returned, only exacerbated fears of Soviet technological superiority.[36] The Alsops were not necessarily critical of the CIA; Stewart Alsop blamed Secretary of Defense Charles Wilson.[37] The political atmosphere that such stories sustained, however, was unfavorable to the CIA because the concerns of the Cold War could easily evolve into criticism of its capabilities. The CIA could not afford to be seen as ineffective.

While the CIA had been challenged by blame for unexpected events as long as the agency had existed, Dulles was better suited to counter that blame than Roscoe Hillenkoetter had been. Dulles played an increasingly public role to demonstrate the CIA's knowledge of the world and to deflect criticism. He gave occasional public talks as early as 1954, both to Congress and at public events.[38] His speeches sought to strike a balance between reassuring listeners that the United States was not losing the Cold War while stressing that the Cold War remained a threat and was not going to end soon. The unspoken message was that the CIA was doing a good job but needed to be maintained against the continuing threat. This feature of his statements at times led to divergent coverage of those statements in the press. For example, following the Soviet crackdown on the Hungarian uprising that occurred concurrently with the Suez crisis, Dulles argued in a speech that the uprisings in Poland and Hungary demonstrated the weakness of Soviet rule. The *Tribune* chose to stress the weakness of Soviet rule, whereas the *Times* focused on Dulles's warning that the Cold War was not over.[39] Dulles's real goal, meanwhile, was to convince Congress that stronger oversight of the CIA was not required.[40]

Dulles also used the CIA's mystique to answer criticism, as he sought to leave the impression that the CIA always knew more than the public might guess.[41] This strategy became increasingly prevalent in the 1960s as the CIA came under greater criticism. Dulles continued to insist that the CIA was better than "we can publicly advertise."[42] There is some basic truth to the point Dulles made, as the CIA did have a legitimate need to protect its sources and methods. Dulles's willingness to leak information, however, reveals a certain level of hypocrisy behind such statements, as he clearly sought to ensure that CIA successes were both known and celebrated.

Dulles's cultivation of friendly relationships with the press proved useful in his efforts to defend the agency. At various points in 1958, reporters friendly to the CIA produced positive profiles of Dulles and the agency. These stories tended to be longer and more substantial than the brief notifications of congressional activity regarding the CIA. Three such stories deserve particular attention because of their ability to illuminate the value Dulles gained from relationships with specific reporters and companies. The earliest story was by Chalmers Roberts, who reported that Dulles and the CIA had known about Sputnik before its launch; the problem was that they were unable to impress on U.S. policy makers the gravity of that development.[43]

A month after the Roberts story, Russell Baker of the *New York Times* wrote a profile of Dulles remarkably similar to the profile that had emerged in the Harkness articles. Dulles was, in the Baker article, a friendly, humble American civil servant. Baker also defended the CIA from its critics. He wrote that the agency was a victim of political cynicism, and that "in casual conversation one is told vaguely that C.I.A. crawls with incompetents and poseurs, that it is inefficient and bungling, that it is not headed by the policy-makers." Baker assured readers that this portrayal of the CIA was inaccurate; its morale was strong and its intelligence gathering of high quality.[44]

Finally, only a few weeks before the Iraq coup, an AP reporter, John Scali, wrote a story on the CIA emphasizing the importance of its mission in the atomic age, "when the merest scrap of information could mean the difference between survival and annihilation." Scali complimented the CIA's decision not to justify itself "when Congress grumbles over failures, real or imaginary," as it was more focused on its important mission and protecting its sources than petty congressional politics. Scali then provided a list of recent intelligence issues, rating the CIA as good to excellent in its performance on Soviet rocket capabilities, Latin American unrest, and the Hungarian revolt. The only shortcoming Scali acknowledged was the CIA's failure to predict the seizure of the Suez Canal.[45]

There is no evidence of CIA involvement in the Roberts or Scali articles, but the CIA had access to Baker's article several months in advance of its publication and had the opportunity to comment on it. The CIA's reviewers objected to the article because it seemed too frivolous. Lyman Kirkpatrick, one of the commentators, believed that the article "seems trite more because of its style than actually what is said. . . . A good deal of the lightness seems to appear in the descriptions of the Director." That being the case, Kirkpatrick recommended trying to persuade Baker to include additional material on Dulles's efforts to make the CIA a real career service and improve training.[46] Baker's response to these suggestions is not available, but his finished article does not reflect any of Kirkpatrick's desired additions. Though the CIA had an opportunity to comment on the article, it did not have the opportunity to shape the article into something useful for the agency beyond support for Allen Dulles himself.

Scali and Roberts, meanwhile, had their own connections with the CIA that had been useful to them in the past. Both reporters were privy to briefings from CIA officials. Scali was one of the members of the press whom Dulles met with before the release of the Hoover Commission report, and he had previously received information from the CIA when preparing an article for *Collier's*. Though Roberts's first documented meeting with a CIA official was not until 1965, when he met with Deputy DCI Ray Cline, he knew

Dulles socially, and their correspondence suggests Roberts was one of the reporters who enjoyed access to Dulles's private briefings.[47] Dulles continued to hold off-the-record meetings, such as one with James Reston and several other reporters to give his views on the world situation.[48] It is unclear whether Dulles prompted these positive stories himself, but he would not necessarily have needed to take direct action for these friendly stories to be released because of the mutually beneficial relationships he had cultivated.

The treatment of the CIA by the press in the late 1950s was thus mixed. Many in the press supported the Mansfield proposal, and journalists dutifully reported congressional criticism of the agency. These problems were overshadowed, though, by positive relationships with the press. Scali, Roberts, and Baker all supported the agency and its reputation. The increasingly hostile environment of the late 1950s resulted primarily from fears that the Eisenhower administration was stagnant and thus falling behind a rapidly advancing Soviet Union. The CIA's relationships with some members of the press mitigated that hostile environment and, as would be seen in Indonesia, helped it keep its covert activities secret.

Indonesia

Unlike U.S. relations with Mossadegh and Arbenz, relations with the government of Sukarno in Indonesia had not taken on a hostile edge before Eisenhower took office. Nor, indeed, did Eisenhower immediately oppose Sukarno. The American effort against Sukarno was not as focused as the effort against Arbenz had been, and U.S. policy toward Indonesia was often uncertain.[49] The relationship shifted radically more than once, defined by what one scholar has called a "curious combination of hope and fear of impending disaster."[50]

In late 1956 several colonels on the outer islands of Indonesia, most notably Sumatra, declared their opposition to Sukarno. The CIA provided support to these colonels. While the U.S. press, especially the *National Review*, condemned Sukarno as a communist dictator few hints of the CIA's presence in the area appeared.[51] Sukarno's forces attacked the rebels in February 1958, rapidly putting them to flight. Eisenhower, much as he had tried to stave off defeat in Guatemala, authorized the use of airpower against Sukarno through the CIA-controlled Civil Air Transport CAT). Though these air strikes enjoyed some initial success, on 17 May a CAT pilot, Allen Pope, was shot down and captured before he could destroy evidence of his connection with the United States and the CIA. By the time the Indonesians announced that they had captured Pope alive on 27 May, the CIA had ceased its operation and sought to explain away Pope as a mercenary. The Eisenhower administration rapidly shifted course to promote friendly relations with Sukarno. Sukarno desired good relations himself, and he did not challenge Pope's status as a mercenary. He released Pope in February 1962.

The U.S. press provided significantly less coverage of Indonesia than it had of Guatemala. The CIA wanted desperately to clamp down and prevent the release of unflattering information. Sukarno, having retained power, attempted to establish a modus vivendi with the United States. In an off-the-record meeting with James Reston in November 1958, Allen Dulles reported that he was optimistic with regard to Indonesia. He predicted that Indonesia would be more inclined to be friendly with the United States.[52]

Few outlets picked up the story of CIA activity in Indonesia. Periodicals commented more critically on U.S. actions in Indonesia than newspapers, but they did not produce substantially more articles.[53] Despite this limited coverage, the CIA was concerned about potential exposure of its activities in Indonesia. When agency officials learned, while operations were ongoing during 1957, that Stewart Alsop was preparing an article on Indonesia, they saw danger. One official warned that "it would be no great trick for an alert writer to read the newspapers and realize that something is going on in Indonesia." The CIA decided to restrict any Indonesian-related information from being leaked to the press to prevent exposure. Alsop did not produce the proposed article.[54]

The greatest amount of coverage of the rebellion itself came from the *National Review* and *Saturday Evening Post*.[55] The *National Review* did not take a pro-CIA stance. It voiced support for the rebels, while doubting that the CIA would be able competently to assist them.[56] The *National Review* fiercely criticized the CIA's "activist wing" for not adequately aiding the rebels and questioned whether the CIA was worth the dollar investment put into it.[57]

Coverage of Indonesia remained low-key even at the height of CIA bombing operations. *Time* ran a piece on "the mystery pilots" in Indonesia, ultimately supporting Eisenhower's contention that the pilots were mercenaries. The capture of Pope and capitulation of the colonels resulted in little immediate coverage. The *Saturday Evening Post* set the tone, a little over half a year after Pope's capture. Harold H. Martin reported, "We may have given the rebels sympathy. We gave them no real help."[58]

Even in 1958 the CIA apparently could conceal a significant and embarrassing failure. The willingness of some congressmen to criticize the CIA did not yet translate to an inability to maintain secrecy. The extremely limited coverage of Indonesia was similar to the situation in Iran in 1953, in that both countries were geographically distant from the United States, open only to the wire services and truly international publications. It is likely that major outlets like the *New York Times* at least had some inkling of what was happening, though that is uncertain. If they heard reports, they did not publish them. The CIA would not be as fortunate with another downed plane, this one in the Soviet Union.

The U-2 Incident

The Soviet interdiction of Francis Gary Powers's U-2 spy plane on 1 May 1960 exposed the CIA and the Eisenhower administration to considerable embarrassment, which was exacerbated by the initial U.S. reaction. After contact with Powers was lost, the CIA assumed he was dead. The CIA, in fact, relied on the assumption that a pilot would not be able to survive the destruction of a U-2, as the craft was very fragile.[59] In response to Russian reports that a plane had been brought down, the State Department released a statement that a civilian pilot on a weather research plane may have lost oxygen and then drifted into Soviet airspace. Following the release of the weather research cover story, the Soviets produced Powers.[60] Eisenhower was forced to acknowledge U.S. espionage, and when he refused to apologize or punish intelligence leaders, Nikita Khrushchev, the Soviet premier, canceled an upcoming summit meeting. The U-2 incident, however, ultimately redounded to the agency's favor. Aerial spying had been a fairly successful program, the goals of which most Americans supported. The CIA's report on the remarkable results of the program impressed Congress. After briefing Congress, Allen Dulles was reportedly met with a standing ovation.[61]

The U-2 had actually begun as a way to mitigate another CIA failure, its inability to penetrate the Soviet Union with human intelligence. Left without reliable intelligence from the ground, the CIA could reliably monitor the Soviet intercontinental ballistic missile (ICBM) program only through the air. The program was spearheaded by Richard Bissell, who had earlier distinguished himself with his role in the operation against Arbenz in Guatemala.[62] Bissell was well-suited to such a technical project, as he had worked in logistics during World War II and taught at MIT before joining the CIA. The first U-2 mission, on 4 July 1956, directly overflew the Soviet Union. Subsequent U-2 missions most often occurred at the edges of Soviet airspace, but another twenty missions were direct overflights. From these flights Eisenhower and the CIA knew that the missile gap of which the Alsops so loudly warned was a fiction. Because of the sensitivity of its source, however, Eisenhower could not reveal that information.[63]

At least two reporters knew of the U-2's existence before 1 May. Hanson Baldwin included the U-2 in his list of stories that he had refrained from printing out of respect for the national interest. Baldwin's *Times* colleague James Reston similarly knew of the existence of the U-2.[64] It is unclear how they discovered it. Dulles or some other member of the CIA might have leaked the information in an attempt to mitigate criticism of the CIA's strategic intelligence capabilities; while the information could not be disclosed to the public, it might at least have been used to convince two prominent commentators that the CIA had a notion of what was going on inside the Soviet Union.

Once the Soviets revealed that Powers was alive and in custody and Eisenhower acknowledged that the U-2 was a spy plane, immediate press coverage was consistent with earlier criticism of the CIA.[65] Because Allen Dulles's salutary appearance before Congress was closed, reporters had to rely on public statements, from which they gleaned that Congress unanimously felt that the 1 May flight was poorly timed, given the upcoming summit planned with the Soviets.[66] Henry Howe Ransom, an early and prolific commentator on intelligence issues, wrote an in-depth article on aerial surveillance and called for strong oversight of intelligence.[67] The CIA successfully countered such proposals, but the refrain that the CIA needed strong congressional oversight had grown throughout the 1950s from the voices of just a few people to a regular point of discussion.

The public soon learned about Allen Dulles's positive reception from Congress when he admitted the U-2 capability. Hanson Baldwin wrote that the U-2 flight was properly planned and approved by the appropriate governmental figures outside the CIA. Commentators in the *Washington Post* defended the necessity of U.S. espionage and rejected any criticism of U.S. action.[68] The *Chicago Tribune* published an unusually friendly story by

Willard Edwards defending the CIA. While arguing that early charges against the CIA for incompetence probably had been justified, Edwards wrote that the U-2 demonstrated the maturation of the CIA into a more capable organization. Edwards wrote that the reaction from Congress when it was shown the U-2 results was "Thank God, we're finally getting something for our money."[69]

Edwards's reporting was not isolated. The *Tribune* consistently reported favorably on the CIA in regard to the U-2. In June, for example, it noted that the CIA had gained good intelligence on Soviet missile-building programs through aerial surveillance. Another *Tribune* reporter explained that the initial confusion over the U-2's mission and the embarrassing cover story was due to some interagency miscommunication at NASA.[70] The *Tribune*'s shift toward praise for the CIA was not a definitive change; the paper would still occasionally criticize the agency. This criticism was muted, however, in comparison to the *Tribune*'s earlier reporting.

By the end of June, the coverage of the CIA in relation to the U-2 incident was almost entirely positive. The *Washington Post* and *U.S. News and World Report* ran columns and editorials supporting the U-2 flights. Allen Dulles's personal reputation was also burnished; the spate of stories about the U-2 prompted more positive biographical portraits of Dulles that emphasized his integrity and hard work in behalf of the United States.[71]

The coverage of the CIA and the U-2 in the wake of Powers's capture was so voluminous that Martin Sommers decided not to run a story on the incident in the *Saturday Evening Post*, as he felt that his publication would have nothing new to say about the CIA. Sommers remained skeptical even when Stewart Alsop informed him that Richard Bissell would be more than willing to talk about the U-2 now that the operation was blown. Bissell had been a go-between for the CIA and the *Saturday Evening Post* earlier that year, when the CIA had hoped to get a story published disputing critics of the CIA's budget. Alsop decided to drop the idea of doing the story only when he approached Allen Dulles on the subject; Dulles saw no reason to keep the issue before the public and suggested any U-2 story ought to wait.[72]

The U-2 exposure had not been a significant threat to the CIA because there was a consensus that the program was valuable and in line with what the agency should be doing. Beyond that, reports that the U-2 had been remarkably successful in providing intelligence on the Soviet Union were reassuring in an environment of widespread fear over Soviet technological capabilities. In addition to the plaudits the CIA received for the success of the U-2, the agency could also take comfort from the fact that it had a new ability to spy on the Soviet Union from above, as Richard Bissell in August 1960 oversaw the launch of the first spy satellite into space.[73] The CIA would have no such comfort or positive reception in 1961, however, when it attempted to overthrow Fidel Castro.

The Bay of Pigs

The operation against Castro began on 15 April 1961, after B-26s attacked Cuban airfields. The U.S. hand was immediately tipped, as one of the planes made an emergency landing in Key West. Early in the morning of 17 April, a brigade of Cuban exiles landed at Playa Girón and Playa Larga and began advancing inland. The Exile Brigade quickly experienced severe difficulties as Cuban resistance did not dissipate, and by 19 April the brigade was forced back to the beaches. Allen Dulles and the CIA seem to have believed erroneously that once forces were on the ground, President John F. Kennedy would authorize any action necessary to prevent the operation's failure. While attempting to evacuate as many brigade members as possible, however, Kennedy did not authorize further air strikes in support of the operation. On 21 April Kennedy was forced to accept responsibility for the total failure of the invasion. At the same time, he also called for greater press self-censorship.[74]

Kennedy's call for press self-censorship stemmed from the fact that the press reported significant details about the upcoming invasion in the months leading up to its execution. Indications emerged in late 1960 that the United States supported Cuban exiles in a planned invasion of Cuba. Dr. Ronald Hilton reported to the *Nation* that the CIA had a large, heavily guarded tract of land in Guatemala that was widely assumed to be a training ground for Cubans opposed to Fidel Castro. These revelations, one *Nation* writer observed, showed that "Fidel Castro may have a sounder basis for his expressed fear of a U.S.-financed 'Guatemala-type' invasion than most of us realize."[75]

Carleton Beals, a veteran freelancer who had been writing about Latin America since the 1920s, charged in the *Nation* even before the reports arrived from Hilton that Cuba had good reason to fear the United States. He argued after Hilton's report that the United States was clearly preparing intervention. The *Nation* also published an article in January 1961 by Don

Dwiggins that revealed the existence of an airstrip in Guatemala built by the United States for use against Castro.[76]

Increasingly, the *New York Times* and the *Washington Post* also reported on Cuban accusations of U.S. activities directed against the regime.[77] Hilton had also informed the *New York Times* reporter Herbert Matthews that some kind of activity was being prepared against Castro.[78] Another *Times* reporter, Paul Kennedy, wrote a front-page story on 10 January on the Guatemalan air base and the charges that the United States was planning an invasion.[79] Kennedy had some experience, from having been in Guatemala in 1954, of seeing the preparations for a CIA intervention. In March 1961 a *Washington Post* article by Karl Meyer examined the political divisions among the exile groups, in which he reported that leftists were concerned that "some agencies of the U.S. government" seemed to think Cuba would be another Guatemala.[80]

The *Saturday Evening Post* and the *New Republic* featured stories that indicated an invasion was being prepared and advising, in the words of the *Saturday Evening Post* writer Harold Martin, that the United States remain a "silent partner" in ousting Castro. How, precisely, the United States would do that in the face of persistent media coverage, Martin did not say. Stewart Alsop had known Martin was being sent to the Caribbean, but either he did not realize the potential consequences of free reporting about Cuba or he felt no obligation to warn the CIA about Martin's presence.[81]

Tad Szulc became involved in the story in March. He had taken on the Latin America beat for the *Times* but been sidelined by a plane crash in 1960 that left him seriously injured.[82] Szulc returned to the United States for a vacation through Miami, where he met with a friend and fellow journalist on a social call. That friend informed him about events to come in Cuba. According to Szulc's later account, a young Cuban, overhearing their conversation, approached them and bragged that he and his friends would be overthrowing Castro with the support of the U.S. government. An interested Szulc discovered that the Miami community was very familiar with the upcoming invasion. A cursory investigation found many recruits more than happy to reveal that the CIA was supporting them.[83]

Szulc enjoyed a good story, so it is possible his details were embellished; however, the amateurishness with which the invasion was prepared means that it is not inconceivable for the events to have occurred as Szulc described them. Regardless of how he got the story, Szulc informed his superiors of what he learned and they assigned him to investigate further. This assignment for Szulc demonstrates that the *New York Times* already was moving toward a greater willingness to report on U.S. covert activities; the story could easily have been dismissed. Reston, having gotten the story from Szulc, then went to ask Allen Dulles about the imminent invasion. Dulles did not deny that something was in the works.[84]

Szulc's story, titled "Anti-Castro Units Trained to Fight at Florida Bases," was published on page one of the *New York Times* on 7 April. Szulc reported that for nine months a 5,000–6,000-man army had been preparing to attack Castro. "United States experts" provided training and direction. Szulc also reported that the plan of the army was to invade and, with an expected internal uprising, rout Castro. Szulc informed readers that the invasion was near, as the Florida camps that had been way stations for the guerrillas were empty.[85]

Szulc's draft had originally said the invasion was "imminent," but the draft was changed. Dryfoos was concerned about the implications of the *Times*'s running the story. It was a delicate time for *Times* management. The de facto publisher, Dryfoos, would not formally assume his father-in-law's position until the end of the month. James Reston advised that references to the upcoming invasion's timetable be removed.[86]

Turner Catledge proposed that rather than remove any reference to the nearness of the invasion, only the word *imminent* be cut. Catledge later reflected that the difference between him and Reston was merely one of degree, but it was a consequential degree.[87] Whether Sulzberger would have published is uncertain, but his previous pattern of reporting provides reason to suspect that he would have decided much more decisively than Dryfoos to avoid the story.

Also absent in Szulc's article was the identification of the CIA as the responsible agency. According to Catledge, that identification was left out not to protect the CIA, but simply because the *Times* could not be sure which part of the U.S. intelligence community was running the operation.[88] Even so, the *Times* had effectively passed on the location and preparations of the suspiciously well-equipped exile force.

Controversy later arose regarding whether the *New York Times* suppressed important details of the story. Arthur Schlesinger claimed that both Szulc's account and a story by Karl Meyer in the *New Republic* were quashed at the request of the president. Clifton Daniel, one of the *Times* editors in

New York in 1961, vigorously rejected that claim. He insisted that the important thing was that the Szulc story was run, even without the word *imminent.*
Daniel would later insist to several of his colleagues that no suppression of
the story had occurred.[89]

Daniel appears, however, to have been somewhat ambivalent about the
Times's choice. He acknowledged that the decision to strike an important
part of a story, even if it was one word, was unusual. The two editors responsible for printing the 7 April issue refused to remove the word *imminent* until
they heard personally from Dryfoos.[90] Daniel wrote privately that "in the
case of the Bay of Pigs invasion, the *New York Times* and other publications
tried, but not resolutely enough, in my opinion, to keep the American public
informed. . . . My [opinion] is that the invasion might have [been]canceled if
enough publicity had been given to it and to the fact that the C.I.A. was par-
ticipating in it. And, certainly, that would have been a net gain for the
Republic."[91]

The ambivalence and confusion involved in the *New York Times*'s decision illustrate that, even with a publication that was generally friendly to the
CIA, issues regarding intelligence reporting were often contentious. The
Times was torn between what was clearly a vital news story and its sense of
concern for national security. The *Washington Post* also demonstrated the
biases of Washington reporters: aside from Meyer's reporting, it neglected
the story. Chalmers Roberts later admitted that the *Post* "had performed mis-
erably" during the Bay of Pigs. Philip Graham was apparently so loyal to
John Kennedy that he specifically ordered his newspaper to overlook the
invasion preparations.[92] Those outside Washington, like Catledge, were less
sure that discretion was always appropriate.

Once the invasion failed and Kennedy was forced to take responsibility,
fierce discussion ensued in the press about the methods and morality of the
intervention. The *Nation* castigated the invasion, noting it was clear the CIA
was involved from the beginning. The *New Republic*, which had supported
discreet U.S. intervention, argued that the United States should have carried
through an attack against Castro. Soon, however, it leaned toward criticizing
the CIA for not supporting genuine Cuban reformers. The *National Review*
followed a roughly opposite trajectory, shifting blame from the CIA to Kennedy.[93] A general anticommunist consensus remained strong in the press;
most criticism was not focused on the ethics of intervention. Questions about
the CIA's efficiency, though, were quite dangerous to the integrity of the CIA.

The CIA was not without its defenders. David Lawrence condemned attacks on the CIA as blunting a key weapon in the battle against communism. Douglass Cater and Charles Bartlett of the *Reporter* criticized Dulles as "a man who likes his part in the flow of news that leaves Washington," but the general tone was not anti-CIA.[94]

Cater's pro-CIA stance was in the minority, however, and the damage to the CIA's public image led to increasing calls from pundits to break up the agency. By 26 April, John Norris of the *Washington Post* reported that unnamed government officials were seriously discussing dividing the agency between its intelligence and operations functions. The refrain that the CIA could be broken up along these lines was picked up in many periodicals and newspapers. Some of the more openly partisan periodicals such as the *New Republic* actively advocated for such a course. The call to separate the CIA's various functions remained a regular staple in CIA reporting.[95]

Though the CIA weathered these calls, the post–Bay of Pigs environment was considerably less congenial, which became immediately clear in reporting on an attempted coup in France. From 21 to 26 April a putsch led by General Maurice Challe attempted to unseat Charles de Gaulle. A week later, the *New York Times* reported that rumors were rife in Paris that the CIA had supported Challe. According to Marquis Childs, many Frenchmen felt that, while it was probably not an official action, the CIA may have aided Challe on its own initiative.[96] There was nothing to the story; that it was reported at all, however, demonstrates the more powerful microscope under which the CIA found itself.

The CIA had generally done very well for itself in the 1950s. Its success in Guatemala and Iran had bolstered its reputation, especially because the negative consequences of those interventions for the United States were still in the future, and the United States generally was unconcerned or unaware of the negative consequences for the people living there. There was greater congressional criticism of the CIA and increased support for oversight of the agency in 1958, but the CIA was able to weather such agitation and maintain secrecy about its foreign activity in Indonesia. Even the public failure of the U-2 ultimately redounded to the CIA's benefit.

There were countertrends in the 1950s, however. Greater prestige for the CIA also meant greater attention to the agency. By the time of the Bay of Pigs invasion, newspapers and periodicals no longer felt the need to explain to their readers what the CIA was. Greater awareness of the CIA's previous covert activities, especially in Guatemala, informed press expectations about Cuba. Younger reporters like Szulc were not as hesitant as their elders in reporting on CIA activities. The press leadership under which the CIA had flourished slowly but surely changed. This altered press environment was not responsible for the failure of the Bay of Pigs operation. Even had the press acquiesced, it is profoundly unlikely that the Bay of Pigs invasion could have been successful. Ultimate responsibility for the Bay of Pigs must go to the poor planning and arrogance of the agency.

The Bay of Pigs invasion did not mark the definitive break in relations between the CIA and the press. There were still off-the-record meetings and public defenders of the CIA. Soon after the Bay of Pigs, however, Dulles resigned. The end of the Dulles era was significant because Dulles had been a key part in the relations with the press during his tenure as DCI. His contacts and his savvy had served him and his agency well. The relationships between the press and the post-Dulles CIA would change over the course of the 1960s, often to the agency's detriment.

4

The Fracture of the 1960s

The public failure of the Bay of Pigs invasion was an embarrassment for the CIA, a threat to its reputation for competence, and a source of significant criticism. Richard Helms, a future director of Central Intelligence, complained privately, "One gets the distinct impression that this Agency is a sort of fire hydrant available to all the stray dogs in the area."[1] A few reporters and commentators moved beyond concerns with the CIA's competence and asked more fundamental questions about the agency's place in American society. It was the end of what has been termed the "golden age" for the CIA's covert actions.[2] In this environment, the CIA sought to protect itself by drawing on past relationships with members of the press and attempting to forge new ones. By providing select reporters with information, leaders in the agency hoped the press would be more sympathetic to the challenges and triumphs of U.S. intelligence. One of the best examples of such efforts is the work of Ray Cline, the head of the CIA's Directorate of Intelligence during the early 1960s.

In September 1965 an anonymous CIA official prepared a report on Cline's relationships with the press. The report explained, "With rising clamor impairing public confidence in the Agency as an institution and in the competence of some of its personnel . . . there is a need to explore new approaches to methods of restoring faith in the Agency's competence." One of those "new approaches" that Cline attempted was to meet with prominent reporters and brief them on world events. The report explained that Cline, since 1957, had met with reporters "without self-interest and purely in the interest of the Agency." Cline believed these meetings "benefit[ed] the general *rapport* of the Agency with these newsmen."[3]

Cline provided a list of press figures with whom he had contact. Joseph and Stewart Alsop, Tad Szulc, Walter Lippmann, Cyrus Sulzberger, Chalmers

Roberts, and Katharine Graham were among those listed.[4] Cline reported that Joseph Alsop was the only newspaperman with whom he met regularly. That regular contact began three years before the report was issued, in 1962; Cline explained that he had maintained this contact at the request of DCI John McCone, Dulles's successor.[5]

The report indicated that, in addition to Alsop, Cline had regular contact with Chalmers Roberts and Murrey Marder of the *Washington Post,* Jess Cook of *Time,* and William S. White of the United Feature wire service. Cline apparently provided no classified information during these meetings with the press. The report concluded that Cline's work should continue. His efforts were "worthy of praise."[6]

The report's note that Cline was exploring "new approaches" in CIA relationships with the press seems to refer to his regular contact with Alsop, Roberts, Marder, Cook, and White, dating from 1962 to 1965, rather than those contacts with the press that dated back to 1957. To call such approaches new was inaccurate, as Cline was essentially following the example of Allen Dulles: meet with newspapermen privately and demonstrate the competence of the agency by providing access to information. In Cline's case, this information apparently did not include CIA activities, but only general world information helpful to members of the press that was not to be attributed to the CIA. In this way, the relationship for journalists leaned toward standard practice.

Cline's meetings were far from the only contact the CIA had with the press during the 1960s. The agency attempted to address the problem of its public image with an effort to continue, expand, and formalize its relationships with prominent representatives of major press institutions. Many of those representatives, such as the members of the *Washington Post* and the Alsop brothers, continued during the 1960s to be supportive of the agency.

These CIA methods, however, proved increasingly ineffective, for two reasons. First, the relationships with the press that the CIA enjoyed did not totally shield it, because those reporters remained independent actors whose interests were not always aligned with those of the agency. Reporters' searches for information could occasionally cause complications; the reason for the report on Cline's activities, for example, was the aggressive fact-finding of the reporter Joseph Kraft. Kraft had called William Raborn, who had in April 1965 replaced McCone as DCI, to get information on Soviet leadership clashes. Kraft claimed that if he received no help from Raborn, he could find other sources in the CIA, such as Cline. This incident led Raborn to demand an accounting of CIA contacts with the press.[7]

The second reason was that, while the agency enjoyed good relationships with some major reporters, the anti-CIA currents that predated the Bay of Pigs invasion grew more prominent. The *Nation* devoted an entire issue to the activities of the CIA. Hints about the CIA's involvement in ostensibly private institutions increasingly crept into the press. In 1967 a small, radical leftist periodical called *Ramparts* exposed the CIA's long covert entanglement with the National Student Association. Once *Ramparts* exposed this relationship, major publications quickly followed in covering the scandal regardless of their relationships with the CIA.

While the press-CIA relationships of the 1950s remained largely intact in the 1960s, the environment in which those relationships existed changed dramatically. In this new environment, those earlier relationships were increasingly ineffective for the CIA's purposes. This became most apparent in 1966 and 1967, which were watershed years for reporting on the CIA.

The Retirement of Allen Dulles and the Appointment of John McCone

Allen Dulles's retirement was the most obvious public sign that the CIA was changing. Dulles had played a key role in defining the CIA's relationships with the press as he sought to present the CIA as an essential, effective force. He had intended to retire before the Bay of Pigs operation, at least according to rumor. When Dulles's retirement was announced in August 1961, the White House stressed that he had informed the president he would leave the post after serving an additional year in the new administration. White House Press Secretary Pierre Salinger did not mention the Bay of Pigs in the statement on Dulles's retirement.[8]

The White House's statement was a polite fiction. Whether or not Dulles had intended to retire before the Bay of Pigs, he did not have an option to remain afterward. He participated in the committee called to review the Bay of Pigs invasion, and he was allowed to stay on until the dedication of the new CIA headquarters at Langley.[9] After his retirement, Dulles continued to defend both his agency and his legacy. For example, he gave talks in which he discussed intelligence operations with which he had been involved, including covert operations such as PBSUCCESS.[10] The historian Simon Willmetts observes that Dulles understood that the CIA had become a celebrity by the time of his retirement, and "perhaps just as concerned with his own individual reputation as the CIA's—although the two had always been contingent upon one another during his tenure—embarked in his retirement upon a public relations campaign to promote his former agency."[11] The results of these efforts were mixed.

Dulles made several appearances on television. He went on *Meet the Press* to discuss Cuba, where he defended his reputation by demonstrating that he did understand the situation there. He still enjoyed a friendly reception; Richard Harkness, with whom he had collaborated to celebrate the CIA's exploits in 1954, asked several questions that gave Dulles the opportunity to speak at length about the CIA's strengths. He also appeared on a show hosted by Hanson Baldwin, which provided a similar opportunity.[12]

Dulles's ability to project a positive image declined over the years, as he became more distant from power and influence and as the CIA came under increasing criticism. A later television appearance went particularly poorly, from Dulles's perspective. He appeared on an NBC special entitled "The Science of Spying," hosted by John Chancellor of NBC News. Produced by Frederick "Ted" Yates, an early Cold War skeptic, the program provided defenders of the CIA the opportunity to make their case, but it also provided space for critics such as Senator Eugene McCarthy (Democrat of Minnesota). Yates apparently revealed some details of the program at a dinner party attended by Frank Wisner, but the CIA was unable to influence the ultimate product.[13] Chancellor's conclusion was, by the standards of the time, especially concerning for the agency. He argued: "The problem we have is how to reconcile the necessity of the CIA with its secret offenses against our public morality. It's getting more and more difficult to be an American these days, and there doesn't seem to be much that we can do about it."[14]

The program gave significant attention to CIA activities in Laos at the time, while also reviewing past CIA activities in Iran, Guatemala, and Indonesia. The Guatemalan operation was not portrayed in a positive manner, as it once had been. Chancellor noted that Castillo Armas had been assassinated in 1957, and his successor, Miguel Ydígoras Fuentes, had been driven into exile. Fuentes spoke at length about Guatemala's involvement in anti-Cuban operations. By 1965 continuing chaos in Guatemala meant that the agency's intervention there was no longer considered an unequivocal success.[15] Dulles wrote to a friend: "I was led to believe . . . the [show's producers] were seeking an opportunity to put in its true and proper light the work of the CIA. In fact, their purpose and intent was quite the opposite."[16]

Dulles remained active in print in addition to television. He engaged in lengthy conversations with Stewart Alsop about working with the *Saturday Evening Post* on a story regarding the U.S. intelligence system. Dulles offered Alsop an article calling for the creation of an Official Secrets Act in the United States, akin to the British system.[17] Alsop was not enthusiastic about Dulles's proposal, but he hoped that, by playing along with Dulles in the moment, he could obtain more exciting stories from him in the future. When Dulles finally produced the article in April 1963, it was rejected, despite Alsop's advocacy.[18] Dulles was no longer in high demand.

The greatest single project that Dulles embarked on was a book on the history of intelligence in the modern age, *The Craft of Intelligence*. A team of former CIA officers, some of whom had only temporarily left the agency, ghostwrote the book. Despite some internal pushback from current CIA officers who were concerned it would set a bad precedent, publication proceeded.[19] Dulles emphasized the importance of the CIA to U.S. national security and defended the CIA from charges that it had or sought to have undue influence in the U.S. government.

Dulles stressed also an argument that, while true, had also become somewhat rote by the 1960s: that the CIA was much more effective than it appeared. He explained, "Since generally only unsuccessful ones [covert operations] become advertised, the public gains the impression that the batting average of intelligence is much lower than is really the case."[20] The book received generally poor reviews; even the friendliest review, by Chalmers Roberts, suggested Dulles's assertion that the CIA sought no policy-making role in government was unlikely.[21] Another effort by Dulles, to turn a book about his negotiations to bring about an early German surrender in Italy in 1945 into a film, met with failure.[22]

As Dulles promoted the CIA, his successor established his own policies with the press. Unlike Dulles, John McCone did not come from the world of intelligence. He was an unexpected choice.[23] McCone was from California, which set him apart from many of the Establishment figures in Kennedy's administration. A graduate of Berkeley, McCone had established himself as a businessman in the 1920s, and he first entered government service during the Truman administration. Before assuming the DCI position, McCone was best known for his stint as the head of the Atomic Energy Commission (AEC) from 1958 to 1960. McCone began to take over responsibility for the CIA in November 1961, though he was not formally appointed until January 1962.

Most news coverage of McCone's nomination was positive, especially from the *Los Angeles Times*.[24] He was controversial, however, among some liberal writers. While head of the AEC, the politically conservative McCone had claimed that atomic scientists in favor of a test ban treaty were unduly influenced by Soviet propaganda.[25] The *New Republic* was especially critical of him and repeatedly published stories criticizing the choice and celebrating McCone's congressional opponents.[26]

That congressional opposition to McCone was objectively minimal but significant by the standards of 1962. Twelve senators, including both Democrats and Republicans, voted against his nomination, in contrast to the voting on McCone's three predecessors, who had experienced no resistance. The reporting of Drew Pearson, who wrote that potential conflicts of interest existed because of McCone's business concerns, influenced some senators. Others cited McCone's lack of intelligence experience. Some voiced concern beyond McCone himself; Eugene McCarthy felt the CIA played too great a role in American foreign policy, especially given that it lacked strong congressional control.[27] The unexpected opposition shook McCone, as did the recent death of his wife, Rosemary. McCone offered his resignation, but it was rejected.[28]

Ultimately, McCone proved to be an effective DCI. Unlike Dulles, McCone emphasized intelligence gathering over operations. Despite his unfamiliarity with intelligence, McCone was an effective absorber and communicator of complicated information.[29] He had not moved away from covert operations entirely; he supported "dynamic action" against Castro, for example, in the various attempts to kill the Cuban leader or destabilize his regime known as Operation MONGOOSE.[30] The CIA conducted aggressive operations in Laos and Vietnam during his tenure. No single event during his tenure, however, captured public attention or catalyzed opinion in the way the Bay of Pigs had.

McCone's approach to the press was different from Dulles's. He did not completely change past practice. As noted at the beginning of this chapter, he permitted Ray Cline to continue briefing members of the press. As will be discussed later, he also established a relationship with the Washington Bureau of the *New York Times*. McCone, however, kept tighter control than Dulles on the information shared through such relationships. In trouble spots like

Vietnam, McCone shut down the exchange of information between foreign correspondents and CIA station personnel. David Halberstam of the *Times,* in Vietnam in 1963, complained that the reporting in Saigon had become more difficult because "the CIA is tight as a drum (orders not to talk to newsmen)."[31]

A sign of McCone's greater caution is the absence of complimentary news stories on him like those that had appeared on Dulles. The sole exception was an article written by Stewart Alsop for the *Saturday Evening Post* in July 1963 on intelligence in policy making, in which Alsop praised McCone's leadership.[32] McCone agreed to an interview, but he insisted that no reference be made to the interview in Alsop's article. The point was important to McCone because he had successfully prevented cover stories on the CIA from appearing in *Time* and *Newsweek* by personally imploring the editors of these publications to ignore the subject, and he did not want to appear hypocritical.[33] McCone was also embarrassed by the article's assumption of a conflict between the CIA and the Defense Intelligence Agency (DIA), and he explained that he had tried to convince Alsop that the assumption was flawed, but Alsop "totally ignored the facts given him in the respective interviews."[34]

McCone and Dulles both provided information to reporters on world situations, with the hope that such access would lead to an understanding of and sympathy for the CIA. McCone differed from Dulles, however, by limiting himself to that kind of deep background arrangement. Dulles, on the other hand, had at times gone beyond deep background to publicize CIA successes and burnish his own image. The philosophy of McCone is best captured in a statement he made to two authors discussing a book on the CIA with him: "Any article or book about intelligence were undesirable from the viewpoint of an intelligence officer."[35]

Reporting on CIA Activities Abroad, 1961–1965

McCone's influence can be seen in the limited reporting on the CIA's operations abroad during his tenure. What reporting occurred tended to focus on Laos. American operations in Laos, and press coverage thereof, predated the Bay of Pigs. By 1961 the United States had committed hundreds of millions of dollars to Laos in an attempt to build an anticommunist bulwark in the region.[36] The political situation there was confusing. The Laotian government originally sought to establish a neutralist stance in the region, but foreign pressure resulted in several changes in the Laotian government, including one military coup supported by the CIA.[37] The most exposure of the CIA's participation in this chaos came in a critique in the *New Republic*, which accused the CIA of attempting to radicalize anticommunists in the country, when accepting Laos as neutral would have been the easier, surer course of action.[38]

In April 1961 the *Saturday Evening Post* reported that millions of dollars in foreign aid to Laos were wasted, partly as the result of clashes between the CIA and Winthrop Brown, the U.S. ambassador to Laos.[39] An article critical of the CIA was unusual for the *Saturday Evening Post*. Despite Stewart Alsop's continued presence, the close relationship between the CIA and that periodical declined. Arthur Krock, Walter Lippmann, and Marquis Childs also weighed in against the CIA's Laotian activities.[40]

The CIA improved its ability to act covertly in Laos after 1962, when a truce was established. Neither that truce nor opprobrium for meddling in Laotian politics prevented continued U.S. clandestine actions there. The CIA came to cooperate closely with ambassador William Sullivan after his appointment in 1964, and it armed the Hmong mountain people of Laos through the Air America airline and the International Cooperation Agency.[41] Throughout the 1960s wide swathes of Laos in which the CIA operated were closed to the press. The photographer Jane Hamilton-Merritt, on location in Laos at the time, recalled that the press knew the ban related to CIA bases in Laos and air bases in Thailand.[42] Most of the press respected this ban. As would be demonstrated in 1969, when three reporters simply hiked fifteen miles to the largest base operated by the CIA in Laos at Long Chen, it would not have been difficult for the press to gain access.

Though precise details were absent from 1962 to 1969, more of the CIA's activities made it into the press than in the pre-1961 period. It was apparent that something, at least, was going on. Peter Grose of the *New York Times* reported in October 1964 that teams trained by the CIA in Vietnam were fighting in Laos, though such actions were "not discussed by responsible officials."[43] The pattern of U.S. reporting on Laos demonstrates that, while there was fraying in press self-censorship with regard to U.S. clandestine activities, the standard that covert U.S. operations not be made the subject of significant attention remained.

A similar pattern held in Vietnam. While there was, of course, increasing attention paid to U.S. military involvement in Vietnam, the same could not be said of CIA activities. The only real revelation of CIA activities in Vietnam during McCone's tenure came during the civil unrest in that country in the summer of 1963, which led to the coup against the South Vietnamese leader Ngo Dinh Diem. Reporters revealed in September 1963 that the CIA had trained the Special Forces being used by Ngo Dinh Nhu, Diem's brother. Those forces had been used to suppress protesters.[44]

During McCone's tenure, the CIA also conducted covert activities in Latin and South America. For example, the CIA funded conservative candidates in the Brazilian presidential elections in 1962, as it had in the Italian elections in 1948. This effort failed, and, following the unexpected resignation of the victorious president, the leftist João Goulart came to power. Fearing Goulart was a communist, the CIA supported agitation against him, and he was eventually overthrown in a military coup in 1964. Coverage in the United States was insubstantial.[45]

These various CIA actions did not draw attention as the Bay of Pigs had because no single decisive moment focused attention on the CIA. McCone did not support activities as difficult to conceal as invasions in Guatemala or Cuba, though less obvious activities continued in Cuba. In some cases, press coverage of CIA activity during 1961–1965 was almost completely absent. For example, though it is now known that the CIA was active in supporting its clients in the Congo and had plotted to assassinate the Congolese leader Patrice Lumumba, these activities carried minimal significance in the U.S. press. The agency's presence in hot spots around the world was attested to in scattered and frequently unreliable stories.

Growing Domestic Concern with the CIA, 1961–1965

The relatively low profile of the CIA abroad did not translate to lack of coverage of the CIA. Most CIA reporting emerged from coverage of congressional hearings on the CIA, or during criticism of the occasional perceived failure by the CIA to predict some troublesome event, a pattern the CIA had experienced since its early days.[46] More important, a new group of commentators began to question whether the CIA unduly influenced or distorted the U.S. government. Some authors began to accuse the CIA of essentially usurping the democratically elected government of the United States.

Part of this more critical coverage of the CIA emerged, as the reporting on Laos had, in the aftermath of the Bay of Pigs invasion. The *Nation* made one of the earliest attempts to produce an exposé of the CIA, in the summer of 1961. An entire issue of the *Nation* was dedicated to the agency. The investigative journalist Fred Cook wrote the whole issue; he confined himself to using what had been published previously on the CIA. What he produced was thus one of the most complete documents of press coverage of the CIA's operations up to 1961.[47]

Cook began with what had, in the weeks after the Bay of Pigs, become a shibboleth of any author on the left commenting on the CIA; he wrote that as the agency was currently a "two-edged sword," it needed to be divested of its operational capacity. Cook charged that Allen Dulles had been able to "*disorientate not only the President and Congress, but also the People of the United States.*" Cook accurately hypothesized that the Harknesses' *Saturday Evening Post* stories had been planted by Allen Dulles, and that especially in the case of Guatemala, "the CIA showed a tendency, if not to brag, at least to chuckle in public about this wily and triumphant coup."[48]

While providing a relatively complete account of the CIA's activities, Cook suffered from several hindrances that prevented his article from gaining further attention. First, without new evidence, there was no real hook. Second, while much of what Cook wrote was correct, he did have a tendency to see conspiracies that strained credulity. His portrait of Allen Dulles was especially hard to believe, as it presented a much more sinister and more competent spy than the recent Bay of Pigs debacle would have suggested. Cook ended somewhat melodramatically with the conclusion that the CIA was "a Frankenstein monster dominating the Congress that created it."[49]

Since he confined himself to what had been previously published, Cook did not have access to an important CIA story: its connections with ostensibly private institutions. These connections were organized by the CIA's International Organizations Division, which had been set up in 1950 by Thomas Braden. Braden judged that simple anticommunism would not be effective in enlisting European intellectual elites against the Soviet Union. He sought, instead, to marshal a noncommunist left to counter Soviet cultural propaganda. In addition to more well-known programs, such as those supporting the Congress for Cultural Freedom and intellectual periodicals in Europe, Braden organized support for modernists like Jackson Pollock and purchased the rights to George Orwell's *Animal Farm* in order to make an animated movie.[50]

The CIA's attempts to influence public opinion included efforts to recruit Americans to report from abroad. A first hint of this emerged in a humorous piece written for *Harper's Magazine* by Hughes Rudd, a CBS News correspondent. Rudd wrote that while in school in California under the GI Bill, he was approached by the CIA. He was offered a job writing "reports from . . . certain countries in Western Europe." While he was not directly stating that he would be writing news reports, Rudd had experience at that point as a reporter; it was this experience, he said, that interested the CIA. Rudd accepted, but he was not contacted again until some years later, after he had a wife and child, at which point he refused to work for the CIA and became entangled in a nightmarish bureaucracy as the government secretly insisted he work for it.[51] The story was told as a farce; Rudd reported with an ironic and humorous slant. In hindsight, however, elements of the story ring true. The CIA's international organizations program was active in 1952, which matches the time line of Rudd's story.

By the time the next major criticisms of the CIA emerged, in 1964, few critics found the agency funny. Eugene McCarthy, in the *Saturday Evening Post,* charged that the CIA usurped and warped U.S. foreign policy. He especially criticized the CIA for its interventions against foreign governments. By January 1964, it was commonly known that the CIA had intervened against Mossadegh and Arbenz in 1953 and 1954; McCarthy suggested, incorrectly, that this had been done without oversight from the executive branch.[52]

In addition to McCarthy's article, two books were released examining the CIA in 1964. Henry Howe Ransom published *Can American Democracy Survive the Cold War?* Ransom was a member of the Harvard Defense Studies Program from 1955 to 1961, author of an early book about the CIA, *Central Intelligence and National Security* (1958), and an occasional contributor to the *New York Times* and the *New Republic.* In *Can American Democracy Survive the Cold War?* Ransom traced the major U.S. national security institutions that developed after World War II. The CIA was dangerous because, Ransom explained, "secret knowledge can become secret power."[53]

More sensational, and more publicized, than Ransom's writing was the collaboration of David Wise of the *New York Herald Tribune* and Thomas B. Ross of the *Chicago Sun-Times,* published in May 1964. In their work, *The Invisible Government,* they charged that the United States had two governments. The first, public government was the duly constitutional order of executive, legislative, and judicial power. The second and more powerful government was composed of the nondemocratic institutions dedicated to fighting the Cold War.[54]

Ross and Wise provided a fairly accurate history of the agency. They wrote that, whatever he might protest, Harry Truman had directed the CIA to conduct covert actions. Ross and Wise examined what were, by 1964, well-known examples of CIA interventions, such as Cuba and Iran. They dug further, however, and wrote that Allen Pope was working for the CIA when he was shot down in Indonesia. They also accused the CIA of operating the ostensibly private Radio Liberty station in Europe.

What made Ross and Wise distinctive was not their coverage of CIA foreign interventions, but their coverage of CIA domestic activities and their willingness to refer to agency officials by name. They revealed, for example, that the CIA regularly debriefed tourists and other foreign travelers when returning to the United States from areas of interest. They also wrote that the CIA was heavily involved in private institutions. They accused the agency of being involved in these private institutions primarily to manipulate not foreign opinion, but the U.S. citizenry.

Ross and Wise were generally accurate in the specific details they provided on the history of the CIA. Like Fred Cook, however, they overestimated the agency's independence from the executive branch; many liberal critics of the CIA would, in the coming years, adopt the point of view of Ross and Wise and argue the CIA was a force unto itself. The evidentiary record, however, demonstrates that U.S. presidents were well aware of the CIA's operations and were the main force in directing its activities. Ross and Wise, still in the minority, were roundly criticized for including the names of CIA officers.[55] Even Ransom criticized them for overstating CIA influence in cultural and academic programs, noting, "Taking this book in all seriousness, one may suspect that his corner grocer is a CIA agent."[56]

While Ross and Wise may have overstated their case on some points, they were more accurate than their contemporaries who insisted there was nothing to their stories. The concerns voiced by Ross and Wise reflected a real and growing segment of opinion. Marquis Childs and Gilbert Harrison both represented this shift. Earlier, they had supported the CIA. Harrison had, as editor of the *New Republic,* reportedly decided not to run a story on the preparations for the Bay of Pigs invasion at the request of President Kennedy. But he and Childs found the implications of *Invisible Government* disturbing and plausible.[57]

Invisible Government also represented the CIA's failure to prevent or mitigate criticism using its connections with journalists and publishers. McCone had asked Wise and Ross not to proceed with the book. The CIA apparently considered buying the entire first run of the book, until it was observed that the publisher would then just print a second run and use the CIA's reaction to raise interest. McCone's efforts to prevent publication made it to the press in 1964, a rare failure of his careful efforts to keep a low profile.[58]

The CIA struggled to keep other secrets as well. In September 1964 it experienced a near miss. An investigation into the nonprofit Kaplan Fund, which was used by the CIA in its program to covertly support nonprofit organizations, almost revealed the CIA's role in the fund.[59] A little over a year later, Dan Kurzman, a writer for the *Nation,* contributed a story to the *Washington Post* that reported that Jay Lovestone, the organizer of the American Federation of Labor and Congress of Industrial Organizations' (AFL-CIO's) overseas activities and a member of the Congress for Cultural Freedom, used his foreign contacts to further U.S. foreign policy and probably had ties with the CIA.[60] While in themselves minor, the articles represented a steady accumulation of possible CIA activity available to any interested parties. All that was required for the stories to draw greater attention was for an interested party to be a representative of a major news organization.

A story published in April 1965 demonstrates this phenomenon. Spurred by a *Ramparts* story, the *New York Times* and the *Washington Post* both reported that Michigan State University had employed CIA agents in its overseas program to train police officers for Diem's regime in Vietnam. MSU's president claimed that his university had not known the men were affiliated with the agency. An aide, on the other hand, explained that MSU knew the men *had* been CIA agents, but it was under the impression that they were not still affiliated with the agency when employed by MSU. Further reporting revealed a similar program at MIT.[61] The story provided the impetus for the publication of a long-gestating *New York Times* series on the CIA.

The *New York Times,* 1961–1965, and the 1966 CIA Series

When The *New York Times* published a major, five-part series on the CIA in April 1966, it was a milestone in CIA reporting. While not the first publication to write extensively on the activities of the agency, the *Times* was the largest, most influential publication to that date to consider seriously the questions of the appropriateness of CIA operations abroad and the influence of the agency in the United States. It was especially noteworthy because of the *New York Times*'s previous interactions with the intelligence community during John McCone's tenure at the CIA. The *New York Times* Washington Bureau entered into an agreement with McCone to obtain access to CIA information.

The Washington Bureau's agreement with McCone began some time before July 1964. During that month, James Reston, the Washington Bureau chief, informed managing editor Clifton Daniel of the arrangement. Reston explained that the *Times*'s Washington reporters were given access to special briefings, where they received information about world events. None of the information was to be attributed to the CIA. Reston felt he needed to inform the home office of the arrangement because it was important that New York editors not add attribution to certain stories, as that might violate the "ground rules" established by the CIA.[62]

Reston's decision to go forward with the arrangement is an interesting departure from his earlier stance. He had, after all, been the one to sound the alarm with *Times* senior management in 1954 that the CIA sought to spread false information in the Otto John case. The main difference between 1964 and 1954 was that the information the CIA provided to the *Times* was general background on world events and not specifically related to CIA activities. Reston also assured Daniel that he and his fellow Washington reporters were cautious with the material they received. His impression was that the CIA was not trying to use the *Times* to spread disinformation.[63]

Daniel feared that the arrangement could compromise the integrity of the *Times*. His reply to Reston demonstrated the *Times*'s official position with regard to the CIA:

> This letter raises a very serious problem in our minds. We are, of course, eager to have any information we can get from the CIA, but, as a general rule, we cannot publish such information without some kind of attribution. This is particularly true, I think, because the CIA is by its very nature an organization that is not averse to planting stories and putting out misinformation on purpose. I realize that these purposes are noble and patriotic, but they are not necessarily the purposes of a responsible, independent, democratic newspaper. . . .
>
> One thing we certainly want to know is what ground rules the CIA has laid down. These must, of course, be understood by and acceptable to the New York office, as well as the Washington Bureau.[64]

Records of Daniel's subsequent in-person meeting with Reston do not exist, but the outcome can be presumed to have been positive, as the arrangement continued.

In addition to the CIA's newly formalized relationship with the *New York Times* Washington Bureau, one of the *Times*'s most experienced reporters on intelligence entered into his own extraordinary relationship with the U.S. government. Szulc apparently consulted with the Kennedy and Johnson administrations on anti-Castro efforts between 1963 and 1965, despite resistance from the CIA to his presence. It seems that Kennedy personally requested Szulc's involvement. Szulc and the CIA clashed on what to do; Szulc supported trying to foment an internal coup, rather than using outside forces to bring down Castro. Szulc, however, agreed not to publish anything on the CIA while engaged in the administration's work. When the operations were halted, Szulc went to Spain and Portugal as a *Times* correspondent.[65] It does not appear as though he informed his employers at the *Times* of these activities, nor did he mention them in his later reporting on the CIA in the 1970s.

Meanwhile, two personnel changes occurred that significantly influenced *Times* reporting on the CIA. In May 1963 the *New York Times* editor Orvil Dryfoos died of heart disease. His successor was Arthur Hays Sulzberger's only son, Arthur Ochs "Punch" Sulzberger.[66] This leadership transition proved consequential because Punch Sulzberger was willing to reject government claims of national security when he thought it necessary. In the beginning, he was influenced by Turner Catledge, who was generally an advocate for disclosure. After Catledge retired and Sulzberger grew more experienced, he continued to allow *Times* reporting that, in previous years, would have been unthinkable.

Unlike Dryfoos, Punch had not spent years preparing for the position and had served in the Marine Corps during World War II and the Korean War.[67] While he would eventually be highly regarded for his decades-long tenure as the *Times*'s publisher, the younger Sulzberger faced a challenging situation in 1963. The *New York Times* had been struggling financially, especially after a New York newspaper strike in early 1963 that lasted a painful 114 days. The severity of the strike drove several other New York papers into closure. Punch Sulzberger played an important role in meeting this problem and expanding the *Times* to a larger national audience, and he made the paper the center of a larger media company. Early on, however, many were suspicious of the young Sulzberger because of his inexperience and willingness to lay off staff to cut costs.

One of the *Times* reporters who brought national security material to Sulzberger was Thomas "Tom" Wicker, the other important addition to the *Times*. A member of the *Times* Washington Bureau, Wicker became a major opponent of government secrecy and national security claims against reporting. Born in 1926 in North Carolina, Wicker served in the navy during World War II and then went into reporting. He joined the *Times* Washington Bureau in 1960 and soon became a White House correspondent.[68] In this capacity he had been in Dallas the day Kennedy was assassinated, when his reporting drew attention for its accuracy and clarity. After that, he was quickly promoted. In 1964 he succeeded James Reston as Washington Bureau chief. In 1965 he took on Arthur Krock's regular column, In the Nation, after Krock retired.

Wicker was considerably more aggressive as a reporter than Reston. He believed good reporting required a willingness to risk losing access to high officials. He was also a major critic of journalistic objectivity, in the sense that a journalist should present both sides of an issue. He felt that all too often "objective journalism required less that the contradictions [between government pronouncements and reality] be noted than that the official record be kept."[69] Over the course of his career, Wicker became convinced that national security arguments against reporting were almost entirely specious. He decried the "National Security Mystique" that prevented reporters from fulfilling their duty to accurately report the news and keep a check on power.[70]

In 1965, though, his reticence toward official contacts was not yet fully developed. As Washington Bureau chief, Wicker inherited the arrangement with McCone that James Reston had established. Like Reston, though, Wicker stressed that the Washington Bureau journalists accepted nothing from the CIA on faith, and they authenticated the information they were given.[71]

Assistant managing editor Harrison Salisbury recommended that Wicker prepare a "real digging story" on the CIA in April 1965, but Wicker did not consider the time right. Wicker did not explain why he felt so, but a reasonable supposition is that the decision stemmed from a desire not to lose access to the CIA. Such a supposition would also answer a question posed by the historian Tity de Vries regarding the CIA's ties with private organizations— if by 1964 there were already stories about the CIA's relationships with such organizations, why were they not pursued more aggressively?[72] Maintaining access was an incentive for reporters where the CIA was concerned. Though Wicker never publicly commented on the arrangement, his later statements concerning the dangers of access indicate that he came to rethink his participation in the arrangement with the CIA.[73]

The understanding with McCone did not continue past McCone's tenure as DCI. Judging by the report on Ray Cline's activities discussed earlier in this chapter, McCone's successor, William Raborn, was not aware of McCone's interactions with the press on behalf of the CIA. Then, in September 1965, a story about the CIA's efforts to bribe the prime minister of Singapore emerged. Turner Catledge was disturbed by the story and suggested the *Times* study the CIA.[74] This time, Wicker agreed.

The reporters Max Frankel, Jack Raymond, Robert "Bob" Phelps, John Finney, and Edwin "E. W." Kenworthy joined Wicker in a comprehensive survey of the CIA. Wicker asked a host of *Times* foreign correspondents to send him information about their interactions with the CIA, their familiarity with the CIA's activities, and their evaluation of the quality of CIA personnel. They also requested foreign correspondents provide their evaluation of the CIA's goals and methods compared to public U.S. policy.[75] Wicker's central thesis was that the political machinery to control the CIA already existed, but that the political will to exercise the machinery was lacking.[76]

Out of respect for the sensitivity of the issues involved, the *Times* allowed McCone to read the series before its publication and make suggestions for changes. Most of McCone's suggestions, however, were ignored.[77] Punch Sulzberger was wary of the series, but Catledge assured him that every point raised by McCone was carefully considered, and that he was confident the series was appropriate to run. Catledge noted, "Articles involving much greater consideration of national security . . . have been published without the extreme care which we have taken in this case." Catledge advised that the series be published. It awaited only "an adequate news peg."[78]

The CIA's involvement with MSU provided such a peg. As that story began to fade, the *Times* released the five articles beginning April 25. Each article, published on page one, addressed a different facet of intelligence. The first presented the basic questions the series explored. Was the CIA, "which was known to have overthrown governments and installed others," out of control of its supposed political masters? Did covert action harm the national interest? Did the CIA influence American political leaders to such an extent that it could properly be called "an invisible government"?[79]

Wicker and his colleagues concluded that the CIA was not out of control. They argued that "for all its fearsome reputation, [the CIA] is under far more stringent political and budgetary control than most of its critics know or concede."[80] Similarly, the authors concluded that the CIA did not constitute an "invisible government." Their chief concern was covert action; the authors believed that there was a danger in the United States' relying too much on "dirty tricks" in foreign policy. The reputation of the agency was so horrendous abroad that, regardless of the reality of its activities, the CIA had become a burden to U.S. interests. The authors concluded that the main problem with covert operations was that the CIA could always promise "action, if not success." The danger, then, was not in control but in the effect clandestine activities had on foreign policy.[81]

The rest of the articles provided an extensive examination of CIA structure, capabilities, and activities.[82] The third article discussed the CIA's electronic spying, its spy satellite capabilities, and its cultural programs. Wicker and the others revealed that the CIA had close ties to academia and to private organizations like the Congress for Cultural Freedom and the British publication *Encounter*.[83] The fourth and fifth articles discussed, respectively, a CIA plot to contaminate Cuban sugar that was halted because it would harm the United States' reputation, and the importance of the qualities of the DCI in determining the conduct of the agency. The series concluded with a reiteration of their main point: concern with the CIA should not be that it was out of control, but with how the "real government of the United States" decided to use it.[84]

The series drew angry denials from some of those mentioned as having ties with the CIA. Nicholas Nabokov, a member of the Congress for Cultural Freedom (CCF), denied his organization received any support from the CIA. This was a lie; Nabokov was a witting participant in the CIA's support of the CCF.[85] In England, Melvin Lasky of *Encounter* also denied any connection to the CIA and threatened the *Times* with legal action. Frankel, who had discovered *Encounter*'s ties to the CIA by interviewing McGeorge Bundy, insisted the report was accurate. The *Times*'s management decided to stand by its reporting, and Lasky did not sue.[86]

Raborn resigned shortly after publication of the series, something that Harrison Salisbury believed the *Times* could take credit for.[87] The *Times* did not, though, follow up on the series. Richard Helms, Raborn's successor, convinced the *Times* not to adapt the CIA series into a book.[88] Salisbury himself remained cautious; while celebrating Raborn's resignation, Salisbury revealed that during his reporting in Vietnam, he had discovered that the CIA was using other governmental organizations as a cover. In Laos, the American Agency for International Development and the CIA "are so intertwined that it is almost impossible to separate one from the other." This information did not appear in the *Times*.[89]

While limitations in reporting remained, the CIA series was an important turning point for the *Times*. During the early 1960s, the *New York Times* had been closer to the CIA through its arrangement with McCone than at any other time in its history. During the course of the arrangement, the *Times* did not run major stories on the CIA, probably for fear of losing access. After their access ended, however, the *Times* still went forward with the series despite CIA protests.

The *Times* continued to be cautious in reporting on CIA activities, but it had published and not suffered for it. As more information about the CIA's connections with private institutions was released, the *Times* was joined by many in the press in reporting on the CIA in greater depth.

The 1967 National Student Association Scandal

The question of the CIA's involvement with ostensibly private actors and groups persisted after the *Times* series appeared.[90] In early 1967 all the various hints and insinuations about the CIA's role in private foundations would be replaced with real, tangible evidence. A former National Student Association (NSA) member named Michael Wood told the editors of *Ramparts* that the CIA was heavily involved in the NSA and gave them financial records to prove it. The editors then matched those records to a CIA front group accidentally revealed in the press in 1964, providing confirmation of Wood's story. The *Ramparts* editors took out advertisements in larger newspapers announcing their upcoming story. In February the CIA involvement in the NSA was publicly acknowledged when Eugene Groves, then the president of the NSA, admitted his organization's past ties with the CIA in an ultimately vain attempt to contain the controversy. By the time "A Short Account of International Student Politics and the Cold War with Particular Reference to the NSA, CIA, etc." was published in *Ramparts* in March 1967, the story was a month old.[91]

The CIA had defenders such as William White, one of the reporters with whom Cline regularly met.[92] The tone of most newspaper commentators, though, was moral outrage.[93] The revelations also continued. Reporters confirmed the CIA's role in labor in May.[94] E. W. Kenworthy, who had been a contributor to the 1966 *Times* CIA series, revealed that the Hobby Foundation, run by William Hobby Jr., owner of the *Houston Post,* extensively funneled money for the CIA. Richard Harwood of the *Washington Post* identified eight private foundations that had funneled CIA money: five operating out of New York, one from Detroit, the Hobby Foundation from Houston that Kenworthy had uncovered, and one from Boston. Andrew J. Glass, also of the *Washington Post,* expanded on the institutions involved even further, locating more in Lexington, Kentucky, Columbus, Ohio, Philadelphia, and Baltimore. Donald "Don" Irwin of the *Los Angeles Times* also dug further, revealing CIA links with Boston-based foundations.[95]

Journalists also revealed the identity of the current head of the CIA's International Organizations Division, Cord Meyer Jr. By the end of February, President Johnson ordered an investigation into the CIA's involvement with ostensibly private groups, headed by the former attorney general Nicholas Katzenbach. The controversy extended internationally as students in a partially U.S.–funded university in West Berlin demanded an investigation into potential CIA involvement in their university. India expelled an American foundation on the grounds that it could be a tool for CIA infiltration. Closer to home, the Woodrow Wilson School of Public and International Affairs sent a letter to all graduate students that stressed the need to avoid any entanglements with intelligence. The school forbade students to participate in covert activities, and it required that any attempted recruitment be immediately reported.[96]

A new wrinkle in the story appeared toward the end of April, when word began to leak that in a May issue of the *Saturday Evening Post,* Thomas Braden would write about his CIA activities. Braden had left the CIA in 1954 and served as president of the California Board of Education and editor-publisher of the *Oceanside (CA) Blade-Tribune.* Reporters wondering if Braden had anything interesting to say in his article would not be disappointed.

In an article titled "I'm Glad the CIA Is 'Immoral,'" Braden laid out in considerable detail the genesis of the CIA's cultural projects, along with specific names of people involved. He opened by noting that he still had the receipt confirming "Warren G. Haskins" had given "Norris A. Grambo" $15,000—and that he was Haskins and Grambo was Irving Brown, a member of the AFL and a direct subordinate to Jay Lovestone. Braden decried recent criticism of the CIA by the labor leader Walter Reuther by noting that he had personally given Walter's brother Victor $50,000 to bolster European labor unions. Braden then went on to give further examples of his own actions, such as funding a trip of the Boston Symphony Orchestra through Western Europe, funding *Encounter* magazine in the United Kingdom, and funding Jay Lovestone's labor activities.[97] Furthermore, Braden reported that, while he had conducted these activities, the CIA's cultural operations enjoyed the firm support of Allen Dulles. Braden's revelations in many cases confirmed things long suspected, but they also revealed CIA activities the press had had no indication existed. It was, in the words of the journalist Alexander Werth, a "Literary Bay of Pigs."[98]

Cord Meyer told Dulles on 1 May that Braden's story had already been set in type, and that Braden had not told the CIA he was writing the article until it was too late to stop it; the main revelations of the article were already reported by 7 May.[99] Meyer wrote to Dulles that "Tom meant well but obviously it is going to be very damaging." Dulles was furious, rejecting any efforts to defend Braden. Dulles's suspicions were confirmed for him when he discovered from a contact that Braden had a book deal. There was no further communication between the two.[100]

Frances Stonor Saunders proposes another theory about Braden's motives. She suggests Braden was directed to reveal what he did by CIA officers unhappy with their alliance with the noncommunist left; this revelation would then break the seventeen-year-long CIA–noncommunist left alliance. She observes that Braden was never penalized for breaking his employee contract with the CIA by revealing what he did, and that the CIA did not prevent the publication of the article despite knowing it existence before its publication date.[101]

There is some support for Saunders's theory. Braden met with Richard Helms shortly after the initial story broke in February.[102] If Helms instructed Braden to purposefully blow the CIA's private-group activities, it would probably have been at that meeting. Additionally, Helms did have a copy of the story in advance that he provided to Katharine Graham in late April, though from Graham's reply it seems when discussing it in person he had expressed considerable anger to her over the article.[103]

Likelier than the plot, though, is that Braden's article was unwelcome by the CIA. Helms had an apparently early edition because, as he explained to Graham, though it was dated 20 May, the article appeared much earlier. Production was rushed because the *Saturday Evening Post* faced an imminent strike.[104] The *Saturday Evening Post*'s relationship with the CIA had become uncertain, and the CIA also had not succeeded in preventing the publication of other stories in the past inimical to its interests in the *Saturday Evening Post.* The periodical also was in dire financial straits in 1967, and it would have been hard-pressed to give up a sensational story on the CIA even had it wanted to.

It was also not out of character for Stewart Alsop to seek exciting CIA stories to publish. Alsop had also earlier sought to get information on blown operations for the *Saturday Evening Post* from Allen Dulles. Alsop and Braden had also collaborated in the past in writing on the OSS; Alsop had even recommended that the *Saturday Evening Post* hire Braden on several occasions. Alsop was also frustrated by attacks on the CIA and the impression that he was too tightly connected with the agency.[105] He may well have seen the article as a defense of both the CIA and himself.

Braden was himself a liberal, with no deep loyalty to any CIA officers who wanted to destroy the CIA-NCL link. Though Saunders's theory is not implausible, it is at least equally likely that Braden simply badly misjudged the reception his article would receive, and the CIA chose not to punish a well-established, respected veteran of the agency. The agency would develop a reputation for being much more accommodating to senior members who had left on good terms than to lower-level employees. Additionally, as the historian Christopher Moran argues, leaks from "apostates," who not only revealed information but also rejected the CIA's view of itself, were treated more harshly. Moran observes that the CIA dealt with leakers and critics like Victor Marchetti, Philip Agee, and Frank Snepp with an almost emotional, and ultimately counterproductive, backlash resulting from a feeling of betrayal.[106] Braden, in 1967 at least, was still a CIA loyalist, if one who behaved poorly. Rather than writing a book on the CIA, he went on to write *Eight Is Enough* (1975), which inspired the later TV series, and cohosted *Crossfire* with Patrick Buchanan.

In May the Katzenbach Committee concluded that the CIA's activities were useful but ought to have been done openly. It recommended the creation of a state-private mechanism for future activities. The committee was hardly unbiased; Katzenbach himself had written for the periodical the *Reporter,* which probably received funding from the CIA, and the committee included DCI Richard Helms. In retrospect, the CIA seems to have taken the committee's findings to mean mainly that it needed to be more discreet.[107] Senator Mansfield, one of the earliest supporters of increased CIA monitoring, did an about-face and agreed with the conclusions of the Katzenbach Committee.

Rather than a permanent congressional watchdog being created, three members of the Senate Foreign Relations Committee were added to the CIA subcommittee of the Armed Services Committee. Mansfield was one of those senators.[108] There were consequences for the CIA, however, the most immediate of which was the destruction of nearly twenty years' worth of work in building connections with anti-Soviet cultural activities in the United States and around the world.

Another consequence of the NSA scandal was an internal investigation by the *New York Times* to determine whether the CIA had unduly influenced it. The management of the *Times,* of course, knew about the arrangement for information with McCone, and that CIA officers were often sources of information for foreign correspondents. It wanted to discover, as a missive to past and present foreign correspondents explained, any relations with the CIA "aside from normal" contacts, or about reporters suspected of having ties to the CIA.[109] The reports sent back did not result in a story in the *Times,* but they do offer a valuable window into CIA efforts to use the press.

Most of the responses were negative, but there were exceptions. Henry Tanner, a reporter with the *Times* Paris Bureau, reported that when he had worked for the *Houston Post,* the CIA and his managing editor had requested he interview foreign visitors under the auspices of the National Education Foundation. Tanner reported that he complied and had never been approached again after he conducted several interviews.[110] Another journalist had a similar story, explaining that he was approached to provide a briefing to CIA officials on Korea after a trip there, whereas another provided a briefing on Cuba. One reporter had, as a student, participated in an NSA program, though he claimed no knowledge of the CIA's influence on the organization. One had been approached during the strike of 1962–1963 to teach journalism abroad and keep an eye on the students for possible recruitment opportunities. Another was approached about employment with the CIA, but in a full-time, official position. Peter Grose, a future biographer of Allen Dulles, informed the *Times* that a close personal friend of his was a CIA officer, but he had never worked on stories with him. The officer in question informed Grose that the CIA would probably tend to avoid career correspondents and, if anything, approach stringers.[111]

Several *Times* journalists had suspicions about other reporters. Two suspected that representatives of *Reporter* magazine had CIA ties. Malcolm Browne, a photojournalist in Vietnam, suggested that the *Times* investigate possible CIA activity in the Saigon press club. A Latin American correspondent reported that the CIA approached reporters for information, supported newsmen writing pro–United States books, and used some newsmen as agents. A Hong Kong correspondent, Tillman Durdin, knew that in the early 1950s a CIA officer named Edward Hunter had posed as a reporter in Hong Kong, and Hunter supposedly then later accused many correspondents of being communists to Joseph McCarthy.[112]

One journalist reported being approached to do work for the agency covertly while maintaining his public affiliation with the *Times.* That reporter, Edward A. Morrow, revealed that, when in Berlin in 1948, he had been approached by the CIA and offered an arrangement in which he would obtain access to CIA information in exchange for conducting various intelligence tasks. The CIA officer who made the approach also informed Morrow that, if he agreed, he would be assigned a secret government rank. Morrow refused.[113]

Of sixty-four foreign correspondents questioned, twenty-one reported that there were other journalists they suspected of having ties to the CIA. Most of those suspected were either stringers or wire reporters. Six reported they had either done some work for the CIA or been offered work. One reported being approached to serve as both an intelligence operative and a reporter.

Some of these contacts were fairly routine. The reporters who provided briefings based on their travels, for example, were communicating what they had learned on stories related to their jobs and had not been tasked by the CIA. The approach to Morrow is suggestive, though, of the practice of the CIA's use of journalists in formal relationships. There was a regular procedure, a clear gain for both parties, and an established system that existed for formal relationships. These responses suggest, however, that such practices were relatively rare at a major publication.

As the 1960s went on, more and more of the CIA's activities were aired to the American public in an increasingly open forum. While punctuated by dramatic and attention-consuming controversies, CIA activities were also revealed in a slow, steady stream. With each progressive revelation, the next crisis became more damaging. The 1967 *Ramparts* disclosures would help lead to even greater problems for the CIA; the historian Hugh Wilford observes that the largely toothless Katzenbach Committee established a prec-

edent for congressional investigation of the agency.[114] Shortly after the dissolution of the CIA's ties with the NSA, the agency began surveillance on the
organization and *Ramparts*.[115] Intensified internal surveillance would have
important ramifications for the CIA.

The 1960s did not see a definitive breaking of the early Cold War relationship between the press and the CIA, but the environment was much less
friendly and predictable. The ability of a small publication such as *Ramparts*
to strike a sizable blow to the CIA demonstrates that the agency's position had
deteriorated in the 1960s, to the extent that some of the members of the organizations it supported could no longer countenance being part of its agenda.
Rather than cooperating for a common task, many interpreted the CIA's
front organizations as dishonest and corrupting. The *Ramparts* flap also
showed how much the CIA had counted on a friendly press and friendly organizations in broad agreement with its goals to function covertly. Publications
that previously might have turned their gaze away from *Ramparts'* reports
instead investigated further. These changes represented a decline of the early
Cold War press-CIA relationships, though not their final dissolution.

5

The Clash of Intelligence Advocates and Critics

In 1974 *Harper's Magazine* editor Taylor Branch wrote a scathing account of the CIA's efforts to censor a book written by the former CIA officer Victor Marchetti. Marchetti's *The CIA and the Cult of Intelligence* was extremely critical of the agency, and the CIA fought a lengthy legal battle to prevent its publication. On the basis of their bumbling efforts against Marchetti and the details revealed in Marchetti's book, Branch concluded that the CIA was not the supremely competent, effective organization its members claimed. This reputation for effectiveness was the CIA's "best protection against the meddlesome notions of outsiders."[1] In reality, Branch argued, the CIA struggled to gain useful intelligence against its primary opponent, the Soviet Union. Instead, the CIA focused its efforts on the Third World because of the agency's need to find a mission in light of its other failures. The CIA intervened abroad just to find something to do. The CIA, Branch observed, was "drawn to the Third World like a lonely derelict to a porn shop, where the salve for dreams is cheap and available."[2]

Branch argued that incompetence did not make the CIA safe. The legal case against Marchetti demonstrated the problems of legally sanctioned government secrecy. The government argued that it could restrict publication on the grounds that, as a CIA officer, Marchetti had sworn a legally enforceable oath of secrecy. Branch feared that the precedent legitimized the CIA's efforts to censor former employees' writing on the basis of their sworn secrecy oaths. This kind of censorship, he warned, could establish two classes of citizens: the ignorant masses, and those deemed dependable enough to be trusted by the government to participate fully in U.S. political life. Ultimately the presiding judge ruled that while many of the more than 300 deletions requested by the government were not required, 168 deletions were justified and would be withheld in the final print.

By 1974 Branch's criticism and ridicule of the CIA were not unusual in *Harper's Magazine,* but such criticism was a marked departure from the publication's early coverage of intelligence. Hanson Baldwin had written one of his earliest articles on intelligence for *Harper's,* in which he praised the NIA/CIG arrangements that had recently been created.[3] Over the years, though, that stance had shifted, as *Harper's* published stories such as Hughes Rudd's humorous writing on CIA efforts to influence the news from Western Europe, or, more seriously, accusations that the CIA was heavily involved in the heroin trade in Southeast Asia. As a writer and editor, Taylor Branch did not give the agency the benefit of the doubt.

The distance between Baldwin and Branch was a microcosm of the changes that had occurred in the United States from the early days of the Cold War to the Nixon administration. As the United States was wracked by division over Vietnam, and as challenges to the Cold War consensus that had governed earlier Cold War policy increased, the CIA frequently found itself portrayed in a negative light. Meanwhile, as Nixon pursued détente with the Soviet Union and the People's Republic of China, many writers saw the CIA increasingly as a dangerous relic of an earlier era.

The fundamental tipping point against the CIA was Watergate. The CIA was embarrassed to find some of its former employees, most notably E. Howard Hunt, directly involved in the break-in at the Watergate Hotel and other illegal activities on behalf of the Nixon administration. The collapse of the Nixon presidency opened further possibilities for congressional investigation and further motivation for those who wanted to explore the more secretive parts of the U.S. government.

Richard Helms, the *New York Times,* and the Growing Press-CIA Strife

The relationships between the CIA and the press during the late 1960s and early 1970s did not evolve uniformly. Generally positive relationships persisted. Members of the press still at times sought out the CIA as a source of information. Members of the CIA, including DCI Richard Helms, cooperated with the press at times to further their ends. Helms combined elements of both Dulles and McCone in his approach to the press, as he cultivated relationships similar to Dulles's but, like McCone, was cautious when making public statements and releasing information on agency activities.

Helms was, in many respects, the embodiment of the first generation of U.S. career intelligence officers. Sophisticated and witty, he felt at home both in the Washington social scene and when he testified before Congress. While not a graduate of the Ivy League like many of his colleagues, Helms had a cosmopolitan background. Educated in Switzerland at a young age, he graduated from Williams College in 1935. His first career was journalism. He wrote for the United Press, putting his French and German skills to use as a foreign correspondent. He was fond of mentioning that he had, in his capacity as a correspondent, interviewed Adolf Hitler.[4] Helms's time as a journalist left him with a familiarity with members of the press, and with the way the press operated. He enjoyed friendships with several members of the press, including Hugh Sidey and Hedley Donovan of *Time,* Cyrus Sulzberger of the *New York Times,* the Alsop brothers, and the Grahams of the *Washington Post.*

Following a postwar interlude in intelligence work, in 1947 Helms joined the newly created CIA. He worked in the Office of Special Operations conducting espionage in Central Europe, and was able to boast of several achievements, such as a successful effort to tap East Berlin cable messages.[5] Though he avoided close involvement in the Bay of Pigs, Helms became involved in the infamous Operation Mongoose, an effort to kill Fidel Castro. Helms later admitted that intense pressure from the Kennedy administration resulted in some "nutty schemes."[6]

Helms established a solid reputation for discretion and loyalty. In 1966 he became the first career intelligence officer to become director of Central Intelligence. He was a formidable leader. Peter Fenn, a member of the Church Committee that would investigate many of the activities that Helms was involved in, recalled that "Helms . . . was one of the biggest snakes . . . He is in his nice suits and his suave, debonair ways, and he's at every frigging Georgetown cocktail party schmoozing with everybody. He had them snowed! Not all of them, but a lot. He was a consummate insider."[7]

Helms was involved in a minor flap early in his tenure when he endorsed an article that criticized William Fulbright. He was, however, quickly able to smooth out any bruised feelings.[8] Given his good relations with Congress and his positive reputation, Helms was a valuable DCI for a CIA that found increasingly stressful public attention directed its way. Helms was, unsurprisingly, concerned with news stories that discussed his agency. He took care to thank both supportive members of the press and former CIA officers who sought publicly to defend the agency from press attacks. He promoted what he referred to as "the cause" of American intelligence.[9]

Helms maintained regular contact with select reporters. For example, he regularly met with Cyrus Sulzberger. While still Raborn's deputy, Helms had apparently aided Sulzberger with a story by leaking a report. The following February, it was Helms's turn to thank Sulzberger for a column that defended the CIA. During a lunch in March, Helms provided Sulzberger with "comments on various matters." Such episodes of cooperation continued after Helms became DCI, as evidenced by a June 1969 report on the Soviet military buildup that Helms provided to Sulzberger. Helms advised Sulzberger to "attribute it to something like 'reports from diplomatic circles in Moscow and Europe.'"[10] There is no indication from their correspondence that Helms and Sulzberger had a formal quid pro quo arrangement of information in return for public support of the CIA, but both clearly obtained practical benefits from the relationship.

Helms's ability to maintain consistent contacts should not be taken for granted. Other veterans in the CIA despaired of their contacts while Helms continued to enjoy his own. For example, by the late 1960s, already facing the dissolution of the division he had worked on for most of his career, Cord Meyer reflected that the most important contacts he had with the American press were dead or retired.[11] Helms, though, was able to maintain and build his network.

Helms's relationship with Benjamin Welles of the *Times* demonstrates what Helms gained from the press. Welles approached Helms to seek his cooperation for a profile piece on the DCI in the *New York Times,* despite a deterioration of the *Times*-CIA relationship. Helms offered to cooperate and assured Welles that he bore the reporter no ill will regarding earlier stories.[12] McCone was also approached and did not cooperate; he advised Helms that he believed cooperation would not be beneficial.[13] Helms disregarded the advice. In the article, delayed in publication until April 1971, Welles was very complimentary to Helms.[14] Welles's friendliness to Helms may have been related to Welles's own past service in the OSS during World War II, which gave him some common ground with Helms.

While valuable to Helms, however, the article by Welles also highlights some of the clashes over proper reporting that were under way in the

New York Times in 1970. Welles, a thirty-year veteran of the *Times*, valued his relationship with Helms for reasons beyond one particular article. He considered the CIA a valuable source of information. When a story he had written on CIA activities in Vietnam had been altered by an editor to include a reference to My Lai, he complained vigorously and explained that he and Tad Szulc had spent "hours—days—weeks—months—years building up contacts of friendship with CIA and other intelligence community people. From these contacts we derive useful intelligence for the *New York Times*. We don't accept it at face value ever—but often it checks out, belatedly, as totally accurate."[15] More than maintaining access to sources, Welles thought the *Times* was being unfair to the CIA. "We can't have it both ways: we can't expect cooperation when we want it—and then find our sources ridiculed or exposed to inaccurate charges read by the million-odd Times readers."[16]

Welles's frustration with the *Times* with regard to the CIA paled in comparison to the frustration of Hanson Baldwin, who had finally retired in 1968. Baldwin, once the most frequent commentator on intelligence and often a critic of the CIA, was thoroughly dissatisfied with the modern *Times*. He believed the paper was increasingly unpatriotic and inclined to ignore his conservative position. Baldwin reflected morosely that the ethos at the *New York Times* could be summed up simply: "The reporter and the press owes no responsibility to anyone except this rather anonymous and vague figure 'the public,' and that there is no other responsibility higher than that."[17]

Despite Welles's and Baldwin's criticisms, *Times* management still wanted access to CIA information if possible, and occasional luncheons with CIA officials were held.[18] Many reporters, however, seemed to share the growing skepticism of government in light of the Vietnam War, providing impetus to further reporting. Joseph Treaster, a *Times* correspondent in Saigon, recalled in an interview after returning to the United States: "There was no subject in Vietnam that I knew to be tabu. . . . And that would include a discussion of Central Intelligence activities, the C.I.A., operations of special forces."[19]

Wicker, never having been shy in challenging governmental authority, went a step further. In 1971 he wrote an article in the *Columbia Journalism Review* arguing that seeking "objectivity" in the press resulted mainly in repeating the official position of the government. Though "comprehensiveness and objectivity" were watchwords of the *New York Times* since the days of Adolph Ochs, Wicker argued that "the newspaper that served his [time] is quite different [from] the newspapers that will serve our time."[20]

The *Times*'s increasing support for investigative reporting was apparent in its decision to hire Seymour Hersh, who had already gained renown as a "scoop artist." Having reported on the massacre of civilians by U.S. soldiers at My Lai as an unaffiliated reporter, Hersh was hired in April 1972 by managing editor Abraham Rosenthal so that the *Times* could keep up with its competitors.[21]

When he hired Hersh, Rosenthal had been managing editor for only three years. Rosenthal had begun his career at the *Times* 1943 and had traveled extensively for the *Times* as a foreign correspondent. He was extremely well regarded by most of his colleagues. Clifton Daniel believed Rosenthal was "probably the most talented newspaperman of his age on the staff of the *New York Times.* He has great ambition, energy, imagination, flair, and charm."[22] Rosenthal was appointed *Times* managing editor in 1969 and proved extremely effective in the position.

Rosenthal was willing to publish the high-profile, controversial reporting that Hersh and other journalists brought to him, but he was committed to maintaining the traditional high standards of the *Times*. Rosenthal's commitment to maintaining the *Times*'s objectivity led to frequent clashes with Wicker. Rosenthal, along with Turner Catledge and Clifton Daniel, had tried to maneuver Wicker out of the Washington Bureau in early 1968, both because they felt Wicker was a poor administrator and because they wanted to bring the Washington Bureau more closely under the direction of the main office. The attempt failed, but it produced bitter acrimony.[23]

The clash between Rosenthal and Wicker continued into the 1970s, as Rosenthal complained to Punch Sulzberger about Wicker's statements in the *Columbia Journalism Review:* "What Tom's piece adds up to is a public statement by an associate editor of The Times. . . . That objectivity and comprehensiveness . . . journalistic foundations of this paper, are no longer valid."[24] Rosenthal found such an approach unacceptable.

While Rosenthal struggled to hold a middle ground, the Nixon administration's policies and antipathy for the press did not ease press-government relations. Policy makers in the Nixon administration certainly felt specific members of the press were unacceptably unfriendly. Kissinger laid down a general rule to H. R. Haldeman that no one in the administration was to talk with anyone from the *Washington Post* or the *New York Times*. Kissinger had, however, already met with the senior staff of the *Post* himself.[25]

Thus, while Helms proved adept in his relations with the press, to the benefit of both his agency and his own personal reputation, this adeptness was increasingly irrelevant. Helms was unable to enjoy good relations with the *New York Times* as an entity despite his good relations with individual *Times* reporters because the *Times* itself was deeply divided. The practical outcome of this challenging atmosphere can be seen in the increased reporting of the CIA's activities in Southeast Asia.

Reporting on the CIA in Southeast Asia

Stories concerning the CIA's activities in South Vietnam and surrounding countries were only a small part of the flood of Vietnam stories in American newspapers and periodicals. The CIA's two most substantially investigated activities in the region were its support of the anticommunists in Laos and the program to eliminate the Vietcong's infrastructure in South Vietnam. All the while, the CIA remained consistently skeptical of U.S. chances for success in the conflict, a fact that emerged with the publication of the Pentagon Papers. I will examine each of these disparate strands in its own context.

Following the hostilities in 1962 that briefly brought Laos to the attention of the U.S. public, the CIA became engaged in large-scale clandestine activities against the communist Pathet Lao and North Vietnamese soldiers in Laos. The CIA, through Air America and the International Cooperation Agency, armed the Hmong people of Laos for the fight against communism.

The inaccessibility of large portions of Laos made it difficult for reporters to provide reliable news of the CIA's involvement, though isolated stories occasionally emerged. In September 1969, however, the long-gestating issue came before the Senate Foreign Relations Committee, which acknowledged the CIA's "deep penetration of Laos." Premier Souvanna Phouma denied that the United States had any combat role in his country, but the *Times* refused to accept this claim, reporting that Thai troops fighting in Laos were there at the United States' request and that Laotian military leaders were advised by CIA agents.[26] Further reporting revealed that the CIA had extensively trained Hmong tribesmen to fight the communist Pathet Lao.[27]

T. D. Allman, writing for the *New York Times,* reported that a massive military installation at Long Tieng, south of the strategically vital Plaine des Jarres, was a base not just for Hmong tribesmen, but also for heavily armed Americans. Allman had discovered this fact by hiking fifteen miles into a restricted zone off-limits to reporters, accompanied by John Saar of *Life* and Max Coiffait of Agence France-Presse. The three reporters walked around the base for two hours until a military patrol noticed that they did not belong there. In that time, Allman reported, a plane landed or took off every minute on the base's airfield. Allman described many non-Laotian, heavily armed men, whom he identified as "former" Green Berets. They were technically contractors for the CIA because, Allman explained, "the fact that they are temporarily C.I.A. personnel and no longer connected with their Army units allows the United States Government to say that it has no soldiers fighting in Laos."[28] This level of detail was unprecedented.

Continued congressional interest in CIA activities triggered further press coverage.[29] The dynamic between Congress and the press that was taking shape was an important one. Each institution reinforced the other's probes of the CIA. Congressional revelations on activities in Laos provided more material than had previously been available for reporters covering the wars in Southeast Asia. Reporters filed stories confirming previously vague rumors of U.S. clandestine acts. Members of the press could also shape a story depending on which congressmen they paid attention to. Different papers gave weight to different senators. While the *New York Times* reported on Fulbright's comments and activities, which were critical of the CIA, the *Washington Post* reported on Stuart Symington's comments that the CIA had become an easy whipping boy whenever foreign developments went poorly.[30] The increase in coverage continued past 1971. In 1972 periodical pieces especially contributed to keeping the story alive.[31]

From a practical standpoint, communist forces in Laos certainly knew that U.S. forces were there, and that U.S. airpower was being used against them. It does not appear as though the reports had an immediately negative effect on U.S. operations. Comments on CIA operations could also be positive, as some stories approved of the CIA's activities. The environment, however, was one in which it was more and more difficult to overlook stories about what the CIA was doing; though the CIA's fight against communists in Laos might not be inherently objectionable to some members of the U.S. audience, the reporting also brought to light other supposed activities that were more disconcerting.

One such disconcerting activity was involvement in drug smuggling. In a *Harper's* story titled "Flowers of Evil," Alfred McCoy accused the CIA of involvement in the heroin trade. William Colby, a CIA officer and future DCI, wrote to *Harper's* to dispute the accusations; McCoy responded by citing specific Laotian officials he had interviewed and an account of the investigative reporting he had performed.[32]

Roughly concurrent with the increasing coverage of Laos in 1969 was an incident that was initially shorter-lived than the Laos coverage but that attracted brief, intense attention. In the summer of 1969, members of the Green Berets, in contact with the CIA as a part of the CIA's counterinsurgency program targeting members of the Vietcong infrastructure, abducted and murdered an informant for Army Intelligence, Chu Van Thai Khac. The Green Berets believed Khac was a double agent feeding information to the North Vietnamese, though the accuracy of the charge is not known. There was some suggestion that the CIA tried to prevent Khac's death, and that CIA officers in Vietnam possibly believed Khac was a triple agent; because of a miscommunication, this information was not provided to the Green Berets. The commander of the Green Berets in Vietnam, Colonel Robert Rheault, initially lied to General Creighton Abrams, commander of U.S. forces in Vietnam, about the whereabouts of Khac. In August eight Green Berets, including Rheault, were arrested for Khac's murder.

The case spawned competing narratives. As the story broke in August, the *New York Times* reporting included allegations that the CIA was involved.[33] A week later, *Time* expanded on and defended the role of the CIA. The CIA, it explained, had ordered the Green Berets to terminate Khac "with prejudice," meaning to fire him, but the order was interpreted as "terminate with extreme prejudice," meaning to kill him.[34] *Life,* meanwhile, ran a profile sympathetic to Rheault and skeptical of the CIA.[35] Others did not even try to provide a definitive answer, seeing in the affair only an inexplicable morass.[36]

The case against the Green Berets eventually fell apart because of the refusal of the CIA to allow its officers to testify in the case. Rheault, though the charges against him were dropped, was unable to continue serving as commander of the Green Berets. He left the army and moved to Maine. Culturally, though, Rheault would continue to have a significant influence even if many did not know his name, as he was reportedly the inspiration for Colonel Walter Kurtz in Francis Ford Coppola's *Apocalypse Now* (1979), a film that popularized the phrase "terminate with extreme prejudice."[37]

The *New York Times* columnists and its editorial page writers tended to be hostile to the CIA in the case.[38] In contrast to the *Times,* the *Washington Post* editorial page was generally sympathetic.[39] The accusation that the CIA had either participated in the murder of an agent ostensibly working for the United States, or participated in covering up the murder, or both, did not make the task of defenders of the agency any easier. Robert Boddington, who briefly served in the CIA at the time, reflected that the Green Beret affair was an early step in "the harmful snowballing effect of the Agency taking on the appearance of a thug organization. . . . Since then, it has became attractive for a wide variety of criminal types to allege possible Agency involvement in their activities."[40] Victor Marchetti, a former CIA officer and the author of an exposé of his former agency, told the *Post* reporter George Lardner that he believed the agency was probably more involved than it officially let on. He observed, "The Agency was very goosey about that."[41]

The CIA had good reason to be concerned. Its interest piqued by the Green Beret murder case, the press then examined the Phoenix Program, an effort to eliminate Vietcong infrastructure in South Vietnam. To its defenders, Phoenix was a counterinsurgency program that, despite some problems in implementation, was a smarter way to wage the war than using previous blunt-force tactics. Phoenix's critics derided it as an assassination program.[42]

Phoenix reemerged in the press in 1970–1971, concurrent with the intensification of conflict in Laos.[43] William Colby, who coordinated the Phoenix Program while stationed in Vietnam, was given space in the *Times* to argue that Phoenix was not an assassination program, but the *Times* published a rejoinder to Colby that argued that Phoenix was essentially used by South Vietnamese officials as a way to eliminate their personal enemies. A larger number of "nurses," the *Times* reported, appeared on Phoenix casualty lists because that was the only way to explain the large number of civilian women murdered.[44] Colby's testimony before Congress drew attention, in part because of the unexpected honesty on Colby's part that would prove divisive when the congressional investigations into the CIA began in 1975. Colby admitted, "I would not testify that no one has been killed wrongfully. . . . It is a fact that in Vietnam various unfortunate things have happened."[45]

The increasing assertiveness of the *New York Times* reached its most famous moment with the publication in June 1971 of the so-called Pentagon Papers. Leaked to the *Times* reporter Cornelius "Neil" Sheehan by Daniel Ellsberg, the papers were a collection of documents compiled by the Department of Defense that served as the history of U.S. involvement in Vietnam. Temporarily restrained by a court order, the *Times* halted publication. The *Washington Post* and the *Boston Globe,* however, began publishing documents leaked to them by Ellsberg. They, unlike the *Times,* refused to suspend publication until the matter was settled in the courts. The Pentagon Papers were an important milestone in the willingness of the press to publish in opposition to the government, a culmination of the press's rejection of close cooperation with the government that had evolved over the previous decade.

It is noteworthy that, by 1971, the staff of the *Times* appears to have been in general agreement that they would publish the papers. It was not necessarily an easy decision; an interview with the foreign editors at the time of publication refers to serious debates.[46] In the end, though, they all agreed to publish. Even James Reston, often unfairly lampooned as a mere mouthpiece of the Establishment, supported publication.

The Pentagon Papers, and the discussions engendered by their release, focused more on the revelations of presidential dishonesty and the problems of American military strategy than on the role of the CIA. Some members of the intelligence community were concerned that the papers would reveal sources and methods. A man identified by Salisbury as a "top spook," a representative of the National Security Agency, met with the *Times* Vice President Harding Bancroft and other *Times* representatives to discuss limiting publication of stories that might alert the North Vietnamese army to U.S. Signals Intelligence capabilities. The *Times* staff, Bancroft explained, were already taking precautions, but they would contact the "spook" if the *Times* needed advice on security matters.[47]

In the long run, the Pentagon Papers were not a positive development for the CIA. They triggered a greater aggressiveness on the part of the media and gave ammunition to critics of government secrecy, a sensitive topic to the CIA for obvious reasons. In the short term, though, the papers actually boosted the CIA's reputation. The CIA had long been pessimistic about the outlook for the United States in Vietnam. The CIA's December 1970 report to Nixon on the situation in Vietnam prompted one of its critics, the *Progressive,* to display rare gratitude to the agency. Acknowledging that the *Progressive* had, in the past "attacked the policies, methods, and credibility of the Central Intelligence Agency," the article praised the CIA's report to Nixon on the situation in Vietnam and argued that it provided an opportunity to press the administration for speedier troop withdrawals from Vietnam.[48] The papers revealed more of the CIA's evaluations on Vietnam, which led to greater praise for the CIA for accurate analysis. The show of support for the CIA on the basis of its Vietnam analysis was hardly overwhelming, but it did continue in occasional articles throughout 1971.[49]

More than three years after the Pentagon Papers were released, as the CIA began to face calls for investigation, Frank Starr of the *Tribune* would hark back to the CIA's apparent success in analysis. He wrote that the CIA's covert operations in Cuba, Laos, and Chile, not its analytical function, were what embarrassed the agency. It was this analytical function, Starr argued, that the CIA should return to.[50] Coming during a period of intense investigation of the CIA, Starr's reminder points to the mixed legacy of the Pentagon Papers for the CIA. While the papers served to bolster the agency's reputation as an intelligence analyzer, they also represented the kind of break between government and the press that led to negative attention being paid to the CIA.

Generally, the *Times* staff looked back on the decision to publish with pride. Rosenthal, though, did not let victory in the Pentagon Papers case blind him to the continued efforts of government to suppress reporting it did not appreciate. He had been disappointed that the Council on Foreign Relations had not put up more of a fight to resist a government subpoena for information on Daniel Ellsberg's talk to the council.[51] Rosenthal took the opportunity of another council meeting to warn that the Nixon administration was generally successful in its campaign to stifle reporting.[52]

Punch Sulzberger, as the man who made the ultimate decision to publish the papers, recalled the stress of the event in a later letter to Rosenthal. Sulzberger wrote to instruct Rosenthal to put a marriage announcement in the *Times* for the son of one of his doctors, a Dr. Saxe. Sulzberger reminded Rosenthal, "You owe me that [announcement] as a favor for publishing the Pentagon Papers. If you don't understand why, I'll give you a clue—Dr. David Saxe is a proctologist."[53]

Chile and the Overthrow of Salvador Allende

Praise for the CIA for its accurate prognostications on Vietnam never outweighed criticism for its counterinsurgency and covert warfare activities. In addition to its involvement in Southeast Asia, the CIA came under fire for its actions in Chile when it was revealed in March 1972 that the agency had sought to prevent the election of the socialist Salvador Allende to the Chilean presidency during the 1970 presidential election. After Allende was ousted in a bloody coup in September 1973, the CIA was an immediate suspect. A year after the coup, more details on the CIA's role in Chile emerged to confirm that the agency had been working to undermine Allende since his 1970 victory. Unlike the media's response to the CIA's intervention in Guatemala nearly twenty years earlier, few in the U.S. press congratulated the CIA for Allende's fall.

CIA activities in Chile were driven by the profound antagonism Nixon and Henry Kissinger felt toward Allende. They were convinced that Allende, an avowed socialist, would threaten U.S. interests in South and Latin America, possibly becoming another Fidel Castro. Rejecting Allende's plurality in a democratic election, Kissinger infamously commented that he did not "see why we need to stand by and watch a country go communist due to the irresponsibility of its own people."[54]

With this philosophy guiding the CIA, the agency funneled nearly $10 million to Allende's opponents to prevent his victory in a runoff election in the Chilean legislature, a requirement imposed by the fact that Allende had won only a plurality. These funds represented what was known as Track I. Track II involved laying the groundwork for a military coup against Allende. The details remain murky, but the CIA apparently provided aid to right-wing extremists in their effort to kidnap General René Schneider, the commander in chief of the Chilean army well known for his loyalty to Chile's constitution. Schneider was killed in the kidnapping attempt.[55]

The initial response in the U.S. press to Schneider's death was muted.[56] Many assumed that the CIA would not be so blatant as to attempt to move against Allende. Even William F. Buckley, while condemning Allende for being part of a "communist-socialist-radical coalition," advised against interference with Allende's government.[57]

Graham Greene, writing in *Harper's,* was less sure that intervention was not being considered. Some kind of blow was coming against Allende, Greene predicted, though the question was whether it would be an economic blockade "or a disguised attack by the CIA with the help of the Right extremists who murdered General Schneider."[58]

The same month that Greene's article was published, the columnist Jack Anderson revealed that such suspicions were well-founded. Anderson had taken over Drew Pearson's old column, The Washington Merry-Go Round, and Anderson proved himself adept at breaking the same kind of stories about the U.S. government that Pearson had.[59] Memos passed on to the muckraking journalist revealed that the International Telephone and Telegraph Company (ITT), which had substantial business interests in Chile, had approached the CIA about taking action against Allende. Corporate officers at ITT proposed that their company attempt to destabilize the Chilean economy to open the way for an army coup. A director of ITT was the former DCI John McCone.[60] Anderson's story quickly made the rounds of the *Times*, the *Post*, and the *Tribune*; condemnation fell particularly on ITT.[61] Only more conservative publications such as the *National Review* and the *Chicago Tribune* were willing to defend ITT's activities.[62]

Though ITT received most of the scorn, the CIA's past involvement in foreign interventions was increasingly raised by reporters when discussing its possible involvement in Chile. In April, Victor Marchetti published one of his first critical writings on the CIA, in an article in the *Nation*. As Marchetti explained, "The CIA . . . is exactly what those who govern the country intend it to be—a clandestine mechanism whereby the executive branch influences the internal affairs of other nations."[63] Marchetti additionally alleged that the CIA was able to maintain a soft facade because it had successfully tamed the media. Tad Szulc made explicit connections between what were, by 1973, well-known CIA activities in Latin America and the CIA's current behavior. Szulc recalled the experience of the United Fruit Company and Guatemala as a parallel to ITT and Chile.[64] Szulc himself was familiar with U.S. efforts against Castro, given his participation in them.

By the summer of 1973, a U.S.-led informal economic blockade strangled Chile's access to foreign credit and resulted in an increasingly tense domestic situation for Allende. A truckers' strike, supported by the United States, strangled the country's internal economic activity. General Carlos Prats, Schneider's successor, resigned in the face of protests from middle-class women, especially the wives of his officers. The CIA may have supported those protests.[65] General Augusto Pinochet took command of the Chilean army. Finally, on 11 September 1973, Pinochet moved to seize power. Allende refused to surrender and, apparently, killed himself, though some of his supporters allege he was killed by Pinochet's order. Pinochet then began a brutal crackdown against potential opposition.

The extent to which Pinochet and the CIA coordinated is unclear, but there was a deliberate objective on the part of the Nixon administration to undermine the Allende regime. Some of the efforts aimed at attaining that objective were not clandestine, such as limiting Chilean access to foreign capital. It is also clear, though, that in pursuit of Nixon's anti-Allende policy, the CIA intervened in Chilean affairs with financial support to Allende's opponents.

The initial tone of reporting on the coup was confused, as the different press outlets struggled to keep track of a changing situation. The *New York Times* reported that the United States had foreknowledge of the coup, but that the CIA had apparently not been involved in Chile since 1970.[66] A theme quickly emerged that Allende was responsible for the coup because of failures of leadership. For example, a *New York Times* editorial argued that Allende was at fault for moving too fast for the Chilean people.[67] Similar stories appeared in the *Chicago Tribune* and the *National Review,* arguing that Chilean hyper-inflation was entirely responsible for the coup.[68] Other outlets, such as *Time, U.S. News and World Report,* and even the *New Republic,* argued that Allende was to some extent responsible for prompting the coup that toppled him.[69] The *Progressive* was one of the few magazines to feature a full condemnation of the U.S. policy toward Chile. Laurence Stern, a regular contributor to the *Washington Post,* noted that the truckers' strike had to have received support from somewhere and observed that, questions of direct intervention aside, the United States had conducted economic warfare against Allende.[70]

The *Washington Post,* normally quite friendly to the CIA, ran an article by Chalmers Roberts observing that the accusations of U.S. involvement were, by this point, inevitable; the CIA had made it hard to argue that the United States did not intervene against governments it perceived to be a threat. Roberts, a veteran *Post* reporter, a friend of Allen Dulles, and one of those correspondents with whom Ray Cline had maintained regular contact, observed that support for a coup would hardly be unprecedented. Guatemala, Iran, Indonesia, and Cuba were well-known examples by this time. It was unclear if the CIA was involved, Roberts wrote, but "for those of us who hope, or even believe, that the CIA has learned some lessons or been reined in, it is not very easy to accept . . . the current CIA denials." Roberts blamed the continued lies of postwar presidential administrations on the lack of trust in U.S. denials of involvement.[71]

With a few exceptions,[72] then, the theme of the first few months of coverage of the coup was that, though the United States had clearly wanted Allende out of power and may have known about the coup beforehand, Allende's fall was his own fault. Even Roberts, while writing that it was difficult to believe U.S. denials, did not actually allege that U.S. involvement had occurred. Suspicions of CIA involvement would be confirmed in September 1974, after the massive collapse of government credibility as a result of the Watergate scandal that consumed Nixon's presidency, and which had threatened to consume the CIA as well.

Watergate

The story of Watergate looms large in modern American history. The arrest of five men caught in the act of burglarizing the Democratic National Committee headquarters at the Watergate Hotel quickly involved the CIA; the former CIA officer James McCord was arrested along with Bernard Barker, Virgilio Gonzalez, Eugenio Martínez, and Frank Sturgis, who had worked with the CIA in previous years against Castro. Quickly arrested also were E. Howard Hunt and G. Gordon Liddy, organizers of the Nixon administration's "plumbers," who ran covert operations against the president's foes in the 1972 presidential election. Over two increasingly painful years, the scandal played out in reporting and in congressional investigations, which led to Nixon's resignation on 9 August 1974.

Eventually, as more evidence of criminal activity on the part of the Nixon administration was uncovered, reports emerged that the CIA had assisted the White House plumbers in their burglary of the office of Daniel Ellsberg's psychiatrist. The CIA gave Hunt, who was in charge of executing the burglary, tools, credentials, and a secretary. Defenders of the CIA pointed to the fact that support to Hunt was discontinued when the CIA realized his activities were directed against Nixon's political enemies rather than real security threats. After Nixon resigned, those defenders held up the fact, with some justification, that the CIA did not give in to presidential attempts use the CIA to throw off the trail of the FBI investigation into the break-in.

Helms was apparently forced out as DCI because of his refusal to cooperate with Nixon on Watergate. He had managed to navigate the CIA relatively unscathed through a very complex and difficult time in the 1970s, but he could not overcome Nixon, who had long distrusted the CIA. Nixon saw the CIA as a bastion of the Ivy League that he hated. He believed that the CIA had cost him the 1960 election by leaking missile gap intelligence to his opponents.[73] Nixon fired Helms in November 1972, just a few months before Helms would reach the official CIA retirement age of sixty.

The DCIs who followed Helms were not as effective as he had been in promoting the cause of intelligence. Helms's immediate successor, James Schlesinger, had earlier served as a member of the Atomic Energy Commission and had no connection with intelligence before becoming director of Central Intelligence. Nixon named Schlesinger director in April 1973 for the apparent purpose of reshaping the intelligence community. Schlesinger soon dismissed 1,500 members of the Directorate of Operations. Schlesinger also ordered his deputy, William Colby, to prepare a report on the CIA's past illegal activities. The report became known as the "Family Jewels."[74] Within five months, Nixon appointed Schlesinger secretary of defense, and Colby became DCI. Colby was an effective intelligence officer but unprepared for the crisis that faced the agency after Watergate. Though Watergate would have been much worse for the CIA if Helms had proven more cooperative with Nixon, the atmosphere after Watergate was still extremely hazardous for the CIA. Questions lingered about what, precisely, Nixon had meant when, on the "smoking gun" tape that confirmed Nixon's authorization of the Watergate cover-up, he remarked, "We protected Helms from one hell of a lot of things."[75]

Though Watergate remained an isolated story for some months, a prominent example of reporting on the CIA and Watergate emerged as early as July 1972, from Tad Szulc. From his original involvement in reporting on the Otto John defection in 1954, Szulc had nearly two decades' worth of experience in reporting on intelligence matters. He had not been entirely antagonistic toward U.S. intelligence and had been more deeply involved in intelligence activities than most reporters owing to his participation in anti-Castro activities. This background was apparent in his reporting in an article titled "From the Folks Who Brought You the Bay of Pigs." Szulc identified the men involved in the Watergate burglary as members of radical anti-Castro groups based in Miami. They were veterans of the Bay of Pigs, which meant they probably had ties with the CIA. Howard Hunt was identified as the chief of this "loosely organized Cuban-American right-wing commando team."

In discussing the motives for the break-in, Szulc noted that the equipment found suggested the group was bugging the Democratic campaign headquarters. He also referred to other suspected activities of the team, such as a burglary at the Chilean embassy. Szulc reported that, though Nixon denounced the break-in, "neither he nor any of his staff explained why Mr. McCord . . . was among the raiders captured. Nor was there any explanation of the relationship between Mr. Hunt and Charles W. Colson, a special counsel to the president."[76]

Aside from Szulc and the famous investigation by Robert Woodward and Carl Bernstein of the *Washington Post*, few reporters initially paid much attention to the story. As Watergate slowly percolated in the American media, repeated suggestions of CIA involvement did not emerge. The removal of Helms as DCI in December 1972 elicited some press attention, but no one had reason to connect the removal with Watergate. Tom Braden suggested in his column that Nixon removed Helms because the CIA's analysis did not support Nixon's desire for an antiballistic missile buildup. Chalmers Roberts in the *Post* took the occasion to remark on the irony of Helms's becoming ambassador to Iran, having played a role in his early career in overthrowing Mossadegh and establishing the reign of the shah. Neither Braden nor Roberts, however, had any reason to suspect the relevance of Watergate to Helms's departure.[77]

That began to change by the end of April 1973, when Nixon asked for the resignations of two of his most important aides, H. R. Haldeman and John Ehrlichman. John Dean, a White House counsel, began cooperating with the special prosecutor investigating the affair. The U.S. Senate, already having established a committee to investigate Watergate in February 1973, began in May to broadcast its hearings on national television.

During this period of intensification, John Crewsdon reported in the *Times* that the CIA was being investigated for its role in the break-in at Ellsberg's psychiatrist's office, which led to a cascade of commentary on the potential abuse the CIA could wreak if misused by the president.[78] Within the agency, there was apparently a great deal of consternation. Years later, James Angleton, the soon-to-be-disgraced chief of counterintelligence, recalled, "There was a lot of panic over in the Agency after Watergate. I'd say in good faith the Agency didn't know what the hell was going on. . . . But the circumstantial evidence was so strong that even some of our best friends at the FBI thought that we were involved."[79]

Some defenses of the CIA proved ineffective and tone-deaf. The *New York Times* provided an outlet to Lyman Kirkpatrick, inspector general of the CIA, to soothe concerns that the CIA was a potential tool of oppression. Kirkpatrick easily admitted that the CIA had interfered with foreign governments abroad, but he insisted that it had not done anything equivalent within the United States. The CIA, Kirkpatrick maintained, did not overthrow governments regularly, and it never did so without executive sanction. These arguments did not, however, address the concern regarding the CIA's potential for abuse from a powerful executive branch.[80] This lack of concern for executive abuse was not helpful in the latter days of Nixon's presidency.

A better defense for the CIA came from the *Washington Post*'s editorial page and the *Chicago Tribune*. One *Post* editorial contended that Watergate demonstrated the trustworthiness of the CIA; it had worked with Hunt only until it realized that his activities were against domestic targets. The real problem was the White House, whose occupants "in their cavalier abuse of power and their contempt for the institutions of American government . . . tried but, it seems, largely failed to compromise or subvert the CIA."[81] Others picked up this thread and pointed to the White House as the core problem.[82]

Some liberal congressmen, much as they had in reaction to the CIA's negative analysis of Vietnam, seized on the opportunity to place their proposals for CIA oversight in a pro-CIA light. Senator William Proxmire (Democrat of Wisconsin), for example, proposed a series of restrictions that would protect the CIA. Proxmire explained that he had "great admiration for the CIA and its directors. It appears that they have resisted pressures of great intensity from the White House itself. . . . It is for the sake of the CIA as well as the American people that I offer this amendment."[83] When Helms was called back from Iran to testify, the *Chicago Tribune* reported, Congress greeted him with relief because by that point it was tired of dealing with the amateurs from the White House.[84]

Szulc eventually added to this picture of CIA professionalism with an article on Hunt. Hunt had been viewed by some as a sinister CIA operative bringing his espionage skills home, but Szulc portrayed him as a pathetic figure, an ambitious scrambler who was never as good an intelligence officer as he thought he was. Apparently some of Szulc's nebulous CIA contacts were able to provide background: Szulc reported that in the CIA, "Hunt syndrome" referred to an officer who had a hard time leaving the thrill and allure of intelligence work.[85]

This portrayal of Hunt fit into the growing narrative of the CIA and Watergate, and it is distinctly possible that Szulc's CIA contacts specifically wanted to portray Hunt as a ridiculous castoff to support its narrative. The CIA, in this telling, was professional, disciplined, and unwilling to violate the Constitution. Nixon's plumbers were amateurs, the rejects from actual professional agencies. Hunt worked for Nixon's plumbers because the CIA refused to indulge his penchant for thrills.

The most direct challenger to this narrative was Senator Howard Baker (Republican of Tennessee), who posited that the CIA was ultimately to blame in Watergate. Baker based this on the account of Charles Colson, who was at the time in prison for his own role in Watergate. Most of the press coverage of Baker's charges was skeptical. John M. Maury, a former CIA officer working in the Department of State, apprised Helms of the investigation and Baker's allegations. Maury remarked, "We are all puzzled as to just what is eating on [Baker], but one theory is that he is trying to drag in references to the Agency as a sort of red herring to keep the full brunt of the investigation from focusing on the Party and the Administration."[86]

When the Baker Report, examining the role of the CIA in Nixon's illegal activities, was released in July 1974, it concluded that the CIA had made several foolish mistakes, but it was ultimately not responsible for Watergate.[87] There were conspiracy theories that the CIA was involved in Watergate to the extent that it actively set Nixon up to be impeached. One *National Review* article, for example, mentioned the theory of the former CIA officer Miles Copeland that James McCord purposefully bungled the Watergate burglary in order to bring down Nixon.[88] Such theories strain credulity, especially since the identity of the legendary "Deep Throat" has been revealed to be the FBI Agent Mark Felt, not a shadowy figure in the CIA.

Though the facts of Watergate would eventually confirm many of the contentions of the CIA and its defenders, Watergate shone an unfriendly light on both intelligence activities and the effect of the Cold War national security state on American life. Even if ultimately the agency's leadership made the rights calls, the attempted illegal use of the CIA, the former CIA officers involved in illegal work, and the continued opacity of the intelligence community raised troubling questions about the effect of the intelligence community on democracy. This question was especially prominent in the *Progressive,* the *New Republic,* and *Harper's.* These periodicals may have been small compared to major newspapers, but they spoke to an emerging generation of liberal critics of the government.[89]

After the release of the "smoking gun" tape in August 1974, however, the CIA had a brief moment to celebrate. Hugh Sidey, keeping up his correspondence with Helms, congratulated Helms on his handling of the affair. Though the CIA had been under attack, Sidey concluded, "the story is plain now. Nixon ordered the CIA used. Dick Helms, without destroying other people or the agency or rupturing the relationship with the White House, pinched it off. I think we can let it rest there."[90] Helms does deserve credit for resisting the pressure of the Nixon administration and preventing or at least mitigating the abuse of the CIA. Sidey was correct that the question of CIA and Watergate would rest; however, other questions about the CIA's conduct emerged almost immediately.

The Road to Chaos

A little over a month after Nixon resigned, the increased willingness of the press and Congress to probe the CIA's activities was amply demonstrated by the confirmation that the CIA had been more active in Chile than had previously been acknowledged. On 8 September testimony by William Colby on U.S. activities in Chile to the House Armed Services Committee was leaked to the press. Seymour Hersh wrote about the leaked information in the *New York Times,* explaining that the Forty Committee, an obscure coordinating group for U.S. intelligence activities, had ordered the CIA to act against Allende.[91] President Gerald Ford attempted to portray the U.S. aid as having been intended only to support democratic opposition to Allende, but this inaccurate description of U.S. activity was not widely accepted.

The *New York Times* emerged once again as a major forum for criticism of the CIA, but at least some level of that outrage was shared by other publications.[92] Kissinger, meanwhile, was especially incensed with the stories leaking into the press concerning Chile. On 20 September, after Hersh reported that the United States had supported the truckers' strike against Allende, Kissinger called Colby. After asking whether the story was true, an angry Kissinger berated Colby, complaining that he was informed the United States supported only political parties, which is what President Ford then publicly claimed. Given his role in driving action against Allende, Kissinger's claim to Colby is difficult to take seriously. Colby, for his part, explained that the money was given to political parties, but that "they did not put it in the bank . . . what they did with it, I don't know."[93]

The reporting on Chile, echoing the coverage of previous CIA activities in Iran, Guatemala, Indonesia, Cuba, Laos, and Vietnam, represented a new normal on reporting on the CIA by 1974. Even in 1969 reporting on the CIA had been more limited, but the flood of stories and controversy, especially after the Watergate scandal, had created a new environment for the CIA.

Part of the evolution in this coverage of the CIA's actions was a number of articles released throughout the 1970s that, unmoored to any particular event, criticized the U.S. intelligence system. Henry Howe Ransom, for example, wrote in the *New York Times* in December 1970 criticizing the intelligence system and its ability to affect decision making.[94] Others wrote to criticize intelligence services for collecting files on American citizens and potentially using information to control citizens' actions.[95] Efforts to prevent Marchetti from publishing, including the lengthy court case, were reported in the *New Times,* the *Washington Post,* and the *Chicago Tribune.*[96] Joseph Alsop, who remained a committed hawk on Vietnam, criticized the CIA for its gloomy estimates in Southeast Asia. He insisted that Helms had known the estimates were wrong but that Helms, "a great bureaucrat if ever there was one," had kept the reports pessimistic to curry favor with the left.[97] The left and the right criticized the CIA for inefficiency and wastefulness.[98]

A phrase that repeatedly came up during Watergate and thereafter was "dirty tricks." Sometimes the phrase was used playfully, other times as an indictment. It was not a novel phrase for intelligence. It can be found in scattered examples before the 1970s; James Reston, for example, wrote about "dirty tricks" in the context of the operations of the U.S. Psychological Strategy Board as early as 1951.[99] The phrase grew considerably in the press in 1972 and especially 1973.[100] Jeremy Stone, writing in the *Times,* reported that one-third of the CIA was part of the Directorate of Plans, and that all those men were involved in dirty tricks. While inaccurate, Stone's reporting reflected increasingly popular assumptions about the CIA. Stone cited Watergate as a demonstration of the damage the CIA's dirty tricks men could wreak on the American political system.[101]

There were defenders of the CIA. Though the *Tribune* was not consistently pro-CIA, its editorials increasingly took a friendly stance toward the agency.[102] One of the most vociferous defenses of the CIA came from Miles Copeland, a former CIA officer. His arguments, however, were ones the CIA probably would have preferred to have gone without. Copeland joked about the CIA's potential surveillance capabilities; he argued that the United States would inevitably have to adopt "police state methods" to secure the country, and that it was better for American society simply to accept this.[103]

Additionally, during Watergate, initial reports of the CIA's connections with the world of journalism began to appear. The *Times* reported in December 1973 that three dozen journalists were reputed to do work for the CIA. Some were full-time CIA agents. The story noted that all the journalists were said to work abroad.[104] The *New Republic* ran a story on the CIA presence among the press in foreign countries, describing it as an open secret.

Anyone who has ever worked as a foreign correspondent is familiar with the type. He lives permanently in a remote capital, say Vientiane or Lagos or Baghdad, as the free-lance representative for an obscure US publication or an occasional "stringer" for one of the better-known American newspapers, news magazines or wire services. His means of support are dubious, yet he has a comfortable apartment, a car and an expense account that permits him to pay for rounds of drinks. . . . Speculating on the motives behind his residence in this faraway place, his more established colleagues usually offer the guess that he works at least part-time for the Central Intelligence Agency. Now, it turns out, their guess is probably correct.[105]

Stuart Loory condemned the practice of intelligence agencies using reporters in the *Washington Post* and the *Los Angeles Times*. He argued that such activities fundamentally delegitimized the press and many of the assumptions Americans held about the strength of their democratic institutions. Loory reflected that in the old days, "the pre-Watergate days," such revelations would have caused a furor. Now they barely merited further attention.[106] Loory then went on to produce the first significant investigation of the press, in the *Columbia Journalism Review* in the fall of 1974.[107] Some members of the press even began to discuss the way in which the CIA leaked in order to change the media narrative or burnish its image; Murray Seeger of the *Los Angeles Times* reported that the CIA was telling a few of its secrets in order offset the disclosures of Victor Marchetti and another former CIA officer-turned-foe, Philip Agee.[108] The press had rarely peeled back the curtain on such reporting methods before.

It was against this backdrop that Seymour Hersh broke another story in the *New York Times*. Published on the front page, on 22 December 1974, the article described a "huge" and "massive" surveillance operation conducted by the CIA on American soil against American citizens. Those under surveillance included antiwar protesters, Civil Rights activists, and anti-Nixon forces in direct contravention of the CIA's statutory authority. The surveillance program, according to Hersh, began as a legitimate investigation into foreign involvement in the United States but ballooned into a coordinated, systematized surveillance policy. It would later emerge that its code name, while randomly assigned, reflected a sinister connotation: it was called Operation MHCHAOS.[109]

Responsibility for the agency's reaction to this breakthrough story fell on DCI William Colby. Looking back on 1975 some years later, Colby recalled his reaction upon learning the program's codename: "Oh, Shit!"[110] It would prove an apt reaction.

The political atmosphere before the prolonged Watergate Scandal had not been friendly to the CIA, or to the national security apparatus more generally. Following the NSA scandal in 1967, newspaper stories had subsided and no congressional investigation was conducted. At the same time, however, the revelations had made many reporters more wary of the agency. As the Nixon administration began, the more extreme claims of CIA critics such as Fred Cook, David Wise, and Thomas Ross were not yet common in the mainstream. Reporters, editors, and many members of Congress grew more concerned, however, about potential CIA subversion and CIA covert actions.

The effects of those growing concerns can be seen in the increasing coverage of the CIA's activities in Laos, Vietnam, and Chile. Topics that had once been safely off-limits, such as the extensive CIA activities in Laos, were exposed in major publications. An agency that was once lauded and respected by most of the mainstream press was regarded with suspicion. Its sheen of invincibility had long since worn off. Many shared the views that Taylor Branch expressed, that the agency was a relic, ineffective at its job and a danger to governments in the Third World and possibly to American democracy. Where once Branch would have been the exception, now he was closer to the mainstream than a CIA defender like Miles Copeland or even an old CIA critic like Hanson Baldwin, whose criticism never included exposure of CIA activities.

As troubled as the CIA's political situation was before the Watergate scandal, it was that scandal that proved truly disastrous for the agency. To its credit, the CIA ultimately exercised laudable judgment with its refusal to aid Nixon in the Watergate cover-up. Despite that refusal, the agency's initial aid to Howard Hunt and the CIA connections of most of the Watergate burglars were damaging. More than any specific decisions made by the agency, however, the political atmosphere created by Watergate was the greatest problem for the CIA. Faith in the American system of government was profoundly shaken, and the crisis empowered critics of government secrecy. When the *New York Times* published Hersh's reporting in December 1974, it finally revealed CIA activities of such undeniable concern that the agency was no longer able to put off the long-forestalled congressional investigation of the CIA.

6

The Year of Intelligence Begins

In late March 1975 the weekend edition of the *Washington Post* included an outline for a new board game called Spook. The game lampooned the world of intelligence, and its board was decorated with CIA-related caricatures. At the top of the game board were cartoon portraits of past directors of Central Intelligence. Game spaces were locations with great significance to CIA history: Greece, Iran, Chile, Cambodia, and Vietnam. Throughout the board, players navigated such challenges as "exposure," which involved rolling a die to determine outcomes such as "your agent is a mole—terminate yourself with extreme prejudice." At the end, if players successfully maneuvered through all the challenges of the game, they were congratulated for reaching retirement "with your thumbs intact" and received the good news that the literary agent Scott Meredith "has gotten you a $100,000 advance on your memoirs!"[1]

Spook focused on what, by 1975, were well-known examples of CIA foreign intervention. On the game board, CIA interventions were not only acknowledged but mocked. Spook reflected the increasing demystification of the CIA in the American press. Rather than a disciplined, professional, and effective force, the agency was portrayed as dangerous, but also ridiculous.

The CIA was open to such criticism and mockery because of its already fragile position, which worsened following Hersh's 1974 revelation of the CIA's domestic surveillance program. The subsequent period, 1975 and much of 1976, would be consumed by the very public investigation of the CIA in what would come to be called "the Year of Intelligence." In January a blue-ribbon presidential committee headed by Vice President Nelson Rockefeller investigated charges that the CIA had overstepped its mandate. Soon the Senate and House both formed their own committees to investigate the CIA; they planned to examine not just the immediate charges against the

CIA leveled by Seymour Hersh, but the longer history of the CIA's activities in the Cold War.[2] Throughout the investigations, the press was an important observer of, interpreter of, and forum for a fierce debate about the future of the CIA. A prominent theme that emerged in CIA criticism was that the agency was dangerous but also ineffective for its intended purpose. Alarm at the CIA's activities was often matched with incredulity about what those activities actually were.

This chapter does not attempt to provide a complete account of the Year of Intelligence.[3] The "year," which in reality stretched across roughly eighteen months, was filled with revelations, negotiations, and bureaucratic maneuvers between and within Congress, Gerald Ford's White House, the CIA, the FBI, and others. This chapter instead examines the way in which the press set the terms of debate for the Year of Intelligence, and the effects that the investigations of the CIA had on the press and its relationships with that agency.

The press was by no means unified in its approach to the CIA. Longtime CIA critics seized the opportunity to criticize the agency. Some charged that the CIA was an existential threat to democracy. Some lampooned the agency. Others defended it and resisted calls to expose past misdeeds and establish meaningful congressional oversight. Many publications, like the *Washington Post,* were home to arguments that represented the entire spectrum of debate, from CIA critics to defenders to those unsure of what to do.[4] Increasingly, the CIA became a partisan issue, and where one fell in the debate on the CIA depended on whether one identified as liberal or conservative. Personal relationships remained relevant, but their importance had declined. These sharp distinctions in the press can be seen in the immediate, at times hostile reactions to Hersh's story.

The Scoop

Hersh first had the idea that the CIA and its activities would be a major story when interviewing sources in relation to Watergate in June or July 1973.[5] A former CIA officer who had joined the Justice Department informed Hersh that some of the worst governmental abuses had come not from the White House but from the CIA. In early 1974 a source in the CIA informed Hersh that the CIA was conducting domestic surveillance.[6] Hersh remained occupied at the time with Watergate and then Chile, but he did not disregard the story. That the CIA was now a clear topic of concern, even if Watergate had ultimately resolved fairly favorably for the agency, demonstrates the long-term damage that the scandal wrought for the agency.

Hersh began to turn his attention to the long-serving head of the CIA's counterintelligence staff, James Jesus Angleton. Angleton was a legendary, intimidating figure in the CIA. As head of counterintelligence, he had directed the agency's domestic activities. Like many of the senior members of the agency, he had gotten his start in the OSS, serving in Italy. He had a reputation for brilliance and eclecticism. For example, he had been an editor of Yale's poetry journal and had a passion for botany. Angleton was also a veteran Cold Warrior. Hersh reported that within the CIA, Angleton was treated with "fear and awe."[7]

Angleton claimed that he never spoke to Hersh, except for an occasion when Hersh briefly ambushed him at a public event. He was aware, however, of "a lot of internal dealings at the Times" that seemed to presage a *Times* story on the CIA.[8] Hersh, though, remembered speaking with Angleton and claimed that Angleton had "standing dates" with many columnists. According to Hersh, Angleton attempted to divert Hersh away from the domestic spying story with the promise of access to an exciting, pro-CIA tale, "a derring-do story."[9] Hersh was not distracted by Angleton and kept working the story, seeking out sources within the CIA; he reported later that he called over fifty people in the agency, but he was not able to get the whole story until he spoke to Director of Central Intelligence William Colby.[10] To understand how Hersh came to speak with Colby on such a sensitive topic, it is important to look both at Colby's background heading into the directorship and at events earlier in 1974, when Colby and Hersh first met.

William Egan Colby, like Helms, fit the profile of a senior member of the CIA in the mid-1970s. Born in 1920 to an army officer father and a mother from a prominent St. Paul, Minnesota, family, Colby graduated from Princeton University in 1940. He served in the OSS, where he organized resistance forces in France. After the war, he completed a law degree at Columbia University and went to work for the law firm of the former OSS chief, William Donovan. Soon thereafter, Colby joined the CIA under the cover of the State Department and by 1963 was chief of the CIA's Far East Division. In 1968 he went to Vietnam as the primary adviser on pacification efforts to the South Vietnamese government. In practice, his position meant that he played a key role in the Phoenix Program.

Colby did not prove as adept in relations with the press as had Dulles, McCone, or Helms. Colby was, according to those who knew him, an intensely private and self-contained man.[11] He had, however, been successful in convincing several reporters not to reveal the details of the CIA's involvement in a ship called the *Glomar Explorer* in early 1974.

Ostensibly designed to extract valuable resources from the ocean, the *Glomar Explorer* was the centerpiece of a CIA attempt to raise a sunken Soviet nuclear submarine from the floor of the Pacific Ocean. The CIA used connections with Howard Hughes to build the ship. Under construction throughout 1973 and early 1974, it was ready for action by the summer of 1974. On 12 August it began the effort to lift the Soviet ship. The submarine broke in half while being lifted from the ocean floor; the CIA recovered some nuclear weapons, half an obsolete submarine, and thirty dead Soviet sailors, who were then buried at sea with full military honors.[12] That modest success would not have been possible had Colby not intervened with the *New York Times* to convince its management to kill a story about the operation. The reporter who found the story was Seymour Hersh. The experience apparently left Colby with a positive view of Hersh's willingness to work with the CIA.

Colby's efforts to prevent the story from emerging are revealing, as they demonstrate that, by this point, there was an established institutional approach to tamping down a story. During the ship's construction, Hersh had received an anonymous tip regarding the project. Hersh's subsequent investigation alerted the CIA to the leak.[13] Colby was unsure of how to go about approaching Hersh, but he was advised by an unidentified official, presumably someone of some seniority and experience, to approach *New York Times*'s management. Colby was counseled to seek out a specific individual, who, while unidentified, was apparently not based in New York, as the CIA official warned Colby that "most of the guys up there [in New York]—a naked appeal will do you no good at all."[14]

Colby did eventually approach someone in New York, probably Clifton Daniel. Colby managed to convince the *Times* to hear out his case in more detail.[15] Colby also spoke, eventually, with Punch Sulzberger. Hersh and Colby spoke on 30 January 1974, and, according to Colby in a later conversation with Brent Scowcroft, Hersh agreed to show Colby whatever he wrote before he printed it. Colby felt he had managed to convey how important keeping quiet was.[16]

Now, in December 1974, Hersh approached Colby and benefited from the fact that Colby thought of him as "a bona fide good guy." Hersh also was disturbed when speaking with Angleton about the carelessness Angleton was displaying, and he informed Colby of that. Another pertinent fact was that no one in the CIA knew how much Hersh himself knew, which Hersh used to his advantage to get details out of Colby. As a result, Hersh was able to meet with Colby, which Hersh later called "a godsend." Colby was fairly open with Hersh, in what Hersh believed to be an effort at damage limitation, coupled with a misunderstanding of how important the story was.[17] Colby confirmed this impression in an interview with George Lardner years later. Colby explained, "I'd hoped I'd damp it down. We'd gone through the Chile thing. We'd gone through the Watergate thing even with the Chuck Colsons of the country trying to put that on us. We'd survived that. We knew what the story was. We knew we'd ordered corrections. . . . I thought there'd be a little scurrying around it—and then it would go away in a few weeks. In fact I told somebody that."[18]

Colby's optimistic view proved to be incorrect. Hersh pulled no punches, and from the first sentence the story was a bombshell. Hersh reported, "The Central Intelligence Agency, directly violating its charter, conducted a massive, illegal domestic intelligence operation during the Nixon Administration against the antiwar movement and other dissident groups in the United States, according to well-placed government sources."[19] Hersh went on to report that 10,000 files had been kept on American citizens, including an antiwar member of Congress, through methods that included wiretapping, burglary, and the illegal inspection of mail. Hersh also reported on the Huston plan, the brainchild of Nixon's aide Thomas Charles Huston, which advocated for the use of illegal activities against antiwar protesters and civil rights activists. Huston believed that domestic turmoil had been fomented by "black extremists."[20] According to Hersh, it was possible the CIA had been involved.

Hersh portrayed the process of surveillance as an example of bureaucracy run amok. Following up on potential external threats, the CIA officers investigating found themselves in the United States. Defenders of the CIA claimed there was a "gray area" in the CIA's charter, as the CIA was not permitted to operate within the United States but was also tasked with protecting sources and methods.[21] This supposed gray area would emerge as a major part of the CIA's initial defense, though the language of the charter appears unequivocal. The CIA, by law, has no "police, subp[o]ena, law-enforcement powers, or internal-security functions."[22] Regardless of the legal issue, Hersh portrayed an agency that not only conducted illegal activities, but was bureaucratically inept.

Angleton felt the effect of the story immediately. By the time Hersh released it, Angleton's position within the CIA was already in trouble. Colby later wrote that he had wanted to remove Angleton for some time. The two had clashed while working in Eastern Europe. Part of that clash was a natural result of their different functions; Colby's job was to gather intelligence, Angleton's to prevent any KGB penetration of the CIA.[23] As the years progressed, though, Angleton had become increasingly paranoid about potential KGB penetration of the agency.

While deputy director of Central Intelligence under James Schlesinger, Colby was surprised that Angleton had survived Schlesinger's downsizing.[24] Colby was disturbed by Angleton's increasingly complex, almost nonsensical theories about KGB penetration. Angleton had, on the sole basis of what Colby called "vague coincidences," penalized good officers whom he suspected of being Soviet agents by posting them to distant, dead-end locales. One friendly foreign intelligence service informed Colby that Angleton had warned it that the U.S. station chief in its country was a Soviet agent, an allegation based on spurious evidence.[25]

By his account, Colby had already planned to maneuver Angleton out of the agency before Hersh's story was published. The story made the question much more immediate and led to Angleton's dismissal in the last week of December. Hersh would later wonder whether Colby's cooperation was part of a miscalculated effort to force out Angleton, an effort that stemmed from Colby's underestimation of the importance of the revelations Hersh would unleash. While theorizing on Colby's motives, Hersh doubted that such was actually the case; regardless of what prompted Colby, the story did definitively end Angleton's career.[26] Angleton became, in the press, the symbol of a Cold Warrior who could not adapt to détente.[27]

The Larger Fallout

Angleton's dismissal was not enough to quiet calls for a wider investigation. Tom Wicker argued soon after Hersh's story appeared that the American public, including Gerald Ford, could not be sure that the CIA had stopped its domestic programs because the agency seemed to be a law unto itself. Wicker argued that a congressional investigation was necessary, and that "radical surgery will be needed just as desperately [as a congressional investigation] if a cancer called CIA threatens American Democracy itself."[28]

Despite some notable exceptions, the *New York Times* was consistent throughout the year. Anthony Lewis, William Safire, David Wise, David Rosenbaum, and the *Times* editorial page argued for investigation of the CIA and for stronger oversight of agency activities. Some reporters feared the investigation would mirror early, toothless investigations, like the Katzenbach Commission after the NSA scandal. One *Times* reporter complained, "Every time there has been an intelligence scandal over the last two decades, the response from Congress has been similar. But the expressions of outrage have produced no concrete action."[29] These sentiments led to great skepticism about any proposal other than a full congressional investigation of the CIA. The *New York Times*'s reporting was also joined, in the early days after Hersh's story, by the *Chicago Tribune*, the *Washington Post, the Los Angeles Times,* and periodicals such as the *Nation*.[30]

Hersh's continued reporting gave further impetus to investigation. On 1 January Hersh reported that "well-placed Government" sources had informed him that Colby confirmed the essential accuracy of Hersh's story in a private meeting with Ford.[31] Two days later, Hersh reported further specific CIA activities in the United States, such as the fact that the CIA had kept a file on the popular singer and actor Eartha Kitt.[32]

This widespread coverage of illegal CIA activities generated more than calls for investigation. It also resulted in practical reporting in the mainstream press concerning the CIA's methods. The *Chicago Tribune* ran a story by John Marks, coauthor of *The CIA and the Cult of Intelligence,* that described in some detail how to determine who at a U.S. embassy was a CIA employee. Marks defended himself against accusations that he had harmed U.S. intelligence by noting that the Soviets and Chinese certainly already knew how to find CIA officers in U.S. embassies. It is still noteworthy, however, that the *Chicago Tribune* agreed to run such an explicit story on CIA practices.[33] Meanwhile, more tawdry details emerged. Jack Anderson reported, for example, that the CIA had hotel rooms in San Francisco and New York for the purpose of luring foreign diplomats into love traps.[34]

Defenses of the CIA appeared soon after the initial criticisms, often in the same publication. One day after publishing a story supporting the investigation of the CIA, for example, the *Washington Post* published an editorial arguing that it was possible that CIA activities were proper, reflecting the "gray area" argument on CIA activities in the United States.[35] Similarly, while some editorials in the *Tribune* called for an investigation, the *Tribune* columnist Frank Starr wrote to defend the agency.[36] There were also defenders of the CIA in periodicals.[37]

Rowland Evans and Robert Novak proved to be two of the most consistent defenders of the CIA. They wrote a nationally syndicated column in which they argued that revealing the agency's past abuses in the Johnson and Nixon administrations would be deleterious to the CIA's morale and destroy its effectiveness as an intelligence agency.[38] They additionally condemned Colby for the dismissal of Angleton, arguing that whatever Angleton had done, his dismissal would lead to fears of a "witchhunt" in the CIA. This fear, they predicted, would lead many in the CIA to begin to disclose much of what they knew to the press.[39]

Time magazine also tended to defend the CIA; Hugh Sidey, Helms's friend, wrote a lengthy article on the CIA sympathetic to the turmoil at the agency and minimizing the seriousness of the CIA's surveillance. Sidey blamed the surveillance controversy on Hoover's FBI. According to Sidey, "To an extent, the new controversy is a jurisdictional question."[40] Sidey also wrote specifically to defend Helms in a later article, observing that the "pointless but relentless assault on privacy" alleged by CIA critics did not make sense given Helms's character.[41]

Besides those who defended the CIA for its own sake, there were those who doubted Hersh specifically. Hersh was seen, according to the historian Kathryn Olmsted, more as a competitor than as a colleague by fellow journalists.[42] Hersh's use of anonymous sources was an oft-criticized element of his work and concerned both his superiors at *the New York Times* and his competitors.[43]

There was private dissension in the *Times*. A few days after Hersh's original 22 December story, the head of the editorial page at the *Times,* John Oakes, wrote to Rosenthal to criticize Hersh's reporting. Oakes, a nephew of Adolph Ochs and a counterintelligence officer in World War II, felt that the standards of the *Times* were betrayed by the "breathless, prejudicial, pejorative and truly-non-objective manner" in which Hersh wrote.[44] Rosenthal, though himself often at odds with Hersh and careful to maintain the *Times*'s objectivity, was outraged that a member of the *Times* would level such criticism. He responded to Oakes with a lengthy rebuttal, writing that "Hersh and *The Times* broke a story that will go down in the annals of American journalism as one that contributed vitally to the understanding of our times and the betterment of our society." Rosenthal criticized Oakes for displaying "almost to a parody . . . the kind of thing you say you object to in others. If . . . you have encouraged investigative journalism in this paper, it has been a well-kept secret."[45]

To defend their record and support Hersh's reporting, the *Times* began looking into the legal options to force the CIA to disclose its surveillance activity. The *Times* legal staff submitted a Freedom of Information Act (FOIA) request on Hersh's behalf for any pertinent CIA files on surveillance. The CIA rejected the initial request on the grounds that "the Agency did not conduct a 'massive illegal domestic intelligence operation' as alleged by you in your articles. Consequently, we are unable to furnish you with documents relating to such an operation."[46]

The day after the *Times* received the rejection, however, William Colby gave testimony to the Senate. Colby repeated the arguments to the Senate that he had made when Hersh first asked him about the surveillance program. According to Colby, the stories about domestic surveillance combined a variety of activities that had all ceased. Importantly, though, Colby did not deny that the activities had happened.[47]

Still, many remained skeptical of Hersh's reporting. Walter Pincus, editor of the *New Republic,* acknowledged that "there was enough truth in the Hersh piece and credibility in the *Times*' presentation to force serious, quick action," but he was critical of the way in which the *Times* had handled the story.[48] Pincus acknowledged some fault on the part of the rest of the press, noting that members of the press had ties with the intelligence community that stemmed from their reporting. "For foreign correspondents . . . CIA station chiefs were often the best men around to give an estimate on local conditions."[49] Pincus added that Philip Geyelin, the editor of the *Washington Post*'s editorial page, had himself been a member of the CIA, which led many to conclude that the *Post*'s perceived pro-CIA slant was a result of Geyelin's loyalty to his old employer. Pincus's rumination on the press-CIA relationships aside, the *Times* was sensitive to the criticism.[50]

Rosenthal was acutely aware of anti-Hersh and anti–*New York Times* sentiment. He believed that the *Times* faced a coordinated campaign intended to discredit its reporting. That belief, and probably also his frustration with critics like Pincus, led him to refuse to print an item from former DDCI Ray Cline that defended Colby. Rosenthal previously had allowed Cline space in the pages of the *Times* to counter criticisms of the CIA, but, as Rosenthal explained to Max Frankel, he felt Cline's most recent piece was just a repetition of Colby's statements before Congress. Rosenthal explained that he did not want the *Times* to join a "carefully orchestrated CIA P.R. campaign against Hersh."[51]

Hersh believed part of the reaction stemmed from the connections Angleton had established with the press. He later told the *Post* reporter George Lardner that after the story ran, "everything in town took a shot at me." Hersh ultimately moved from Washington, D.C., to New York City, chasing a murder story possibly related to the CIA that did not pan out. Nicholas Horrock of the *New York Times* Washington Bureau took over the story.[52] Victor Marchetti at the same time was speaking to Lardner, mentioning rumors of a story that the CIA had killed someone in New York City through the Mafia.[53] Though the story ultimately fell apart, that it was seriously investigated is telling of the decline in the CIA's position after nearly a decade of crises.

As Colby's testimony largely supported Hersh's version of events, the defense that what the CIA had been doing was unimportant, as stated by the columnist Joseph Kraft and the writers of the *National Review,* came to dominate theories that Hersh's reporting had been flawed. By March there was little dispute that the main points of Hersh's story were accurate.[54]

After the early scramble among members of the press to react to Hersh's revelations in January, clear and fairly stable positions among publications emerged in February and March that generally remained unchanged for the rest of the Year of Intelligence, despite additional revelations about CIA activities. These positions reflected the initial reporting on Hersh's story; those who defended Hersh, those who were uncertain over the affair, or those who criticized him tended to transition to those who called for a strong investigation of the CIA, those who were ambivalent in either support of or opposition to the investigations, and those who defended the CIA, respectively.

The most ardent supporters of an investigation hoped that the CIA would be either radically transformed or destroyed. While never a clear majority, they were vocal. Wicker was the most active single member of this group. Hersh refrained from the kind of statements of political opinion that Wicker made, but practically speaking he was also a part of this group. The

Nation and the *Progressive* both were reliably pro-investigation; their only criticisms of the investigation in the early months were that it did not go far enough. They also warned that, if the investigation proceeded too slowly and deliberately, the opportunity for reform would be lost.[55] The *New Republic,* while publishing articles by Walter Pincus critical of Hersh, gradually joined the strong pro-investigation camp.

Some investigation supporters expressed ambivalence about what the ultimate goals of an investigation ought to be. The ambivalent commentators were often of an older generation. Many had connections, either formal or social, to the CIA. Their views in some ways mirrored Colby's, in that they hoped for an investigation that would determine and rectify abuses, mitigate lingering doubts about the CIA, and allow business to return to normal. They also tended to blame the president as the fundamental problem, not the CIA.[56]

The *Washington Post* generally reflected this ambivalently pro-investigation position from the beginning of January. For example, the *Post* provided a forum to Franklin Lindsay, an OSS and CIA veteran and Wisner's former deputy at OPC, who argued for the importance of the CIA, the utility of its past service to the nation, and its continuing relevance in an age of détente. Lindsay claimed to support the investigations, though, as a way to restore confidence in the CIA and return it to a reasonable position within the national security establishment.[57]

People who only tentatively supported investigation and those who only tentatively opposed investigation had more in common with each other than the extremes on either side of the question. James Reston in many ways exemplified this position of ambivalent opposition; he argued in March that investigations could only prolong the nation's embarrassment and further weaken U.S. intelligence. He felt that the best way forward was for the current leadership of the CIA to be fired, the agency rechartered, and strong congressional oversight established that would govern future behavior but not probe the past. Cyrus Sulzberger, who had become largely divorced from the day-to-day activities of the *Times,* was also skeptical of the value of investigating the CIA.[58]

Finally, there were those who rejected any need for investigation into the CIA's activities entirely. Evans and Novak were two of the earliest and most consistent exemplars of this position. The *National Review* was similarly inclined to oppose any investigation of the CIA. Buckley confirmed in April that he had briefly worked for the agency, but he dismissed any suggestions that this affiliation had influenced his reporting.[59] With the sole exception of James Burnham, the *National Review* opposed investigating the CIA; writers for the magazine repeatedly accused the *New York Times* of artificially creating a scandal to bolster its position over those of its competitors.[60]

There were, of course, exceptions to the pattern of solidification. The *New York Times, Chicago Tribune, Los Angeles Times,* and *Washington Post* all provided forums for views opposing the consensus within their papers. George Lardner, though himself suspicious of the CIA, recalled that the *Washington Post* did not really take a single position on the CIA; there was a diversity of opinion in the newsroom.[61]

The Official Investigations Begin

President Ford, not having been briefed on the "Family Jewels" report until after Hersh's story on domestic surveillance was published, publicly supported a limited investigation. In January 1975, as the debate over Hersh's initial reporting continued, Ford announced the formation of a blue-ribbon commission led by Vice President Nelson Rockefeller. The commission's mandate was to determine whether the CIA had exceeded its statutory authority, and whether existing safeguards to prevent abuse by the CIA were adequate.[62] Under Rockefeller were seven men who, while chosen for their apparent lack of connection to the CIA, also tended to be conservative members of an older generation of political elites: C. Douglas Dillon, Lyman Lemnitzer, John T. Connor, Ronald Reagan, Erwin Griswold, Edgar F. Shannon, and Lane Kirkland.[63]

The commission was criticized or at least questioned for its composition, especially by those calling for a real congressional investigation.[64] Hersh revealed that Griswold, who had been the solicitor general who had tried to prevent the publication of the Pentagon Papers, was the possible target of a grand jury investigation for perjury following his testimony on Nixon's campaign finances and fund-raising with ITT.[65] Even though Griswold was never indicted, the presence of an advocate for government secrecy with possible ties to a corporation with known CIA connections did little to inspire confidence among observers.

Other publications such as the *Chicago Tribune* and the *Washington Post* joined the criticism. Frank van Riper, for example, noted that Lane Kirkland had been the secretary-treasurer for the AFL-CIO during a time when that union was known to have cooperated with the CIA in funneling money to Europe.[66] Even Joseph Kraft, normally a defender of the CIA, criticized the commission's composition.[67] The *Nation* enjoyed a rare moment of speaking for the main consensus of the press. Everyone involved in the committee, one *Nation* editorialist observed, had been in a position to know what the CIA had been doing. The commission was "the first bad joke of the year. The obvious purpose of the commission is to put a damper on the charges, not to investigate them."[68]

It would appear that the critics were correct. According to Colby, the committee was not particularly interested in trying to get answers from him. Griswold, who had a well-earned reputation as a Fifth Amendment champion, was the only one Colby reported to be in any way aggressive; while he had argued for the right of the government to suppress the Pentagon Papers, he was not the lackey of governmental power some commentators had assumed he would be. Other members were not as interested in a full investigation into the CIA's activities. By Colby's account, Rockefeller pulled him aside after his first day of testimony to ask if he really had to be so forthcoming. According to Colby, Rockefeller told him, "We realize that there are secrets that you fellows need to keep and so nobody here is going to take it amiss if you feel that there are some question you can't answer quite as fully as you seem to feel you have to." Peter Fenn, a staff member on the soon-to-be formed Church Committee, recalled similar feelings from Senator John Stennis (Democrat of Mississippi) in earlier meetings of the Armed Services Committee when it turned to the CIA.[69]

On 19 January the Senate's response to the Rockefeller Commission was announced with the formation of the Select Committee to Investigate Intelligence Activities.[70] The press's role in the formation of this congressional response was important. Calls for congressional investigation into the CIA had continued after the autumn 1974 revelations about Chile, but a bill that would provide for greater congressional oversight of the agency was defeated. Hersh's story provided impetus to the Senate to act again. From the initial exposure of the CIA's activities by Hersh to the increasingly common calls for congressional investigation to the intense skepticism that met President Ford's response to the scandal, the press generally contributed to an atmosphere in which the long-averted, serious congressional investigation of the CIA could occur.

Frank Church was nominated to chair the Senate's CIA investigation. A Democrat from Idaho, Church began his career in the Senate in 1957 and had emerged as an opponent of many U.S. Cold War policies. Church himself became the subject of considerable press attention, in addition to the material covered by his committee, through 1975 and 1976. The press often portrayed him positively in the early days of his chairmanship, but Church feared that sensational news coverage would delegitimize the investigation; he sought to portray himself as a neutral figure rather than as someone with the intent to destroy the CIA.[71] That did not prevent criticism from Evans and Novak; they complained, for example, that the lead investigator appointed by Church was a Cold War "revisionist" who they felt was too anti-CIA to investigate the agency objectively.[72] Nor was Church himself always capable of restraining a dramatic gesture that undermined his efforts at keeping the investigation focused, especially as he considered a 1976 presidential run.

The staff members of the Church Committee reflected this effort at neutrality, and they succeeded more often than Church himself did. Frederick Baron, the assistant to the chief counsel, Frederick A. O. "Fritz" Schwarz Jr., recalled that the committee members felt they had to be careful that the agencies under investigation did not see the committee as "hot-dogging" and "trying to gin up publicity."[73] Fenn observed, "The integrity of the investigation was very, very important. This was something that Church cared about, that [Senator John] Tower [Republican of Texas] cared about, everybody on the committee cared about. If at some point things looked like it was a circus, like things were being leaked all over the place, the reporters were all over things, then our credibility was harmed."[74] Fenn's sentiment, the fear of chaotic leaks undermining the investigation's legitimacy, was broadly shared.[75]

The House Committee, initially chaired by Lucien Nedzi (Democrat of Michigan), was called in February. The House Committee did not attract as much attention as the Church Committee, but it was potentially more important. Whereas the Church Committee focused on specific instances of abuse, the House Committee examined the more general question of whether the CIA was an effective and useful agency. Most of the news about the House Committee would detail not information about the CIA, but the contentious nature of the committee itself. Nedzi stepped down in June after it was revealed that, as one of the few congressmen to be in a position to know about the CIA's activities before the investigations, he had failed to exercise real oversight. He had been one of the few congressmen to read the Family Jewels report before Hersh's story came out.[76]

Otis Pike (Democrat of New York) replaced Nedzi. Pike's appointment did not end the controversy about the House investigation, and some representatives opposed the investigation entirely. By the time the Pike Committee had finally finished its work, the prospects for opponents of the investigation had improved, and they were able to block publication of the report. Elliot Maxwell, serving on the Church Committee, later complained that the seemingly chaotic nature of the House investigation strengthened the hand of the agencies in not disclosing information.[77]

As it became clear that the Rockefeller Commission would not have the final word, Ford, Kissinger, Colby, and other White House officials grew increasingly concerned about the direction of events. At a meeting in late February, Kissinger warned that Congress would never be able to keep any confidential material under control, as congressmen were "professional leakers." Colby hoped that secrecy agreements could prevent publication of CIA-related materials, but Kissinger noted that such agreements would prevent them from "[publishing] in their own names. You can't keep them from Sy Hersh."[78]

Kissinger argued that, since congressional investigation could not be avoided, their best course of action was to try to draw attention away from the CIA and discredit the investigators. He proposed cooperating with Congress initially with items of small importance; if those then leaked, it would provide a foundation from which to argue that executive privilege was needed to protect sensitive materials. Addressing the question of which materials to begin with, Deputy Attorney General Laurence Silberman observed, "The FBI may be the sexiest part of this. Hoover did things which won't stand scrutiny, especially under Johnson." Silberman believed that the Bureau hoped to protect itself by releasing information as slowly as possible. He argued that, rather than this slow trickle, FBI materials should be "put out in generic terms as quickly as possible. . . . This will divert attention and show relative cooperation with the committee. This relates only to illegal activities." Kissinger agreed with the approach.[79]

A few days after that meeting, Joseph Alsop ran a column in the *Chicago Tribune* that argued the CIA-FBI investigations revealed "only one fact of real importance," that Hoover had been incompetent when it came to counterintelligence, and he refused to allow his counterintelligence agents into certain parts of Washington. The CIA was forced to investigate the antiwar movement because Hoover had refused to do so for petty reasons. Alsop argued that "the foolish may credit the argument that the CIA-FBI rumpus has uncovered a grave threat to our civil liberties. But more sensible people will instead perceive an open invitation to the KGB."[80]

While Alsop's story is not direct evidence that he took an anti-FBI line at Kissinger's behest, the timing is suggestive. Alsop was friendly with Kissinger, as both were active in the Washington social scene. Alsop admired Kissinger, who, he felt, "like Metternich, is a master of playing weak hands with success."[81] Kissinger could easily have pushed Alsop toward focusing on Hoover. Alsop also would not have needed strong motivation to denigrate Hoover's memory, as they had clashed more than once. The Alsops had been critical and suspicious of the FBI, and Hoover perceived them as threats. Regarding intelligence matters, the Alsops had written articles critical of Hoover during the debate over postwar intelligence arrangements and contended that Hoover's FBI was incompetent.[82] At a personal level, Joseph Alsop also had reason to be displeased with Hoover. As mentioned earlier, Alsop, a closeted gay man, had fallen prey to a KGB honeytrap with another man while traveling in the Soviet Union. Alsop alerted a friend in the State Department when the KGB sought to blackmail him with evidence of the encounter. A report on the incident was sent to Hoover, who forwarded it to members of the Eisenhower administration.[83]

Any effort to focus the investigation on the FBI was undermined by a luncheon shared by President Ford, Donald Rumsfeld, and other senior members of the White House staff with the senior members of the *New York Times* in early February. Arthur Sulzberger, Abe Rosenthal, Clifton Daniel, James Reston, John Oakes, Tom Wicker, and Max Frankel were all present.[84] As the conversation turned to the CIA, Ford warned against further investigations, noting that they could reveal things the American people might rather not know. When pressed about what kind of things he was referring to, Ford responded that such things included assassinations. Seeming to realize the danger of his statement, Ford's Chief of Staff Donald Rumsfeld immediately reiterated that the president's comments were off the record.

Though the luncheon was off the record, Rosenthal and Wicker both reportedly wanted to publish. Reston and Oakes opposed publication. Daniel argued that the *Times* was honor-bound not to report on something given off the record but proposed that the *Times* seek permission from Ford to publish his statement.[85] In his notes for the luncheon, Daniel relegated matters related to the CIA to a second "P.S." section and even in his own private record made no note of the assassination comment.[86] The ultimate decision went to Sulzberger, who decided the *Times* could not violate the trust of an off-the-record environment.

Sulzberger had demonstrated in the past that he was willing to confront the government with his paper's reporting. Even for something as serious as Ford's statements, however, he believed the *Times*'s reputation for honest dealing outweighed the incentive to publish such an incendiary story. The *New York Times* and other news organizations also had less idealistic and more practical reasons for respecting the accepted rules concerning things said off the record. To maintain access to sources in government or other sensitive posts, the *Times* had to show it was trustworthy. Sulzberger tried to keep the statement from leaking out even further within the paper; Seymour Hersh, having moved back to New York, claimed that no one at the meeting informed him, but that he heard through other sources what had happened. He called it "a sad day for the integrity of the Times," but he did not publish anything against the wishes of his publisher.[87]

Sulzberger's decision not to publish Ford's statements did not long prevent their release. Someone leaked the information to Dan Schorr of CBS News. In a 27 February interview by Schorr of Colby, Schorr asked if the CIA had ever killed anyone in the United States. Colby, surprised by the question, responded, "Not in this country."[88] Schorr subsequently reported on Ford's remarks.[89] Reactions to this reporting ran from the moral condemnation of the *Nation* to wry cynicism.[90] Faced with the now unavoidable question of assassination, Ford extended the Rockefeller Commission's mandate to consider the question of assassinations in addition to CIA domestic activities. A flurry of assassination-related stories was released in March. The stories were troubling enough that even Braden called for the dissolution of his former agency.[91]

Sulzberger suspected that Tom Wicker had leaked the story to Schorr. In a letter to Wicker, he wrote that he was specifically concerned about a column by Wicker that said Schorr's report "can be unequivocally confirmed here."[92] Sulzberger wrote that "this aspect of what the President said was completely off-the-record. Indeed, the News and Editorial Departments have kept hands off the subject, tempting as it is." Sulzberger asked if Wicker had any way to confirm that Schorr's report on Ford's remarks was accurate aside from having been in the meeting where the remarks were made. If not, Sulzberger wrote, "I am sure you can see how it puts us in a tough spot with one department of the paper confirming something and the other departments being unable to do so. It seems to me that when we all attend an off-the-record luncheon (and whether we should is another matter for discussion) we are equally bound by the same rules. Now, frankly, I am bewildered as to what we ought to do."[93]

There is no record of a response from Wicker, but his later criticisms of the *Times* and the press focused largely on what he saw as the tendency of the press to give in to national security arguments against publishing. Rosenthal disagreed. He wrote to Wicker later to explain: "What killed [the Ford story] . . . was not that national security mystique because I don't think that entered into it at all. What killed it was the journalistic 'off the record' problem. . . . If we had gotten that story on any other basis—say Hersh had brought it in—there would have been no 'national security' problem at all."[94]

Rosenthal, despite his justification to Wicker, felt that the *Times* should have run the story on the assassinations comment. Rosenthal suspected that Ford had manipulated the *Times* by telling its journalists something in a setting that Ford knew would leave them feeling as though they could not report on his comments. This would restrict their reporting on assassination more generally, as any leads that might have potentially come from the luncheon would be contaminated. A year after the incident, Rosenthal wrote to Sulzberger, "We were burned pretty badly, although perhaps inevitably, by President Ford's 'assassination' comment." Rosenthal also felt that Colby had manipulated the *Times* on another story, regarding the *Glomar Explorer*, which reemerged in early 1975.[95]

The *Glomar Explorer* Revelation and Post-Luncheon Investigation Coverage

Rosenthal's feeling on the *Glomar Explorer* case stemmed from the discovery that Colby had used the *New York Times*'s decision not to run with the story as a way to convince other outlets not to run anything. Colby succeeded in quashing the story in 1974, before a bizarre twist to the story led to further complications. Burglars broke into the office of Hughes's California headquarters as part of an unrelated criminal activity. They found documents concerning the *Glomar Explorer*. They then attempted to extort ransom for the papers from Hughes, only to be captured by the authorities. The *Los Angeles Times* learned about the existence of the submarine-recovery operation through the burglary, and it then subsequently learned that the *New York Times* was preparing a story on the submarine. The *Los Angeles Times* prepared a first-page story, but Colby convinced the paper to move the story from the front page to the interior and not to run follow-up stories.[96]

What ensued was frantic activity on Colby's part in mid-February and again in mid-March to maintain the silence; the back-and-forth exchanges involved are worth examining in detail for what they demonstrate about the state of press-CIA relationships as they had developed in 1975. Most reporters were willing to cooperate, but they required assurances that the story in question represented a legitimate national security interest and that their decision to cooperate with the CIA would not harm their market position. If, as ultimately happened, one individual reporter decided to go ahead, the entire effort at suppression would unravel.

Colby and his staff began discussing efforts to maintain the story's secrecy on 10 February; by that evening Hersh had already found out about the *Los Angeles Times* story and tried to get in touch with Colby. Hersh left a message urging Colby to cooperate with him. Referring to one of the several different code names used in the project, Jennifer, Hersh explained that Colby "has a choice again—either he delegates someone . . . to sit down with me and make it as good as I can. It is a positive story. Or else I am in a position of writing what I know, which is more than he thinks I know, about our lady friend program." Hersh predicted that the story was a few days from breaking widely because people in the police and retired CIA officers were talking.[97]

Colby called Hersh that night to discuss the story. Hersh continued to warn about the imminent publication of the story, especially considering that reporters he respected at the *Los Angeles Times* were looking into it. Echoing the kind of argument Joseph Alsop had made two decades before, Hersh gave what he called "free public relations advice"; he urged Colby to consider the possible beneficial effects of the story in light of the CIA's current troubles. "It doesn't hurt," Hersh explained, "to let people know." Colby continued to be reluctant to disclose anything, but he thanked Hersh for Hersh's continuing forbearance. Hersh explained that no thanks were necessary: "I am a citizen too."[98]

Instead of working with Hersh in the manner Hersh suggested, Colby and the CIA's deputy director of science and technology, Carl Duckett, decided after telling the *New York Times* that the *Los Angeles Times* would hold the story to "do vice versa"—that is, use the *New York Times*'s decision not to publish as a way to keep the *Los Angeles Times* from changing its mind about publishing. By 14 February Colby was able to report to Deputy National Security Adviser Brent Scowcroft that he had the *Los Angeles Times,* the *New York Times,* and the *Washington Post* "sewed up on this." Where the *Washington Post* came in is unclear, but, for the moment, Colby's approach seemed to be working. By 3 March Colby even had a written statement from the *New York Times* acknowledging that it would not publish the story, on the understanding that it would be informed if publication from another outlet was forthcoming.[99]

The story continued to spread, however. Hersh had been incorrect about the timing, but he was correct in recognizing that the number of people who knew made it practically impossible to keep it secret for long. If nothing else, journalists would talk among themselves. On 12 March, in keeping with his agreement, Colby told John "Jack" Nelson of the *Los Angeles Times* that a reporter from *Time* had the story. Nelson alerted Colby that he had learned Lloyd Shearer, a columnist for *Parade,* had also heard about it.[100]

The next day saw sustained efforts by Colby to juggle the ever-increasing numbers of reporters who had the story. Colby called both Shearer and the unidentified *Time* reporter, urging them to hold the story. Shearer agreed to hold, and he warned Colby that he might want to look into the Philadelphia and Boston papers, as they might also have the story.[101] Colby explained to a subordinate, "The only way to go is at the top," presumably referring to the management.[102]

Someone at *Newsweek* also called the CIA to warn the agency that a *Newsweek* reporter had the story, which prompted Colby to seek out an unidentified intermediary with Katharine Graham, who at this point was owner of *Newsweek.* Through the intermediary, Colby was able to bring another publication into the agreement not to publish.[103] Colby then reported this to Jack Nelson, to ensure that he would continue to hold off publication.[104] This constant juggling, however, was beginning to wear on Colby and Duckett. When informed that *Time* had agreed not to publish, Duckett was skeptical it would matter. He responded: "Great. There are only ninety-three more [outlets] that I can think of."[105]

The next day, 14 March, Colby reported to Scowcroft on the growing list of publications that had knowledge of the story and told Scowcroft, "I am carrying around a list of phone numbers in my wallet because if it goes I am committed to tell everyone."[106] Colby saw some reason to be hopeful, however, telling Scowcroft: "The fact that we have the other ones locked up is absolutely compelling that the other guys be responsible too. We can end up with an American (conspiracy) here."[107]

A few days later, on 17 March, Colby, Duckett, and Assistant to the Director for Press Relations Angus Theurmer contacted members of ABC, NBC, CBS, NPR, and the wire services.[108] Colby explained to Theurmer that they wanted to try and get ahead of any stories. He instructed Theurmer to tell them that "if you hear (the) word 'CIA' and 'ocean,' we would like to talk to them."[109] The story continued to spread, especially through the social circles of the press. Scowcroft informed Colby that James Schlesinger, the former DCI and current secretary of defense, had heard about the story from his press officer, who in turn had heard about the story at the radio and TV correspondents' dinner, where the topic was discussed freely.[110]

This ever-expanding network of silence had taken on farcical qualities, but it finally reached its end on 18 March. One of the new journalists to pick up the story was Jack Anderson. As he had with increasing frequency, Colby made a personal appeal. Anderson noted that, while he had "never turned you—or Helms, before you—down," he thought that the relationship with Hughes was questionable, and that the story was bound to get out whether or not he was the one to break it. Colby tried, unsuccessfully, to convince him otherwise.[111] Les Whitten, Anderson's partner, later revealed that after that call, when Colby "really laid this national security shit on us," he and Anderson contacted a source in the navy, who told them publication would probably hurt nothing since so many people already knew.[112] Lacking a commitment from Anderson, Colby made a round of calls to alert the members of the press he had made agreements with that the story was breaking.

Colby's approach to different journalists and his internal strategizing in the CIA deserve special attention because they epitomize the essential CIA approach to attempting to keep a story from publication. Colby appealed directly to the publishers and upper management of news organizations, hoping for their patriotic support on a matter of national security. He also continued to stay in contact with reporters such as Hersh to ensure they would continue observing their superiors' directives and not try to get around the suppression. Colby recognized that the press needed to see him as reliable; thus, he was conscientious in alerting them. Finally, Colby was also able to distinguish the ongoing story of CIA domestic activities from the *Glomar Explorer* story. He continued to work with Hersh, for example, even telling one of his deputy directors, "I am going to give H (credit) for (being) a responsible guy on some (things) and not on others."[113]

The press, for its part, was willing to listen to an argument on national security grounds. In addition to listening to these arguments, however, the press also sought to use the occasion to proceed in other areas. Hersh, most notably, worked to wring concessions from the CIA. Members of the press were also motivated to maintain their silence once they agreed to the initial request to keep silent; otherwise, they would face the possibility of losing out when others published before them. Other representatives of the press cooperated in CIA efforts to keep silence, even informing the CIA when they received indications of other reporters working on the story.

As more and more people learned of the existence of the *Glomar Explorer,* however, the chances that someone would publish the story increased dramatically. In Guatemala in 1954, the CIA could use a combination of appeals to patriotism and subtle maneuvering to keep its involvement out of the public sphere, even as fairly significant numbers of the press knew at least part of the story. The chances that no reporter would decide to publish were, by 1975, much lower than in 1954. All it took was for Jack Anderson and Les Whitten not to believe in the seriousness of the "national security shit" that Colby stressed to them for the entire delicate arrangement to collapse.[114] The failure to contain the *Glomar Explorer* story in 1975 reveals the extent to which earlier successes in maintaining secrecy had depended on press compliance.

With the story now out, Hersh in March 1975 published a story on the operation, the break-in at Hughes's office, the blackmail attempt, and the failure to get the Soviet submarine intact from the floor of the ocean. Hersh also told his readers that "a reporter" for the *New York Times* had been asked not to report on the operation by Colby. Hersh did not reveal that he had been that reporter.[115]

While the *Glomar Explorer* affair highlights some of the complications that came from the interaction of the press with intelligence agencies, it should not be interpreted as the symbol of a quiescent press. For men like Rosenthal and Sulzberger, the decision not to publish was probably not, as Kathryn Olmsted has argued, reached out of a desire not to *seem* to be unpatriotic.[116] Rather, they probably felt a legitimate sense of patriotism. This is an important distinction, as publishers or editors would have different incentives if they wished to avoid the appearance of being unpatriotic as opposed to being genuinely patriotic. It is hard to imagine that the *New York Times* would have published the Pentagon Papers had it feared that the publication would seem unpatriotic. It knew that it opened the paper up to such accusations by deciding to publish. Keeping quiet also maintained access they found valuable.

It is also worthwhile to examine the case of the *Glomar Explorer* with concurrent reporting on the CIA. Hersh was holding the story on the *Glomar Explorer*, but he had released a much bigger one. While at times censoring themselves, the mainstream press's increasing attention to the CIA was a significant change and challenge to the CIA.

The decision to hold off led to internal disagreement at the *Times*. Wicker, who had criticized the decision not to report, later contacted Rosenthal for Rosenthal's reasoning behind suppressing the story. Rosenthal insisted he had agreed only to a delay.[117] According to Rosenthal, the *Glomar Explorer* case had been "the first time that I ever felt that the arguments against immediate publication outweighed the arguments in favor." While agreeing with Wicker that in most cases assertions of national security were specious, Rosenthal concluded that "one can be quite aware of the general phoniness of the national security argument and still be confronted with situations where one has to take it into account."[118] Though Rosenthal defended himself to Wicker, he admitted privately to another member of the *Times* staff that he felt he had been manipulated in the *Glomar Explorer* case. Rosenthal noted that, while he feared no prosecution for publishing, he was disquieted by the fact that Colby had apparently used the *Times*'s decision not to run the story to convince other newspapers to act similarly.[119]

An internal CIA memorandum reflected its struggle over its new, more problematic press relations. A CIA officer suggested that the CIA seek to establish "some kind of seminar for members of the press wherein the dangers of . . . disclosures and the losses that they could incur to the U.S. intelligence could be frankly covered." The officer suggested that "Allen Dulles' sessions at the Alibi Club" could be a model, an apparent reference to Dulles's old press meetings.[120] Whether any such meeting was ever held is not known. The positions in the press in regard to the Year of Intelligence that had emerged early in the process remained largely unchanged from March until December. The *Glomar Explorer* briefly attracted attention, but it could not ultimately distract from the investigations into the agency's conduct.

The Year of Intelligence began with a story about the CIA straying from its charter, which prohibited domestic activities. The CIA had over the years opened mail, placed Americans in the United States under surveillance, and maintained files on the activities and associations of American citizens. In the early furor of the stories and the initially confused assemblage of three separate investigations, different segments of the press set down their positions and prepared to pore over the agencies in detail.

This was the culmination of trends that had existed from the beginning of the agency and that had intensified in the 1960s and 1970s, especially after Watergate. A solid record of CIA activities had been built up, and once relatively secret operations like TPAJAX and PBSUCCESS were now all but openly acknowledged by the government and clear points of reference for the press. The mystique of the CIA, and its authority in invoking national security, was no longer a sufficient defense against congressional investigation. Even in this season of inquiry, however, the Central Intelligence Agency still had allies in the press and in Congress that were willing to support it. The call for national security remained strong, even for reporters like Hersh. By the summer of 1975, the competing strains of investigation of the agency and support for its goals, combined with the market demands of media businesses, the strength of long-established relations, and the increasingly partisan post-Watergate environment, had created an uncertain situation. What the outcome of the investigation would be depended on the press's ability to maintain focus on the critical issues of the investigation and the CIA's ability to find enough supporters of its particular view of national security to defend itself from further investigation.

7

The Year of Intelligence's Contentious End

In August 1975 new reporting on the ongoing investigation into the CIA revealed the extent to which all presidents after the creation of the CIA were involved in CIA activities. Taylor Branch and George Crile wrote in *Harper's* that, following the Bay of Pigs invasion, Kennedy was deeply enmeshed in assassination plots against Castro.[1] At least some members of the press were aware of that fact. Earlier that April, Joseph Alsop had written privately to Arthur Schlesinger with comments about a proposed biography of Robert Kennedy. Alsop warned that Kennedy was deeply involved in assassination plotting. "Of course Bobby knew all about these CIA operations. He adored being on the inside of that . . . sort of thing. He undoubtedly knew."[2]

Kennedy's involvement was a sensitive matter. Schlesinger was especially devoted to protecting the Kennedy legacy, which brought him into conflict with agency veterans like Ray Cline. Schlesinger and Cline had both been in contact with George Crile about Cuba; Cline disputed Schlesinger's spin that put the onus on the CIA rather than Kennedy as the force that authorized the operation. Schlesinger struck back that he knew CIA activities against Castro had been prepared during the Eisenhower administration.[3]

Even more details could have been uncovered. Frederick Baron, a member of the Church Committee, recalled that the investigators were given pause when they discovered that some of the connections between the CIA and the mafia might have initially been formed by a connection between Sam Giancana, a Mafia boss, and Judith Campbell Exner. Exner's name appeared multiple times on the White House visitors' logs, which led to the assumption that her relationship to Kennedy was both personal and sexual. To avoid a messy fight between Republicans and Democrats on the committee over whether to reveal one of Kennedy's many affairs, John Tower decided to lead the Republicans in not insisting that the committee make clear that the connection between Kennedy and Giancana was a woman.[4]

As this story demonstrates, recriminations flowing out of the Church and Pike Committee investigations were not limited to the Central Intelligence Agency. The investigations revealed a variety of relationships, activities, and practices that had existed out of the public eye during the early years of the Cold War. The press, too, would not escape without blemishes, as the Church and Pike Committees, and subsequent congressional investigation, confirmed at least some stories of the press's relationships with the CIA. This flow of information was, for many of the participants, exhausting. Many looked forward to mid-1976, when the investigations into the agency were set to end.

Congress Takes the Lead

As the Rockefeller investigation neared its end and the congressional investigations took central focus, pushback against the investigations ratcheted up. Former members of the CIA sought to defend their agency in a variety of outlets. Such activity was not new. Even before the investigations into the CIA began, Ray Cline would defend his former employer on programs such as *The Dick Cavett Show,* on which he appeared with Robert Komer opposite Victor Marchetti and Seymour Hersh.[5] Cline also took a paid position as a consultant for an ABC special on the history of the CIA, though he ultimately was disappointed. The program focused on activities such as interventions in Iran and Indonesia in 1953 and 1958, rather than on the more positive aspects Cline sought to emphasize.[6]

David Atlee Phillips, a veteran CIA officer, took it upon himself to present the CIA's case to the press. Before retiring early from the CIA, Phillips had overseen CIA activities in Chile as chief of Latin American operations. In early May 1975 he publicly denied the CIA's role in the overthrow of Allende.[7] Phillips hoped that the investigations would result in a new consensus that met the demands of those finding fault with the CIA while not damaging its "critical responsibilities for the national security."[8]

Such a consensus did not emerge from the Rockefeller report, which was released on 9 June after some debate about whether any part of it should be published. The report was vague on the question of White House responsibility for the actions of the intelligence community. The sections dealing with assassination were not declassified for the public. The report did reveal for the first time, however, that the CIA's domestic surveillance program was called Operation MHCHAOS.[9] Both the decision to release the report, and the actual report itself, drew criticism; some commentators, though—notably Wicker and Hersh—were surprised by the report's level of candor.[10]

When the Rockefeller Commission finished in June, the congressional investigations became the major focus of the press. Those investigations were more rigorous than that of the Rockefeller Commission. New information continued to emerge from Congress over the summer. In early July the CIA's experiments with LSD in the 1950s emerged in the press, including the fact that an army researcher, Frank Olson, had died after he was dosed with LSD without his knowledge. The story that emerged in 1975 was that after a week of erratic behavior, Olson threw himself out of an upper-story window while under CIA observation. President Ford arranged a meeting with Olson's family in the Oval Office to make an official apology and to promise restitution.[11] That summer also saw renewed attention to a book by the former CIA employee Philip Agee. *Inside the Company* revealed the names of many CIA operatives then undercover; it also alleged that the CIA had assassinated some of its employees. Agee had published the book in Britain, placing it outside the ability of the CIA to suppress it, as it had the work of Marchetti and Marks.[12]

This series of stories did not fundamentally alter the initial positions taken earlier in 1975, especially as the focus had shifted away from the concerns initially raised by Hersh about the CIA's willingness to violate its charter and instead had moved to the more sensational stories contained in the Family Jewels report. Karl Inderfurth, a member of the committee, recalled that the revelations about the agency's activities led to "a constant cascade of stories and reports showing where the intelligence community had made mistakes."[13] This cascade meant that, by the summer, attention was focused on the upcoming report concerning assassinations.

In September 1975 a series of stories came out of the Church Committee regarding the CIA's work with various poisons. What had triggered the stories was the revelation that a CIA officer had apparently refused to destroy a cache of toxins when ordered to do so following a presidential directive to eliminate U.S. stocks of bacteriological weapons.[14] Those stories led to a famous picture of Senator Church displaying a gun capable of firing poison darts. Church, who had been concerned that the investigation would be harmed by a sensational atmosphere, at times could apparently not resist his political instincts to make a dramatic demonstration for the public.

Loch Johnson, a Church Committee member and future intelligence scholar, remembered that he was "appalled" by Church's decision; Church had asked him in his office whether the dart gun was available. When Johnson questioned why, he alleged that Church responded, "We've got to dramatize these hearings. We have to attract the attention of the American people if we are ever going to have any reform."[15] The image provided critics like Evans and Novak an opportunity to accuse Church of sensationalizing the committee.[16] It was not the last time that Church's presentation had unintended consequences; another committee member, Patrick Shea, remembered urging Church not to quote Rudyard Kipling's reference to a rogue elephant; Church decided to do so in the moment, which led to the enduring phrase referring to the CIA as a "rogue elephant," though Church phrased it as a question and not a statement.[17]

The sheer amount of information released by the committees, especially the Church Committee, over the summer and autumn of 1975 was exhausting. An incredible rate of stories and level of commentary were produced. Dozens of articles were available each month. Colby's plan, to admit to what the CIA could not deny and, he hoped, move past the investigations with renewed legitimacy, had clearly failed. He was dismissed in September. He was eventually succeeded by George H. W. Bush.

Despite the staggering amount of coverage, there was very little movement in the positions of major commentators. The Church Committee's report on assassinations was released in November, attracting press attention. The report was the crowning achievement of the investigations. Spanning 1959 to 1972, the report found the CIA had tried to kill the Congo's Patrice Lumumba, had possibly had a hand in the death of the Dominican Republic's Rafael Trujillo, and had supported the attempt to kidnap General René Schneider in Chile, although it claimed that the conspirators who did kill the general were not those who had recently received weapons from the CIA. A possible plot against Ngo Dinh Diem was dismissed. Standing above these other incidents were the numerous efforts to kill Cuba's Fidel Castro. Some publications, such as the *Los Angeles Times* and the *Washington Post,* released a summary of the major findings of the report. The *New York Times* published the actual text of the report.[18] Its details, as the Church Committee itself wrote, "strain[ed] the imagination." Especially noteworthy was the involvement of Mafia figures such as Sam Giancana and Santos Trafficante.[19] The CIA, it was reported, had plotted to kill Castro before the Bay of Pigs invasion and had continued to plot after President Kennedy's death.[20]

After these dramatic revelations, however, the dynamics of the Year of Intelligence began to change. Skepticism emerged in the press about whether the report was useful. A writer for the *Chicago Tribune* argued that the report showed only American "puritanism." *Time* observed that, of the five world leaders targeted for assassination, the four who had died did not appear to have actually died at the hands of the CIA.[21] Hersh, writing in November, predicted that the CIA would emerge from the committee's investigation with its prestige intact, as most people following the story would make the false assumption that everything had been revealed by the Church Committee.[22]

Members of the committee would later reflect some concern with both the time they had and the direction the investigation took. The initial twelve-month time frame, extended to eighteen months, was brief for an investigation looking into decades' worth of questions across the Central Intelligence Agency, the Federal Bureau of Investigation, and the National Security Agency. One of the counsels on the Church Committee, Michael Madigan, observed that "they had the time limit, which is just an invaluable tool for someone who is under investigation, and they used it." He believed that the CIA gave away information such as the assassination material to divert the Church Committee down particular paths so that it would avoid other, critical areas of the agency.[23]

Resistance to the Investigations

By December 1975 CIA defenders began to blame the investigations for apparent setbacks in foreign policy. For example, Congress overrode Ford's attempts to support the National Union for the Total Independence of Angola (UNITA) over the Soviet-backed People's Movement for the Liberation of Angola (MPLA) during the Angolan Civil War, which prompted conservative backlash.[24]

A defining moment of the investigation came on 23 December 1975, a year and a day after Hersh's original story had appeared. On that day, the CIA station chief in Greece, Richard Welch, was assassinated outside his home. Welch's assassination added a theretofore-absent moral component to criticism of the investigations. Welch's body was flown to Washington, to be buried at Arlington National Cemetery in a televised ceremony. Ford was present, along with Welch's family, when the plane landed at Andrews Air Force Base.

To many, the ceremony's purpose was clearly to push against the investigations of the CIA. Fritz Schwartz, a Church Committee counsel, later commented that the executive branch "danced with joy" on Welch's grave.[25] Publications and commentators such as *Time, U.S. News and World Report,* Evans and Novak, and the *Chicago Tribune,* all of which had either been opposed to the investigations or, at least, ambivalent, tended to take the position that the Church and Pike Committees were to blame for Welch's death. Even *Harper's,* which over the course of the late 1960s and early 1970s had established itself as a CIA critic through several prominent stories, published a piece in which the CBS reporter George Crile criticized what he saw as the assumption that CIA leakers like Marchetti, Marks, and Agee were telling the truth. The press, Crile warned, was becoming an advocate against the CIA rather than a dispassionate observer.[26] Though it is unclear if Crile had contact with Helms at this time, he would eventually have some positive communication with the former director of Central Intelligence.[27] He definitely, as we saw at the beginning of this chapter, had contact with Cline.

In the coming months and years, George Bush, Colby, and other agency defenders would invoke the name of Richard Welch as an argument against the revelation of CIA activities or what they perceived as overblown criticism in the press.[28] This interpretation did ignore, however, the complicated political situation in Greece in the 1970s and the hatred that many in Greece felt for the CIA regardless of what was printed in the American media.

Critics of the CIA countered that the investigations were not responsible for Welch's death, and that the Ford administration sought to manipulate the press to turn it against the investigations. The *New York Times* also attempted to rebuff the rising pushback. Anthony Lewis was especially vocal, arguing that there was a media campaign under way "to rehabilitate the CIA, in the public mind, after the uncovering of its secret abuses and crimes." The goal was obvious: to prevent any serious congressional control of the CIA.[29]

Morton Halperin, looking back on the Welch assassination, called it "the only episode I am aware of where there is clear evidence of CIA manipulation of the American press for the purpose of influencing events in the United States." He accused the CIA of exploiting the death of its station chief. He noted that *Counterspy,* a radical magazine, had identified Welch while Welch was still stationed in Lima, Peru. Welch lived in the home in Athens that previous CIA chiefs had lived in, and he was warned by the CIA that he should reconsider his security arrangements in light of anti-CIA and anti-American feelings in Athens. The night of the assassination, the CIA's head of public relations, Angus Theurmer, had called reporters on deep background to tell them that Welch had died because his name had been printed in an American magazine, despite the fact that the details were still unclear.[30] Under questioning, Halperin noted it was entirely possible that Welch had been killed simply because he was living in a house known to be used by the CIA station chief.[31]

Pushback also occurred within Congress even at the time. When called to testify, George Bush began criticizing the investigation and invoked the murder, leading Phil Hart (Democrat of Michigan) to caustically ask, "Mr. Director, don't you think enough people have danced on that grave?"[32] In 1978 Representative Les Aspin (Democrat of Wisconsin) recalled that regardless of the accuracy, most Americans after the initial flurry of reporting would get the inaccurate impression that Welch died because his name was printed in an American paper.[33] Despite efforts to push back against the CIA narrative, however, Welch's name continued to be invoked by opponents of the investigation.

In February the Pike Committee finished its report on the CIA. Congressional opponents of the investigation successfully prevented the release of the final report to the public. Someone, however, leaked a copy to Dan Schorr, who in turn gave it to the *Village Voice.* The leak, especially after Welch's murder, was controversial. One *Time* reporter, for example, argued the leaks discredited the entire probe.[34] Schorr had his defenders, but he eventually was fired from CBS for his conduct.[35]

The Church Committee Final Report was released at the end of April. Coming after the issue of the assassination report and much of its findings having already been made public, the release was not a major event. Strong advocates for reform or dissolution of the agency were disappointed. The Church report provided a history of the Central Intelligence Agency, a theory of American intelligence, and a tally of some of the ways the intelligence community had expanded into questionable activities. The report argued for "an effective legislative oversight that has sufficient power to resolve . . . fundamental conflicts between secrecy and democracy."[36] Tom Wicker agreed that a strong congressional hand was needed to keep the CIA under control, but he saw such a strong hand as unlikely: "It is not the agencies that are under fire for abusing their powers, but members of Congress and the press for airing 'secrets' and supposedly endangering national security."[37]

Those most grateful for the end of the investigations were those who had been ambivalent about them; their writing was increasingly triumphant. A March *Time* article, for example, noted that months of investigation "have produced a dismaying variety of abuses by the nation's intelligence agencies. Yet the probes were so haphazardly and sometimes vindictively conducted and so many secrets leaked that the public has appeared to shift back in support of the embattled agencies." With both sides discredited, the nation could move forward, content that abuses had been corrected and a watchdog was in place.[38] Wicker continued to urge for pieces about the CIA. He argued, for example, that a profile should be written on Helms, who had not yet been charged with perjury despite his clear lies to Congress.[39] Helms would eventually be indicted for lying to Congress regarding Chile. By September, however, even the *New York Times* had, for the most part, moved past the CIA. One *Times* editor wrote to Rosenthal and advised that CIA-related stories seemed to be played out. Hersh should move to other subjects, because "the Times would benefit if he had another string in his bow."[40]

Both advocates for strong reform and those for leaving the intelligence system untouched were disappointed. Congress established permanent committees to exercise intelligence oversight in both houses. In 1978 the Foreign Intelligence Surveillance Court was created, providing a supposedly clearer, more official line for determining the foreign-domestic divide in intelligence responsibilities. With good reason, given the record of presidential activity through the CIA, the main conclusion that many drew was that the CIA's misdeeds were fundamentally an issue of presidential power rather than problems specific to the agency. Commentators like Wicker immediately raised questions about the effectiveness of oversight that emerged after the Church Committee. Those questions have largely remained.

Public Grappling with CIA-Press Relationships

One change that resulted from the committees' work was a growing caution in the press about relationships with the CIA. In January 1976 Walter Pincus reported that the CIA had a journalistic network abroad to gather information and spread stories. John Crewsdon reported that the CIA had tried to recruit a *Times* reporter, Wayne Phillips, in 1953, with the apparent blessing of Arthur Hays Sulzberger. The Church Committee reported that about fifty journalists, who remained unnamed, had been paid to work with the CIA. There was widespread condemnation of the practice, as many reporters argued that such activities delegitimized the press at home and abroad. George Bush announced that the CIA would no longer enter into paid or contractual relationships with the press, but he did say that the CIA would still be accepting information voluntarily proffered.[41]

The revelation that the CIA had paid relationships with reporters was not shocking to reporters themselves, but it was a cause for real concern nonetheless. Within the *New York Times,* at least, the information led to a concerted effort to find out whether any *Times* reporters were connected to the CIA. Rosenthal, following the advice of the *Times's* legal counsel, advised Sulzberger to write to the CIA to request the names of any *Times* reporters who had a formal relationship with the agency.[42] The *Times's* request was denied, but its suspicions of CIA infiltration were confirmed in other ways. A few days later, Rosenthal informed Sulzberger that Nicholas Horrock and John Crewsdon had related to him that a *Times* stringer in Brussels, Paul Kimizes, "has had relations with the CIA."[43] Richard Halloran, who had previously written on U.S. involvement in Laos, wrote to Rosenthal to reveal that he had once been affiliated with the CIA but denied any current involvement.[44]

Sulzberger, in early February 1976, planned to meet with Bush. Rosenthal advised that he should first ask Bush that no off-the-record factual information be discussed. Rosenthal feared that Bush would use the opportunity of an off-the-record meeting to reveal information to Sulzberger that Bush did not want the *Times* to report, compromising the *Times's* position, much as Ford had with the assassination comments. Bush wrote to both Sulzberger and Rosenthal, promising that reporters would not be used "operationally." Bush refused, however, to give guarantees regarding the use of stringers, though he did assure Rosenthal and Sulzberger that stringers would not be used to try to influence information going to U.S. media organizations.[45]

Rosenthal, who was deeply concerned that the CIA could subvert the *Times,* informed Sulzberger in March that every effort had to be made to find out who, if anyone, at the *Times* had connections with the CIA.[46] Clifton Daniel, meanwhile, continued to pursue the legal avenue and to press the

CIA for information.[47] In May Soviet officials accused *Times* Moscow Bureau Chief Christopher Wren of being affiliated with the CIA. Sulzberger wrote to Bush, explaining that the Wren situation was precisely the kind of thing that reporters feared would happen as a result of the possibility that the CIA had infiltrated the press.[48]

For some, the possibility of ties to the CIA remained an awkward and concerning question. The case of Philip Geyelin, the editor of the *Washington Post*'s editorial page, is useful to consider, both for what it demonstrates about the changes that occurred over the existence of the CIA and for understanding the difficulty in discerning the different conceptions of the CIA and reporters of what counted as cooperation.

Geyelin began his career in journalism at the *Wall Street Journal* as a foreign correspondent in 1947. During the Korean War, Geyelin took a leave of absence from the *Journal* and, from December 1950 to December 1951, worked for the CIA in Washington, D.C.[49] By January 1975 Geyelin's temporary stint at the agency had already become common gossip, and he was accused of softening the *Post*'s stance toward the CIA because of his loyalty to his old employer. Former CIA officer David Phillips, the agency's chief defender, even wrote to express his appreciation for "the consistently fair and objective Post editorial position on the current controversy about the CIA and the intelligence community."[50]

Then, during the summer of 1975, a former CIA officer, John Bross, was called before the House Committee on Intelligence. Bross had talked to Stuart Loory when Loory was preparing his exposé on the CIA's use of the press. Bross had told Loory he was aware of only one case in which a journalistic cover was used in covert operations; when asked by the House Committee who this person was, Bross named Geyelin, when Geyelin worked for the *Wall Street Journal* in Europe. This identification prompted an objection from Geyelin, who acknowledged he had met with CIA officers after leaving the agency, but only in the course of checking with sources as standard operating procedure. Bross then wrote to Richard Helms, asking about Geyelin's connections to the agency and expressing confusion about why anyone should care in the first place. Helms remembered nothing about using Geyelin's status for intelligence gathering and recalled only meeting him in Washington in the 1960s. Helms, unlike Bross, seems to have understood the problem. Helms wrote to Bross, "The national attitude of 1955 was obviously significantly different from that of 1975. Since a man is not blessed with a capacity for clairvoyance, it is exceedingly difficult to anticipate at one state in one's career how people might view actions many years later against a different background and in another context."[51]

Bross apologized to Geyelin for apparently naming him in error, but Geyelin had already prepared to make legal arrangements to see his CIA file. Ultimately, Geyelin, his attorney, and a CIA officer met to review his file. It found that after his agency service, Geyelin was listed by the CIA as being in a "collaborator relationship" with the agency; what this meant in practice, though, was that Geyelin was "simply . . . a person who was talking to the CIA." There were three specific items justifying this status for the CIA. First, Geyelin had been cleared to do covert work in 1954–1955 by the CIA, though this clearance noted that Geyelin was not a member of the CIA, and it does not appear Geyelin was aware of it. Second, Geyelin had agreed to be debriefed after returning from pursuing a story in Cuba in the 1960s, which was in line with a policy the *Wall Street Journal* had of allowing its reporters to be debriefed and interviewed by the agency. Finally, Geyelin was listed by the CIA as having written two reports for the agency; upon further investigation, however, these "reports" were in fact interviews Geyelin had given to CIA officers that had been filed for reference by the CIA.[52]

The Geyelin case illustrates the often-ambiguous nature of the CIA contacts with the press. Bross, it appears, most significantly misunderstood Geyelin's involvement.[53] The CIA identified Geyelin as a collaborator and even considered him, for a time, an asset. Because of confusion about the use of his reporting in intelligence analysis, the CIA mistakenly identified Geyelin as having actively provided it material, when in reality he had simply been reporting on his trip. Geyelin, meanwhile, seems to have been unaware that the CIA considered him a collaborator and, apart from his Cuba debriefing, understood his contacts with the CIA to be part of the normal practice of journalism: seeking information from a variety of sources.

Geyelin's case was not isolated. Two major figures at the *New York Times,* Harrison Salisbury and Cyrus Sulzberger, also were forced to confront their past relationships with intelligence. Salisbury, when writing *Without Fear or Favor,* his history of the *New York Times,* portrayed Cyrus Sulzberger as deeply connected to the CIA; this followed an increasingly fraught series of exchanges between the two men.[54] Cyrus Sulzberger insisted that he had traded information with the CIA and had treated the agency as a source as he would have any other potential government source; he maintained that, unlike Joseph Alsop, he had never been tasked by the CIA for a specific goal.[55] Salisbury's refusal to believe this claim fractured his relationship with Cyrus Sulzberger; Salisbury, meanwhile, discovered that he himself was considered a source by the CIA because he had been willing to brief it on his trips behind the Iron Curtain.[56]

The conflict between what was a reporter working as a CIA asset and what was a reporter engaged in standard practice emerged publicly with an article by Carl Bernstein. In the fall of 1977, Bernstein published "The CIA and the Media" in *Rolling Stone*, in which he identified many collaborators with the agency in the press, notably Arthur Hays Sulzberger, Stewart Alsop, and *Time*. He also claimed there were not fifty reporters essentially working for the CIA, but four hundred. In an interview with Tom Brokaw, Bernstein contended that, though much had changed, the fact that no paid relationships existed was of little importance, as cooperation was often on a "strictly volunteer basis."[57] Brokaw questioned whether the relationship might have been misinterpreted by both sides, as had apparently happened with Geyelin, Cyrus Sulzberger, and Salisbury. Bernstein, however, insisted that that was not the case, that the CIA had files on thousands of press-CIA relationships, but that the four hundred he alleged were the ones considered to be "major assets" by the agency.[58] Bernstein claimed to have seen files related to journalistic assets, but those have not been revealed in the decades since. Given the issues that arose in the Geyelin case, it is entirely possible both for Bernstein to have seen CIA files on journalistic assets and for the CIA to have misunderstood its own relationships with the media.

The *New York Times* management was particularly concerned about Bernstein's allegations that Arthur Hays Sulzberger had an official relationship with the CIA. Noting that Bernstein had cited "thousands of files" on the press-CIA relationships but had given no indication of how he had accessed them, Sydney Gruson wrote to Gene Wilson and Admiral Stansfield Turner, then DCI, requesting any information on Sulzberger and the CIA. The *Times*, however, did not receive any such confirmation.[59]

Rosenthal reflected that, if Bernstein's allegations were true, and the CIA did have a substantial program meant to use the media as a weapon in the Cold War, that fact had proven to be of limited use. Rosenthal sent a draft statement to Sulzberger that noted: "It is depressingly obvious that for many years, the CIA carried on a campaign to infiltrate American newspapers, magazines, radio and television and the book-publishing industry. To some extent, they obviously succeeded."[60] Rosenthal dismissed the importance of CIA efforts, however, as "millions of dollars, apparently, were spent in this black propaganda campaign against the American press—and indirectly against the American public. The net result seems to be that a few false rumors were planted and printed, and a few small books that originated in the imagination of CIA officials were printed and distributed, and that a few small journalists, out of thousands, were prostituted."[61] Commenting privately to Sulzberger, Rosenthal concluded, "Considering the fact that the CIA was so active, the *Times* comes out, to my mind, remarkably well."[62]

The same month that Bernstein's article ran, CIA Director Stansfield Turner issued a new directive for relationships with the media. The Turner Directive forbade the CIA from entering into relationships with full-time or part-time journalists, including stringers, "for the purpose of conducting any intelligence activities." The CIA also would not enter into relationships with non-journalist staff of any U.S. media organization, or use media cover for CIA officers. Journalists were still allowed to provide non-intelligence-related services, and voluntary, unpaid contacts between the CIA and members of the press were allowed. The DCI could make exceptions if needed in extraordinary circumstances.[63]

In December 1977 and carrying into early 1978, the newly formed Subcommittee on Oversight of the Permanent Select Committee on Intelligence of the House of Representatives held hearings on the relationships between the CIA and the media. The hearings included witnesses such as Ray Cline, Stuart Loory, Tad Szulc, and William Colby. The hearings focused on general issues and questioned what kind of guidance would be useful in the future. While some details of the relationships were revealed, the naming of names was generally avoided. In his opening statement, Chairman Edward Boland (Democrat of Massachusetts) remarked: "We are not interested in drawing attention to past excesses of intelligence activities. We are aware that access to and knowledge of past excesses are essential to shaping a better future in this field. The important thing to remember as we plunge into what follows is that we want to emerge, if possible, with workable suggestions for a stronger press and a healthy, efficient CIA."[64]

There was some discussion of past activities. David Phillips, the veteran CIA officer who had taken the lead in defending the agency in the press, discussed how he had come into the CIA through his work as a journalist in Chile in the 1950s. The CIA station chief asked for help on a part-time basis. Phillips recalled: "The cold war was hot. Joseph Stalin was still alive. It never occurred to me to say no." Phillips noted he was not employed by a U.S. publication; he himself owned a small, English-language newspaper. He handled agents, recruited, assessed, and spotted, for the salary of fifty dollars a month. Eventually, Phillips entered the CIA as a full-time officer.[65]

Reporters and members of Congress noted that a good deal of contacts between the CIA and the press were part of normal journalistic practice. Joseph Fromm, the deputy editor of *U.S. News and World Report,* commented: "For a responsible journalist, the relationship with intelligence officials doesn't differ fundamentally from his relationship with politicians, diplomats, civil servants or businessmen. All are legitimate news sources. All must be treated with a measure of skepticism when they provide information on a nonattributable basis."[66] Herman Nickel of *Fortune* agreed; reporters realized that sources spoke to them "because they like to put across their side of the story and, thereby, advance their own purpose."[67]

Szulc was similarly inclined; he explained he had swapped information with CIA officers while working on a story, the kinds of contacts that took place over drinks or lunch.[68] Szulc did not, however, mention his own involvement in the plots against Fidel Castro; especially in the post-1975 environment, he had good reason not to include those details. Les Aspin (Democrat of Wisconsin) remarked that the CIA was not unlike the Defense Department or the Department of State, in that it would leak to forward its policy objectives. He noted that Washington "is a town full of people trying to peddle one line or another, and it is not unlike that."[69]

Some issues were disputed; supporters of the CIA wanted the availability of press cover for their officers, especially as the media were so useful a cover. The tenets of the Turner Directive were generally agreed to be sound. The most concerning item was the use of the non-American press, and whether that would be used to try to influence the American people indirectly. No clear resolution to that question was found beyond a pledge that it would not be done. Stuart Loory argued that more investigation into the past was needed; specific names were needed. He argued: "I do not think your committee can perform that oversight function really well without having some kind of base line against which to judge everything. Not only your committee, but the committees that have come before you, have been reluctant to get into the past."[70] His suggestion was not taken.

The Turner Directive was a real change in the CIA's policies with regard to the media. Under it, such activities as Allen Dulles's directing stories in

1954 or efforts to hire *New York Times* reporters in Germany would not have been allowed, at least not without some accountability. The new rules did not change the important unofficial relationships that had played a role in shaping the agency's public persona. Though the rules did not codify such a change, however, the changes in the media landscape since 1947 had already significantly altered how the press and the CIA related to one another.

While not to the extent that critics hoped, the Year of Intelligence fundamentally transformed the Central Intelligence Agency. The CIA's reputation for effectiveness, trustworthiness, and respectability was, for many Americans, severely undermined. Some of the CIA operations revealed were chilling, such as assassination attempts on foreign leaders and the testing of drugs on unsuspecting people. At the same time, many of the agency's activities appeared farcical. To many, the agency appeared to be a relic of the Cold War and was no longer safe or necessary. It was not good for the agency either to be viewed as a threat to American democracy or a foolish, ineffective organization. Practically speaking, the extensive publicity had hindered the CIA's ability to operate abroad and to recruit in the United States. The CIA and its advocates had succeeded in maintaining the agency to some extent, however, by successfully countering the strongest critics of intelligence reform. Wicker, Hersh, Braden, and others were disappointed at the ultimately weak oversight instituted by Congress.

The Year of Intelligence had also solidified the issue of intelligence as a partisan issue in the U.S. press. Political connections between reporters and the agency had proved important in promoting the agency's agenda. Personal connections remained but were diminished in importance. CIA connections with the press continued past 1976, but the social environment, shared politics, and deep personal connections often no longer existed.

Conclusion

On 17 September 1997 the Central Intelligence Agency celebrated the fiftieth anniversary of its founding. At an event held that day for former members of the agency, George H. W. Bush saluted CIA officers for their professionalism and dedication. Bush explained that he had expected chaos when he assumed the post of director of Central Intelligence in 1976. The agency had been "demeaned by the universally negative press coverage stemming from mistakes made by a handful of people."[1] Despite such attacks, Bush told his audience that he found at the CIA a professional, dedicated workforce.

Bush praised the CIA for overcoming the disrespect of Congress and the hostility of the press. Bush gave special tribute to the Directorate of Operations, formerly Plans, for having "largely recovered from the ghastly period of disclosure that cost us much of our liaison, cost us many of our sources around the world, cost us the life of Richard Welch."[2] Bush's remarks indicated that, more than two decades after the Year of Intelligence, wounds remained; they also reflected some popular conceptions held by the agency and its supporters after that investigative year, those of the press as a monolithic enemy of the agency and of Congress as an irresponsible overseer. Bush also refused to acknowledge the argument that Welch's assassination was not the fault of investigations into the CIA's activities.

Bush and the CIA criticized the press and Congress for irresponsibility, but others reflected on the Year of Intelligence with disappointment that it had not truly reshaped the U.S. national security establishment. Tom Wicker, for one, remained deeply critical both of the agency and of the press's coverage of national security issues. He felt that Frank Church had erred by focusing too much on assassinations when the real fundamental questions of the agency, including whether it was even cost-effective in light of its actual product, were overlooked. The drawn-out process and delay by Congress had eventually given the agency and its supporters their chance to counterattack when Welch was murdered in Greece. The CIA and the Ford administration used Welch as a martyr to inveigh against the investigations. Wicker believed that "the American press has been more often hesitant than aggressive in pursuit of its constitutional obligation to act as a check on the power of government. All too often, the press has been a collaborator in the national-security mystique, rather than a challenger of it."[3]

To Bush, the press was a hostile enemy. To Wicker, the press was too often a tool of official power. Both Bush and Wicker erred in simplifying the press as a monolith. In actuality, the press had consistently displayed a variety of perspectives on the agency and intelligence in general, beginning in the postwar debate on intelligence and continuing to 1976. Robert McCormick and many conservatives often criticized the agency in its early days. Joseph Alsop approached the CIA about working with it for American interests early in the agency's existence, whereas the senior management of the *New York Times* sought to prevent any CIA manipulation of its publication. Many publications, especially newspapers, never demonstrated internal consistency in their treatment of the CIA. The *Washington Post* was often friendly to the agency, but revelations and condemnations of agency activity could be found in its pages. Over time, some publications friendly with the CIA grew less so, such as the *Saturday Evening Post,* and the reverse happened with the *Chicago Tribune.*

In different eras, some themes in reporting were more preponderant than others. Criticism, though extant, was less dominant in the 1940s and 1950s than it was in the 1960s and 1970s. As critics grew and more exposés of agency activities were published, however, there were still defenders of the CIA, still reporters who refused to publish stories that might have revealed CIA activities. Even in 1975–1976, when criticism peaked during the Year of Intelligence, *Time* magazine, a publication with several ties to the CIA, supported the investigations as a way to fix problems at the agency and restore faith in it. Wicker's colleague Abe Rosenthal believed that the "the Hersh article saved the CIA from itself."[4] Crises such as the downing of Francis Powers's U-2, the Bay of Pigs invasion, and the NSA scandal of 1967 all produced a variety of reactions in the press.

Though Wicker's and Bush's positions considerably simplified a complex situation, they were telling of the change in the relationships between the press and the agency after 1976. There was still sympathy in some quarters of the press for the CIA, but the kind of easy understanding and personal relationships that had undergirded most of the CIA's positive relationships with the press were relics of the past. Many in the CIA and the press no longer shared the common backgrounds, experiences, and understandings of the world that had facilitated earlier relationships. The CIA increasingly filled its ranks with more diverse personnel, rather than with members of the old Establishment. Reporters more and more entered the press without the "Cold War–era complacency and nationalism" that Wicker believed poisoned efforts to report on national security issues.[5] Whereas once a reporter might not think twice about briefing the CIA or concealing a story about the agency, after 1976 even if some reporters were inclined to do such things, they knew there would be serious concern and possibly criticism from their colleagues.

While firmer controls on CIA-press relationships were in place, though, those controls were dependent on the national mood, as all CIA activities were. When interviewed by George Lardner in 1975, William Colby noted that the environment was different in the 1950s from the 1970s. Where once the American people approved of an aggressive CIA, increasingly they did not. Thus, the agency rolled back. Lardner noted that this left open the opportunity for future CIA active phases. He asked Colby if "following that . . . down the line, are you saying, too, that if in 1984, 1985, opinion is back to 'good idea, go knock off Castro' or 'good idea, go knock off Leader X,' that the agency will go back to that[?]" Angus Theurmer, in the room for the interview, immediately interjected, "Don't answer for 1984."[6]

The point was made humorously and those present laughed, but the point was an important one. The CIA had been prohibited from using the U.S. press to spread propaganda in the United States, or to use the U.S. press operationally. Members of the press began to seek guarantees that their organizations would not be used. The formal arrangements such possibilities would require, however, were always a limited part of the CIA and the press's interaction. Norms had shifted after 1975–1976, but they could shift back.

Dramatic events, such as the 11 September 2001 terrorist attacks, were surely the kind of occurrence that could influence a change in norms. The 2014 case of Ken Dilanian, a staff writer for the newspaper chain that today owns the *Los Angeles Times* and the *Chicago Tribune*, demonstrates the continued possibility of mutual interest between the CIA and the press. Edward Snowden's massive leak of confidential documents revealed that Dilanian sent drafts of some of his stories to the CIA for its approval and sought to project a good image of the agency. Dilanian and the agency had a "collaborative" relationship. Dilanian's former supervisor indicated such contact was considered a breach of protocol, and many reporters condemned Dilanian's actions. Dilanian had already moved to the Associated Press before the revelation, however, and his new employer indicated that it had no qualms about Dilanian's continued employment.[7] Cases such as Dilanian's appear to be rare, though it is difficult to draw firm conclusions with current information.

More recently, the continued controversy over foreign interference in the 2016 presidential election has led to an extraordinary alteration of the media landscape. As of the time of this writing, events are too fluid and contested to draw firm conclusions, but what is undeniable is that Donald Trump's election to the presidency changed the incentives of different partisan groups in their reactions to the CIA and the intelligence community more broadly. The fears of "fake news" having a profound influence on how people think and vote reflect, perhaps, greater media savvy than existed in the early years of the CIA; the use of the term by some to simply dismiss any inconvenient story, however, suggests that the disintegration of any kind of national consensus on priorities or threats to the United States, and the increased awareness of the potential of media manipulation, has not resulted in a clearer picture of how the major figures and institutions of U.S. political life affect events. Instead, the picture has become only more confusing. Where once there could be a mainstream opinion on the threat of the Soviet Union, however potentially damaging or stultifying such a consensus could have been, the divided reaction to potential Russian interference demonstrates just how thoroughly U.S. elite opinion has fractured since the 1970s.

What is clear, however, is that the CIA's approach to its public image has grown considerably more sophisticated in recent years. The CIA now seeks to ensure it is well represented in fiction and popular culture. As Richard Immerman has observed in his recent history of the agency, the CIA's presence on film and television screens increased dramatically during the War on Terror. Those television shows and films often consult with the CIA. The CIA appointed its first official liaison to Hollywood in 1996. Many former employees are allowed to serve as consultants and extras. The CIA even hired the actor Jennifer Garner, known for playing a spy on the ABC program *Alias,* to star in a recruitment video.[8]

The CIA tried to use the domestic press to influence American public opinion. The agency wanted certain stories suppressed and a positive view of the agency to prevail. In this, their efforts were much like those of other, non-secret government agencies. Its methods were relational and often ad hoc. Though the CIA paid some reporters for intelligence-related tasks, the relationships that promoted the image of the agency depended on personal ties and common understanding. There were often murky lines between cooperation and patriotic discretion, between the standard journalistic practice of gathering information and special collaboration to further the interest of a particular agency.

This diverse and varied set of relationships was an important part of the CIA's early history. An interconnected web of OSS veterans, reporters, editors, and institutions such as the Council on Foreign Relations articulated and defined the idea of a civilian central intelligence agency with an active mission. Cooperation or discretion helped rebut or prevent criticism that would have challenged that intelligence idea. Fears of the Soviet Union and the necessities of the Cold War meant many in the press were unwilling to challenge the demands of national security.

The press-CIA relationships in the agency's early years restricted, but did not totally succeed in limiting, the access of the American public to information on the agency's activities. The public's opinions on U.S. activities in the world and the U.S. intelligence establishment were based on heavily mediated information. This mediated press landscape is an important context to consider when examining the development of the CIA. There were alternative models of intelligence systems, such as the CIG's clearinghouse idea. The unified, active system won out, and it was aided in doing so by the press atmosphere.

Despite this early success, the CIA failed to adapt to a changing press environment. Positive relationships did not abruptly end, but countertrends increased. Smaller, political publications like the *Nation* continued to report on agency activities, and they were joined by younger reporters at major publications such as Wicker and Hersh who were less personally committed to the kind of discretion embodied by reporters such as Hanson Baldwin. The positive relationships that had depended on discretion and access to information, rather than actual collaboration, did not prevent reporting on the CIA when the agency's activities came under closer investigation. Above all else, many in the press changed their attitude to government more broadly as a result of the great crises of their era, the Vietnam War and the Watergate Scandal, which deeply shook faith in the trustworthiness of government.

As more reporters challenged the CIA's role in the United States and revealed its activities, the CIA found it more difficult to challenge the kind of congressional oversight it had long tried to stave off. Hersh's revelation that the CIA was conducting illegal domestic surveillance was simply the last of a long series of controversies that attracted attention and finally led to the Year of Intelligence. While the outcomes of the Church and Pike Committees remain ambiguous, and controversy over the U.S. intelligence establishment is a regular feature in political discourse to this day, that year fundamentally changed the relationships between the CIA and the press.

Ultimately, that change was almost certainly for the better. An active, challenging press rather than a quiescent press is a likelier guard against the kind of abuses uncovered by the Church and Pike Committees. George Bush may have blamed a few mistaken individuals for the agency's troubles, but the CIA was undoubtedly involved in a variety of highly questionable activities. The agency was under closer executive control than its critics would have admitted, but with the failure of real congressional oversight for much of the CIA's early years, it fell to the press, in the end, to keep the agency and the executive branch more broadly in check. As the CIA and the larger U.S. intelligence establishment became an extensive and active part of the U.S. government, press attention to intelligence, to its process, activities, and operation within the constitutional system, was vital. As long as the CIA and the intelligence establishment retain their large and active role, such press attention will continue to be vital.

Acknowledgments

This project began with a relatively simple question in a discussion at the Ohio State University: What did the American people know about the Central Intelligence Agency's intervention in Guatemala in 1954? I did not expect that the question would evolve into a project that would consume my next seven years. I also could not have anticipated, but am glad now to acknowledge, the number of people and institutions that would provide invaluable assistance throughout this project.

Peter Hahn, Robert McMahon, and Jennifer Siegel of Ohio State read multiple drafts of this work and provided generous feedback and advice for improvement. They challenged me to sharpen my thinking, observed where I allowed untested assumptions to affect my conclusions, and generally provided patient and wise guidance. David Culbert of Louisiana State University, Hugh Wilford of California State University Long Beach, and Katherine Sibley of St. Joseph's University all gave their time in reading and commenting on different chapters of this work. I also owe a debt of gratitude to the faculty of the Gettysburg College History Department, especially Timothy Shannon and Michael Birkner, for their professional assistance in the revision process.

In addition to those readers, I was fortunate over the course of my research and writing to work with a variety of scholars who assisted me in finding critical sources, advised me on historical approaches, raised questions I had not considered, and provided logistical support in my research efforts. At the risk of leaving out those who ought not be left out, I wish to specifically thank Ryan McMahon, Frank Blazich, Matthew Ambrose, Scott Ward, Kirsten Hildonen, Aaron George, Kate White, Joseph Arena, Mark Sokolsky, and Frank McGough. Aaron Coy Moulton, of Stephen F. Austin State University, deserves special mention as he provided substantial assistance in clarifying some subtle but pertinent factors in the events in Guatemala in 1954.

I was fortunate to receive generous support from the Lynde and Harry Bradley Foundation and the Ohio State University Department of History's grant programs. I would also like to acknowledge and thank the staffs of the New York Public Library's Manuscript Division, Princeton's Seeley Mudd Manuscript Library, the Marshall Foundation, the Robert R. McCormick Research Center, the Library of Congress, the Special Collections Library at Georgetown University, and the Arthur and Elizabeth Schlesinger Library on the History of Women in America. Everywhere I was struck by the patience, friendliness, and assistance that the staff of those institutions demonstrated. George Lardner Jr., retired, of the *Washington Post,* was kind enough to allow me to conduct research in his papers, and to speak with me about his experiences in the *Post*'s newsroom in the 1970s. I would like also to thank my publisher, the University Press of Kentucky, and my editor, Ann Twombly.

Without this personal and institutional assistance, this work would not exist today. Any errors of fact or interpretation are entirely my own.

Finally, I would like to thank my long-suffering family and friends, who have had to listen to me drone on incessantly about this topic while I have been working on it. Special thanks are due to my mother, Marion, my sister, Jane, and my brother, Scott. This book is dedicated to the memory of my father and my maternal grandparents, all of whom, along with my mother, always encouraged and supported my love of history.

Significant CIA and Press Figures

Central Intelligence Agency/Group

Angleton, James J.—CIA officer, 1947–1974; chief of the Counterintelligence Staff, 1954–1974

Bissell, Richard M., Jr.—CIA officer, 1948–1962; deputy director for Plans, 1958–1962

Braden, Thomas W.—CIA officer, 1950–1954; chief of the International Organizations Division, 1950–1954

Bross, John A.—CIA officer, 1951–1971; deputy to the director of Central Intelligence for Programs Evaluation, 1963–1971

Bush, George H. W.—Director of Central Intelligence, 1976–1977

Cline, Ray S.—CIA officer, 1949–1969; deputy director for intelligence, 1962–1966

Colby, William E.—CIA officer, 1950–1975; director of Central Intelligence, 1973–1975

Copeland, Miles A., Jr.—CIA officer, 1947–1953

Duckett, Carl E.—CIA officer, 1963–1977; deputy director for Science and Technology, 1966–1977

Dulles, Allen W.—CIA officer, 1950–1961; director of Central Intelligence, 1953–1961

Grogan, Stanley J.—CIA officer, 1951–1966; assistant to the director of Central Intelligence, 1951–1966

Helms, Richard M.—CIA officer, 1947–1973; director of Central Intelligence, 1966–1973

Hillenkoetter, Roscoe—Director of Central Intelligence, 1947–1950

Marchetti, Victor E.—CIA officer, 1955–1969

McCone, John—Director of Central Intelligence, 1962–1965

Meyer, Cord, Jr.—CIA officer, 1951–1977; chief of the International Organizations Division, 1954–1967

Phillips, David A.—CIA officer, 1954–1975

Raborn, William F., Jr.—Director of Central Intelligence, 1965–1966

Schlesinger, James R.—Director of Central Intelligence, 1973

Smith, Walter B.—Director of Central Intelligence, 1950–1953
Souers, Sidney W.—Director of Central Intelligence, 1946
Thuermer, Angus M.—CIA officer, 1952–1978
Vandenberg, Hoyt—Director of Central Intelligence, 1946–1947
Welch, Richard S.—CIA officer, 1951–1975
Wisner, Frank G.—CIA officer, 1947–1962; deputy director for Plans, 1953–1958

Press

Adler, Julius O.—*New York Times,* 1914–1955 (save for service in World Wars I and II); general manager, 1935–1955
Alsop, Joseph—Columnist, 1946–1975
Alsop, Stewart—Columnist, 1946–1958; *Saturday Evening Post,* contributing editor, 1962–1968
Anderson, Jack N.—Columnist, 1947–2004
Armstrong, Hamilton F.—*Foreign Affairs,* managing editor, 1928–1972
Baldwin, Hanson W.—*New York Times,* correspondent, 1929–1968
Buckley, William F., Jr.—*National Review,* editor in chief, 1955–1990
Burnham, James—*National Review,* editor, 1955–1977
Catledge, William Turner—*New York Times,* aide to the managing editor, 1944–1951; managing editor, 1951–1964; executive editor, 1964–1968
Cook, Fred J.—*Nation,* occasional contributor
Daniel, Elbert Clifton, Jr.—*New York Times,* managing editor, 1964–1969
Dryfoos, Orvil E.—*New York Times,* vice president and director, 1954–1957; president, 1958–1963; publisher, 1961–1963
DuBois, Jules—*Chicago Tribune,* correspondent, 1947–1966
Evans, Rowland, Jr.—Columnist, 1963–2001
Geyelin, Philip L.—*Washington Post,* editor, editorial page, 1967–1979
Graham, Katharine M.—*Washington Post,* publisher, 1963–1979
Graham, Philip L.—*Washington Post,* publisher, 1946–1963
Gruson, Sydney—*New York Times,* correspondent, 1944–1965; foreign editor, 1965–1966; editor, international edition, 1966–1967; executive assistant, director, and vice chairman, 1969–1986
Harkness, Richard—NBC, correspondent, commentator, host, 1942–1972
Hersh, Seymour M.—*New York Times,* reporter, 1972–1979
Hibbs, Benjamin—*Saturday Evening Post,* editor, 1942–1962
Kirchwey, Freda—*Nation,* editor, 1933–1955
Krock, Arthur B.—*New York Times,* correspondent and columnist, 1927–1966
Lardner, George Jr.—*Washington Post,* reporter, 1963–1999
Lawrence, David—*U.S. News and World Report,* publisher and columnist, 1948–1973
Loory, Stuart H.—*Los Angeles Times,* correspondent, 1967–1971; professor of Public Affairs Reporting at the Ohio State University, 1973–1975

Luce, Henry—Time-Life, editor in chief/editorial director, 1930–1964

Marder, Murrey—*Washington Post,* reporter and correspondent, 1946–1985

McCormick, Robert R.—*Chicago Tribune,* president, 1911–1955; editor and publisher 1925–1955

Novak, Robert D. S.—Columnist, 1963–2008

Pearson, Andrew P. "Drew"—Columnist, 1931–1969

Phillips, Wayne—*New York Times,* reporter, 1951–1961

Reston, James B.—*New York Times,* correspondent, 1939–1942; 1945–1953; columnist and Washington Bureau chief, 1953–1964; associate editor, 1964–1968; executive editor, 1968–1969; vice president, 1969–1974

Roberts, Chalmers M.—*Washington Post,* correspondent, 1949–1971

Rosenthal, Abraham M.—*New York Times,* correspondent 1943–1963; editor/assistant managing editor, 1963–1969; managing editor, 1969–1977

Ross, Thomas B.—*Chicago Sun-Times,* correspondent and bureau chief, 1958–1977

Salisbury, Harrison E.—*New York Times,* correspondent, 1949–1962; national editor/assistant managing editor/associate managing editor, 1962–1973

Sidey, Hugh S.—*Time,* correspondent, 1957–1996

Sommers, Martin—*Saturday Evening Post,* associate editor/foreign editor, 1936–1962

Stern, Laurence M.—*Washington Post,* reporter/editor, 1952–1979

Sulzberger, Arthur H.—*New York Times,* publisher, 1935–1961

Sulzberger, Arthur O. "Punch"—*New York Times,* publisher, 1963–1992

Sulzberger, Cyrus L.—*New York Times,* correspondent and columnist, 1939–1978

Szulc, Tadeusz W. "Tad"—*New York Times,* correspondent, 1953–1972

Trohan, Walter—*Chicago Tribune,* reporter, 1939–1971; Washington Bureau chief, 1949–1968

Welles, Benjamin—*New York Times,* correspondent, 1946–1972

Whitten, Leslie "Les" H.—Columnist, 1969–1978

Wicker, Thomas "Tom" G.—*New York Times,* correspondent, 1960–1964; Washington Bureau chief, 1964–1968; columnist, 1966–1991; associate editor, 1968–1991

Wise, David—*New York Herald Tribune,* correspondent, 1951–1963; Washington Bureau chief, 1963–1966

Notes

Introduction

1. William Colby, interview by George Lardner, 20 June 1975, 14, George Lardner Papers (hereafter cited as Lardner Papers), box 18, folder 3: CIA—Chile, undated, Manuscript Division, Library of Congress, Washington, DC.

2. By some estimates, less than 15 percent of the population sought to be "actively informed," meaning they read newspapers and watched televised news. See Ralph Levering, *The Public and American Foreign Policy, 1918–1978* (New York: William Morrow, 1978), 23, 29–32.

3. L. Britt Snider, *The Agency and the Hill: CIA's Relationship with Congress, 1946–2004* (Washington: Center for the Study of Intelligence [Central Intelligence Agency], 2008), xv, 6–7.

4. David Barrett, *The CIA and Congress: The Untold Story from Truman to Kennedy* (Lawrence: University Press of Kansas, 2005), 167.

5. Stuart H. Loory, "The CIA's Use of the Press: A 'Mighty Wurlitzer,'" *Columbia Journalism Review* 13.3 (1974): 9.

6. Victor Marchetti and John D. Marks, *The CIA and the Cult of Intelligence* (New York: Alfred A. Knopf, 1974), 7.

7. U.S. Senate, *Final Report of the Select Committee to Study Governmental Operations with Respect to Intelligence Activities, Book 1: Foreign and Military Intelligence* (Washington, DC: U.S. Government Printing Office, 1976), 196, www.intelligence.senate.gov/sites/default/files/94755_I.pdf, accessed 13 September 2018.

8. Carl Bernstein, "The CIA and the Media," *Rolling Stone,* 20 October 1977, www.carlbernstein.com/magazine_cia_and_media.php, accessed 7 May 2011.

9. Deborah Davis, *Katharine the Great: Katharine Graham and the Washington Post* (New York: Harcourt Brace Jovanovich, 1979).

10. Memorandum to the Executive Secretary, CIA Management Committee, 16 May 1973, available from the National Security Archive at www2.gwu.edu/~nsarchiv/NSAEBB/NSAEBB222/, accessed 18 January 2014.

11. The CIA historiography is extensive; the following list contains some major titles that follow the CIA from its foundations, but it should not be taken as comprehensive. See John Prados, *President's Secret Wars: CIA and Pentagon Covert Operations*

from World War II through Iranscam (New York: William Morrow, 1986); John Ranleigh, *The Agency: The Rise and Decline of the CIA* (New York: Simon and Schuster, 1986); Loch K. Johnson, *America's Secret Power: The CIA in a Democratic Society* (Oxford: Oxford University Press, 1989); George J. A. O'Toole, *Honorable Treachery: A History of U.S. Intelligence, Espionage, and Covert Action from the American Revolution to the CIA* (New York: Atlantic Monthly Press, 1991); Christopher Andrew, *For the President's Eyes Only: Secret Intelligence and the American Presidency from Washington to Bush* (New York: HarperCollins, 1996); Rhodri Jeffreys-Jones, *The CIA and American Democracy*, 2nd ed. (New Haven: Yale University Press, 1998); Timothy Weiner, *Legacy of Ashes: The History of the CIA* (New York: Doubleday, 2007). Weiner does examine some cases of press-CIA interactions, but not in a systematic way. For the most recent survey of the CIA, see Richard Immerman, *The Hidden Hand: A Brief History of the CIA* (Malden, MA: Wiley Blackwell, 2014).

12. For the CIA's social world and connection with private institutions, see Robin Winks, *Cloak & Gown: Scholars in the Secret War, 1939–1961* (New York: William Morrow, 1987); Sigmund Diamond, *Compromised Campus: The Collaboration of Universities with the Intelligence Community, 1945–1955* (Oxford: Oxford University Press, 1992); Hersh Burton, *The Old Boys: The American Elite and the Origins of the CIA* (New York: Charles Scribner, 1992); Eric Thomas Chester, *Covert Network: Progressives, the International Rescue Committee, and the CIA* (London: M. E. Sharpe, 1995); Frances Stonor Saunders, *The Cultural Cold War: The CIA and the World of Arts and Letters* (New York: New Press, 1999) (published in the United Kingdom as *Who Paid the Piper? The CIA and the Cultural Cold War*); Hugh Wilford, *The CIA, the British Left, and the Cold War: Calling the Tune?* (London: Frank Cass, 2003); Hugh Wilford, *The Mighty Wurlitzer: How the CIA Played America* (Cambridge: Harvard University Press, 2008); Elke van Cassel, "In Search of a Clear and Overarching American Policy: The *Reporter* Magazine (1949–68), the US Government and the Cold War," in *The US Government, Citizen Groups, and the Cold War: The State-Private Network*, ed. Helen Laville and Hugh Wilford (London: Routledge, 2006); Larry Valero, "'We Need Our New OSS, Our New General Donovan, Now . . .': The Public Discourse over American Intelligence, 1944–53," *Intelligence and National Security* 18.1 (2003): 91–118; Gregg Herkin, *The Georgetown Set: Friends and Rivals in Cold War Washington* (New York: Alfred A. Knopf, 2014).

13. See John F. Neville, *The Press, the Rosenbergs, and the Cold War* (Westport, CT: Praeger, 1995); Walter L. Hixson, *Parting the Curtain: Propaganda, Culture, and the Cold War, 1945–1961* (New York: St. Martin's, 1996); Nancy E. Bernhard, *U.S. Television News and Cold War Propaganda, 1947–1960* (Cambridge: Cambridge University Press, 1999); Karen Paget, *Patriotic Betrayal: The Inside Story of the CIA's Secret Campaign to Enroll American Students in the Crusade against Communism* (New Haven: Yale University Press, 2015).

14. For a sample of important examinations of the connection between public opinion and foreign policy, see Lester Markel, *Public Opinion and Foreign Policy* (New York: Harper and Brothers, 1949); Bernard C. Cohen, *The Public's Impact on*

Foreign Policy (Boston: Little, Brown, 1973); Levering, *The Public and American Foreign Policy;* Daniel C. Hallin, *The "Uncensored War": The Media and Vietnam* (Berkeley: University of California Press, 1986); Charles W. Kegley and Eugene R. Wittkopf, eds. *The Domestic Sources of American Foreign Policy: Insights and Evidence* (New York: St. Martin's Press, 1988); Nicholas O. Berry, *Foreign Policy and the Press: An Analysis of the* New York Times' *Coverage of U.S. Foreign Policy* (New York: Greenwood Press, 1990).

15. Douglas Foyle, "Public Opinion," in *Routledge Handbook of American Foreign Policy,* ed. Steven W. Hook and Christopher M. Jones (New York: Routledge, 2012), 264–85. See also Douglas C. Foyle, *Counting the Public In: Presidents, Public Opinion, and Foreign Policy* (New York: Columbia University Press, 1999); Richard Sobel, *The Impact of Public Opinion on U.S. Foreign Policy since Vietnam: Constraining the Colossus* (Oxford: Oxford University Press, 2001); Robert M. Entman, *Projections of Power: Framing News, Public Opinion, and U.S. Foreign Policy* (Chicago: University of Chicago Press, 2004); Lance Bennett, *News: The Politics of Illusion,* 8th ed. (New York: Pearson Longman, 2009).

16. Douglass Cater, "The Fourth Branch, Then and Now," in *The Media and Congress,* ed. Stephen Bates (Columbus, OH: Publishing Horizons, 1987), 1–13. See also Robert O. Blanchard, ed., *Congress and the News Media* (New York: Hastings House, 1974).

17. John Foran, "Discursive Subversions: *Time* Magazine, the CIA Overthrow of Mussadiq, and the Installation of the Shah," in *Cold War Constructions: The Political Culture of United States Imperialism, 1945–1966,* ed. Christian G. Appy (Amherst: University of Massachusetts Press, 2000), 160–61.

18. Douglas A. Van Belle, Jean-Sébastien Rioux, and David M. Potter, *Media, Bureaucracies and Foreign Aid: A Comparative Analysis of the United States, the United Kingdom, Canada, France and Japan* (New York: Palgrave Macmillan, 2004).

19. Richard J. Aldrich, "American Journalism and the Landscape of Secrecy: Tad Szulc, the CIA and Cuba," *History* 100.340 (2015): 190.

20. For a good breakdown and analysis of this Establishment, see Robert Dean, *Imperial Brotherhood: Gender and the Making of Cold War Foreign Policy* (Amherst: University of Massachusetts Press, 2001).

21. Matthew Jones, "Journalism, Intelligence and the *New York Times:* Cyrus L. Sulzberger, Harrison E. Salisbury and the CIA," *History* 100.340 (2015): 234.

22. Nancy Bernhard's examination of early television news and Cold War propaganda includes a useful but not extensive consideration of the CIA's connections with William Paley and CBS News. See Bernhard, *U.S. Television News and Cold War Propaganda,* 184–86.

1. The Postwar Intelligence Debate and the CIA

1. The *Washington Post,* as well as other major papers of the day, did not provide the name of an editorial's author.

2. "Choice and Chance," *Washington Post,* 9 January 1953, 20.

3. Ibid.

4. Ibid.

5. The 180,000 figure is somewhat soft, coming from Katharine Graham in her autobiography. See Katharine Graham, *Personal History* (New York: Alfred A. Knopf, 1997), 179. Newspaper circulation figures can be difficult to obtain, but readership practically doubled after Phil Graham purchased the *Washington Times-Herald* in 1954.

6. Deputies' Meeting, 14 January 1953, available from the CIA Records Search Tool Twenty-five-Year Program Archive (hereafter cited as CREST), www.foia.cia.gov /sites/default/files/document_conversions/5829/CIA-RDP80B01676R002300120059 -2.pdf, accessed 30 April 2015. It is unclear where the Soviets commented on the editorial, as that portion of the document remains classified.

7. Immerman, *The Hidden Hand,* 42.

8. Michael S. Sweeney, *Secrets of Victory: The Office of the American Press and Radio in World War II* (Chapel Hill: University of North Carolina Press, 2001), 217–18.

9. Ibid., 3–4.

10. Ibid., 164.

11. Arthur Hays Sulzberger to Turner Catledge, 19 December 1951, the New York Times Company Records (hereafter cited as NYTCR): Arthur Hays Sulzberger Papers (hereafter cited as Sulzberger Papers), series II, box 125, folder 3, New York Public Library.

12. Graham, *Personal History,* 24, 55.

13. Arthur Krock to Joe Richardson, 28 July 1944, Arthur Krock Papers (hereafter cited as Krock Papers), series IIA, box 53, folder: *Saturday Evening Post;* Seeley Mudd Manuscript Library, Princeton, NJ.

14. McCaw to Huston (first names unavailable), 13 November 1941; Edwin L. James to Sulzberger, 14 November 1941, Arthur Krock to Bush (first name unavailable), n.d., all in Sulzberger Papers, series II, box 125, folder 125.5.

15. Richard Norton Smith, *The Colonel: The Life and Legend of Robert R. McCormick, 1880–1955* (Boston: Houghton Mifflin, 1997), 156.

16. Walter Dear to Robert McCormick, 22 August 1941, Robert R. McCormick Papers (hereafter cited as McCormick Papers), series I-60, box 4, folder: ANPA-General, 1927–1953; Colonel Robert R. McCormick Research Center, First Division Museum, Cantigny, IL.

17. Robert McCormick to Joseph Ator, 6 March 1942, McCormick Papers, series I-61, box 8.

18. Sweeney, *Secrets of Victory,* 79.

19. David R. Davies, *The Postwar Decline of American Newspapers, 1945–1965* (Westport, CT: Praeger, 2006), 16, 19, 22.

20. U.S. House of Representatives, Subcommittee on Oversight of the Permanent Select Committee on Intelligence, *The CIA and the Media,* 59th Cong., 1st and 2d sess., 27–29 December 1977, 4–5 January and 20 April 1978, 238, 271.

21. James L. Baughman, *Henry R. Luce and the Rise of the American News Media* (Baltimore: Johns Hopkins University Press, 1987), 2.

22. Robert McCormick to Thomas Morrow, 1 February 1945, McCormick Papers, series I-62, box 2, folder 6: Correspondents, General (2); Henry Wallace to Senior Staff of the New Republic, 18 March 1947, Freda Kirchwey Papers (hereafter cited as Kirchwey Papers), series IIA, box 6, folder 103, Arthur and Elizabeth Schlesinger Library on the History of Women in America, Cambridge, MA.

23. House Subcommittee on Oversight, *The CIA and the Media*, 99.

24. Davies, *The Postwar Decline of American Newspapers*, x.

25. John Dickson, managing editor, *National Cyclopedia of American Biography*, 12 March 1947, Kirchwey Papers, series I, carton 1: folder #1–46, folder 1; Freda Kirchwey to Michael Straight, 7 July 1948, Kirchwey Papers, series IIA, box 6, folder 103.

26. Evans Clark and W. D. Patterson to Freda Kirchwey and Michael Straight, memorandum, 7 July 1948, Kirchwey Papers, series IIA, box 6, folder 103.

27. O'Toole, *Honorable Treachery*, 424.

28. Ibid., 425; Andrew, *For the President's Eyes Only*, 147, 156.

29. Andrew, *For the President's Eyes Only*, 147.

30. Weiner, *Legacy of Ashes*, 6–8; Andrew, *For the President's Eyes Only*, 156–57.

31. Valero, "'We Need Our New OSS'"; O'Toole, a former CIA officer who tends to defend the CIA and the OSS, argues that Donovan was reacting to a "campaign of calculated lies" already active in the press. Donovan was thus responding with "counterpropaganda." See O'Toole, *Honorable Treachery*, 426. Donovan himself wrote an article in *Life* arguing for a U.S. intelligence agency. See William Donovan, "Intelligence: Key to Defense," *Life*, 30 September 1946.

32. Quoted in Bradley F. Smith, *The Shadow Warriors: O.S.S. and the Origins of the C.I.A.* (New York: Basic Books, 1983), 391.

33. Valero, "'We Need Our New OSS,'" 98.

34. Forrest Davis, "Secret History of a Surrender," *Saturday Evening Post*, 22 September 1945, 11.

35. Robert W. Merry, *Taking on the World: Joseph and Stewart Alsop—Guardians of the American Century* (New York: Viking, 1996), 120, 151.

36. Stewart Alsop and Thomas Braden, *Sub Rosa: The O.S.S. and American Espionage* (New York: Reynal & Hitchcock, 1946), 231.

37. Arthur Krock, "In the Nation: The OSS Gets It Coming and Going," *New York Times*, 31 July 1945, 18.

38. Arthur Krock, "In the Nation: General Donovan's Case for Unified Intelligence," *New York Times*, 21 September 1945, 20.

39. William Donovan to Arthur Krock, 29 September 1945, Krock Papers, series IIA, box 24, folder: Donovan, William, 1931, 1945.

40. Valero, "'We Need Our New OSS,'" 97.

41. Chesly Manly, "Move to Purify Byrnes Bureau of Its Red Taint," *Chicago Tribune*, 25 April 1946, 5.

42. Edgar Bundy, "Officer Views War in China as Life of Luxury," *Chicago Tribune*, 6 May 1946, 2; for a later example, see "Developing Crisis," *Chicago Tribune*, 21 July 1948, 16.

43. Hanson Baldwin, "Defense Improvements," *New York Times*, 6 February 1946, 16.

44. Danny Jensen and Rhodri Jeffreys-Jones, "The Missouri Gang and the CIA," in *North American Spies: New Revisionist Essays*, ed. Rhodri Jeffreys-Jones and Andrew Lownie (Lawrence: University Press of Kansas, 1991), 123–37. This was written primarily by Jensen; Jeffreys-Jones finished editing the article following Jensen's death from the lingering effects of an earlier injury.

45. Andrew, *For the President's Eyes Only*, 164.

46. Snider, *The Agency and the Hill*, 4.

47. Joseph and Stewart Alsop, "Matter of Fact: 'FBI' Becomes Secret Service," *Washington Post*, 29 April 1946, 7.

48. Arthur Krock, "In the Nation: The President's Secret Daily Newspaper," *New York Times*, 16 July 1946, 22.

49. Andrew, *For the President's Eyes Only*, 165–66.

50. Hanson Baldwin, "Wanted: An American Military Policy," *Harper's Magazine*, May 1946; "Intelligence Work," *Washington Post*, 4 August 1946, B4.

51. The National Security Act of 1947, 26 July 1947, sec. 102 (d)(3) and (d)(5), in CIA, *CIA Cold Wars Records: The CIA under Harry Truman*, ed. Michael Warner (Washington, DC: Center for the Study of Intelligence, 1994), 131–34.

52. Hanson Baldwin, "Set Up for Intelligence," *New York Times*, 6 April 1947, 38, and Baldwin, "Scope of Intelligence," *New York Times*, 10 April 1947, 13; see also Hanson Baldwin, "Inquiry for Intelligence," *New York Times*, 7 April 1947, 8.

53. "Intelligence Agency," *Washington Post*, 26 December 1946, 4; "Intelligence Chief," *Washington Post*, 4 March 1947, 8; "Civilian Intelligence," *Washington Post*, 29 May 1947, 6; "Civilian Job," "*Washington Post*, 23 July 1947, 10. Though this argument was initially unsuccessful, it did return when questions of the next DCI arose in 1949 and 1950. See "First Line of Defense," *Washington Post*, 21 March 1950, 8.

54. "No Merger but High Costs," *Chicago Tribune*, 3 June 1947, 18.

55. Walter Trohan, "The Budding American Gestapo," *Chicago Tribune*, 23 June 1947, 18.

56. Walter Trohan, "U.S. Set to Pay Super Spies 12.7 Million a Year," *Chicago Tribune*, 20 June 1947, 18.

57. Frederick Sherman, "Admiral Rakes Spying Bureau's Plot to Expand," *Chicago Tribune*, 4 July 1947, 2; "Hoffman Fears Dictatorship in Unification Bill," *Chicago Tribune*, 19 July 1947, 3.

58. Robert McCormick to Leon Stolz, 17 December 1947, McCormick Papers, series I-61, box 10, folder 1.

59. Smith, *The Colonel*, xxi.

60. Valero, "'We Need Our New OSS,'" 107.

61. This analysis of the covert operations question draws from Immerman, *The Hidden Hand*, 20.

62. Delmer Dunn, "Symbiosis: Congress and the Press," in Blanchard, *Congress and the News Media*, 242.

63. Paget, *Patriotic Betrayal*, 98.

64. Arthur Hays Sulzberger to Hamilton Fish Armstrong, 20 August 1940; Sulzberger to Armstrong, 14 May 1942; Armstrong to Sulzberger, 17 November 1947, all in Sulzberger Papers, series I, box 3, folder 3.2; Hamilton Fish Armstrong to Hanson Baldwin, 23 November 1938, Hamilton Fish Armstrong Papers (hereafter cited as Armstrong Papers), series I, box 6, folder: Hanson Baldwin; Seeley Mudd Manuscript Library, Princeton, NJ.

65. For details, see the undated memorandum describing an early meeting of the group on 5 September 1946; Langbourne Williams to Arthur Hays Sulzberger, 19 December 1946; Williams and Hanson Baldwin to Sulzberger, 12 March 1947; Walter Mallory to Sulzberger, 30 April 1947, all in Sulzberger Papers, series II, box 149, folder 149.6.

66. In 1967 Thomas G. Patterson wrote to Baldwin to inquire about the group; Patterson wondered if Baldwin's group was "an unofficial predecessor to the Policy Planning Staff." Baldwin did not remember the group exactly as Patterson described, and when he asked Armstrong about the group, Armstrong reminded him that the group had carried out a series of studies that had been the basis of Baldwin's book *The Price of Power*. Thomas G. Patterson to Hanson Baldwin, 24 September 1947; Baldwin to Hamilton Fish Armstrong, 26 September 1967; Armstrong to Baldwin, 28 September, 1947, all in Armstrong Papers, series I, box 6, Folder: Hanson Baldwin.

67. The publisher at Harper and Brothers, Cass Canfield, a friend of Hamilton Fish Armstrong, wrote to Sulzberger to try to get the *New York Times* to help drum up sales of the book. See Cass Canfield to Arthur Hays Sulzberger, 25 February 1948, Sulzberger Papers, series I, folder 3.31.

68. Hanson Baldwin, *The Price of Power* (New York: Harper and Brothers, 1947), 205.

69. Ibid., 208–11.

70. Ibid., 213.

71. For Dulles's original 1947 quote, see Allen W. Dulles to Hanson Baldwin, 13 November 1947, Allen W. Dulles Papers (hereafter cited as Dulles Papers), series 1, box 7, folder 4, Seeley Mudd Manuscript Library, Princeton, NJ. For its reproduction, credited to an "experienced intelligence officer," see Baldwin, *The Price of Power*, 215.

72. Harry Howe Ransom, *The Intelligence Establishment* (Cambridge: Harvard University Press, 1970), 31.

73. Joseph Alsop to Walter H. Mallory, 12 December 1946, Joseph Alsop and Stewart Alsop Papers (hereafter cited as Alsop Papers), part I, box 2, folder 8, Library of Congress, Manuscript Division, Washington, DC.

74. Merry, *Taking on the World,* 149–50, 155–56.

75. Joe Alsop to "Jimmy," 27 December 1945, Alsop Papers, part I, box 2, folder 7. While the recipient of the letter is referred to only as "Jimmy," mention of the recipient's role as secretary of state definitively identifies him as James F. Byrnes, secretary of state at the time.

76. Joseph Alsop to Martin Sommers, 31 December 1946, Alsop Papers, part I, box 26: Special Correspondence (Saturday Evening Post), folder 1: "Saturday Evening Post," Apr–Dec 1946.

77. Unidentified correspondent to Martin Sommers, 3 January 1947, Alsop Papers, part I, box 26, folder 2: "Saturday Evening Post" Jan–Apr 1947. Though the copy of the letter to Sommers in the Library of Congress does not bear a signature, the letter from Sommers replying to the various story ideas is addressed to Joseph Alsop.

78. Martin Sommers to Joseph Alsop, 16 January 1947, Alsop Papers, part I, box 26, folder 2.

79. Harry S. Truman, "Limit CIA Role to Intelligence," *Washington Post,* 22 December 1963, A11.

80. Andrew, *For the President's Eyes Only,* 172.

81. For a discussion of this uncertainty, see Kaeten Mistry, "Approaches to Understanding the Inaugural CIA Covert Operation in Italy: Exploding Useful Myths," *Intelligence and National Security* 26.2–3 (2011): 246–68.

82. Zachary Karabell, *Architects of Intervention: The United States, the Third World, and the Cold War, 1946–1962* (Baton Rouge: Louisiana State University Press, 1999), 37.

83. Andrew, *For the President's Eyes Only,* 171, 183.

84. Three former OSS officers had apparently tried to organize an overthrow of the government of Romania; see William Lawrence, "U.S. Aides Accused by 3 in Maniu Trials," *New York Times,* 31 October 1947, 19.

85. Bradley Smith, "An Idiosyncratic View of Where We Stand on the History of American Intelligence in the Early Post-1945 Era," *Intelligence and National Security* 3.4 (1988): 111–23.

86. Arthur Hays Sulzberger to Turner Catledge, 19 December 1951, Sulzberger Papers, series II, box 125, folder 125.3.

87. "Italy: 40% or Fight," *Time,* 29 March 1948; "Truman as Leader," *New Republic* 17 May 1948, 23.

88. William D. Patterson to Evans Clark, 20 July 1948, Kirchwey Papers, series IIA, box 6, folder 103; Larry Siegel to Frasier McCann, 18 March 1953, Kirchwey Papers, series IIA, box 6, folder 106.

89. Christopher Andrew and Vasili Mitrokhin, *The Sword and the Shield: The Mitrokhin Archive and the Secret History of the KGB* (New York: Basic Books, 1999), 105, 109.

90. Hanson Baldwin to Roscoe Hillenkoetter, 5 August 1949, CREST, www.foia .cia.gov/sites/default/files/document_conversions/5829/CIA-RDP80R01731 R001300130025-1.pdf, accessed 30 April 2015.

91. Joseph Alsop to Martin Sommers, 13 January 1948, 1–2, Alsop Papers, part I, box 26, folder 5.

92. Roscoe Hillenkoetter to Joseph Alsop, 16 January 1948, Alsop Papers, part I, box 3, folder 2; Joseph Alsop to Martin Sommers, 23 May 1949, Alsop Papers, part I, box 26, folder 8; Stewart Alsop to Martin Sommers, 28 September 1950, Alsop Papers, part I, box 27, folder 3.

93. See, for example, "The X at Bogota," *Washington Post,* 13 April 1948, 14; see also Marquis Childs, "Washington Calling," *Washington Post,* 13 April 1948, 14.

94. See, for example, "Colombia—the Aftermath," *Time,* 26 April 1948, and "Pearl Harbor Lesson Wasted," *Chicago Tribune,* 17 April 1948, 10; "Brown Assails Envoy Power of 'Censorship,'" *Washington Post,* 17 April 1948, 7; "An American Un-Secret Service," *Los Angeles Times,* 2 May 1948, A4.

95. "Infiltration and Espionage," *Chicago Tribune,* 23 April 1948, 11.

96. Snider, *The Agency and the Hill,* 11.

97. Assistant Director OPC to Hillenkoetter, 13 September 1948, CREST, www.foia.cia.gov/document/cia-rdp86b00269r000200010010-7.pdf, accessed 30 April 2015.

98. Report from the Intelligence Survey Group to the National Security Council, 1 January 1949, in U.S. Department of State, *Foreign Relations of the United States, 1945–1950: Emergence of an Intelligence Establishment, Retrospective Volume,* ed. C. Thomas Thorne Jr. and David S. Patterson (Washington, DC: Government Printing Office, 1996), document 358.

99. Hanson Baldwin, "Intelligence-II," *New York Times,* 22 July 1948, 2.

100. Hanson Baldwin, "Intelligence-III," *New York Times,* 23 July 1948, 5; Hanson Baldwin, "Intelligence-IV," *New York Times,* 24 July 1948, 5.

101. Hanson Baldwin, "Intelligence-V," *New York Times,* 25 July 1948, 15; Hanson Baldwin, "Bureaucrats Foul Up Intelligence Services," *Los Angeles Times,* 4 August 1948, A5.

102. Stewart Alsop to Martin Sommers, 27 April 1948, Alsop Papers, part I, box 26, folder 6. The letter is misdated 27 April 1948, but from the context of his reference it can be inferred that it is probably in fact 27 July 1948.

103. Martin Sommers to Stewart Alsop, 4 August 1948, Alsop Papers, part I, box 26, folder 6.

104. Weiner, *Legacy of Ashes,* 46.

105. Joseph Alsop, "Lovett Top Choice for CIA Head," *Washington Post,* 14 August 1949, B5; Robert S. Allen, "Presidential Advisor Accused," *Washington Post,* 1 September 1949, B15; Marquis Childs, "Johnson's First Year: Economies and Empire-Building," *Washington Post,* 22 March 1950, 13.

106. Stewart Alsop to Martin Sommers, 26 May 1950, Alsop Papers, part I, box 27, folder 2.

107. Martin Sommers to Stewart Alsop, 1 June 1950, Alsop Papers, part I, box 27, folder 2.

108. Drew Pearson, "Diplomats Beat Army on Korea," *Washington Post,* 29 June 1950, B13; Robert F. Whitney, "Capital in Dispute on Korean Attack," *New York Times,* 26 June 1950, 3; "Eyes and Ears," *Washington Post,* 27 June 1950, 10; "Half-Way Intelligence," *Washington Post,* 3 July 1950, 8; "Pearl Harbor All Over Again," *Chicago Tribune,* 3 July 1950, 8; Hanson Baldwin, "U.S. Errors in Korea," *New York Times,* 10 July 1950, 7; "Watchdog Group Set for Korean War," *New York Times,* 18 July 1950, 10.

109. "National Defense—for Small Fires," *Time,* 1 July 1950.

110. "Smith Scaled Army Ladder Rung by Rung," *Washington Post,* 17 February 1946, B1; "Tough Man for a Tough Job," *New York Times,* 17 March 1946, SM8. The installments of Smith's account of his time in Moscow appeared in twenty-seven segments throughout late 1949.

111. Arthur Krock, "In the Nation: No.2 Man in the Central Intelligence Agency," *New York Times,* 25 August 1950, 20; "The Nation: Smith for CIA," *New York Times,* 20 August 1950, 118; "CIA and Its Chief," *Washington Post,* 20 August 1950, 118; "General Smith's New Job," *New York Times,* 22 August 1950, 25; "Gen. Smith and Secret Service," *Los Angeles Times,* 22 August 1950, A4.

112. See, for example, "The Admiral Tells a Fishy Story," *Chicago Tribune,* 9 January 1946, 18; "Where Were You the Night of December 6?" *Chicago Tribune,* 28 February 1946, 16; "What a Diplomat and What Diplomacy!" *Chicago Tribune,* 1 October 1947, 20; "Horsey George's Fumbling Friend," *Chicago Tribune,* 20 March 1948, 14.

113. Though only one account of an off-the-record meeting with Smith is available in Arthur Hays Sulzberger's papers, the reporter at the meeting, James Reston, mentions he had been present at other such meetings Smith held. See James Reston, memorandum, 4 January 1954, Sulzberger Papers, series I, box 69, folder 69.27.

114. Stewart Alsop to Martin Sommers, 25 November 1950, Alsop Papers, part I, box 27, folder 3.

115. Martin Sommers to Stewart Alsop, 28 November 1950, Alsop Papers, part I, box 27, folder 3.

116. Stewart Alsop to Martin Sommers, 15 December 1950, Alsop Papers, part I, box 27, folder 3.

117. Joseph Alsop to William H. Jackson, 22 January 1951, and Jackson to Alsop, 26 January 1951, CREST, www.foia.cia.gov/sites/default/files/document_conversions /5829/CIA-RDP80R01731R001300130088-2.pdf, accessed 30 April 2015.

118. Daily Staff Meeting Memorandum, 12 June 1951, and Daily Staff Memorandum, 22 August 1951, CREST, www.foia.cia.gov/sites/default/files/document _conversions/5829/CIA-RDP80B01676R002300040030-2.pdf, and www.foia.cia.gov /sites/default/files/document_conversions/5829/CIA-RDP80B01676R002300060029 -2.pdf, both accessed 30 April 2015.

119. Daily Staff Meeting Memorandum, 19 February 1952, CREST, www.foia .cia.gov/sites/default/files/document_conversions/5829/CIA-RDP80B01676 R002300080003-8.pdf, accessed 30 April 2015.

120. Joseph Alsop to Martin Sommers, 17 March 1948, Alsop Papers, part I, box 26, folder 5.

121. Steven Casey, *Selling the Korean War: Propaganda, Politics, and Public Opinion in the United States, 1950–1953* (Oxford: Oxford University Press, 2008), 57.

122. Ibid., 155.

123. James Reston, "Millions for Defense behind the Iron Curtain," *New York Times,* 9 December 1951, 169; "The Week," *New Republic,* 7 July 1952, 7–8; "The Administration—Apology for a Fantasy," *Time,* 7 July 1952.

2. Allen Dulles and Covert Intervention

1. This chapter is derived in part from an article published in *Intelligence and National Security* on 13 January 2015, www.tandfonline.com/10.1080/02684527 .2014.989685. Used by permission.

2. Hanson Baldwin, "Myopia on Intelligence," *New York Times,* 3 June 1954, 13.

3. Ibid.

4. Allen Dulles to Hanson Baldwin, 1 August 1953, and Dulles to Baldwin, 28 June 1954, both in Dulles Papers, series 1, box 7, folder 4.

5. Allen Dulles to Hanson Baldwin, 28 June 1954, 2, Dulles Papers, series 1, box 7, folder 4.

6. Hanson Baldwin to Allen Dulles, 6 July 1954, 1, Dulles Papers, series 1, box 7, folder 4.

7. Allen Dulles to Hanson Baldwin, 28 June 1954, and Baldwin to Dulles, 6 July 1954; for the article with the revised budget, see "C.I.A. and Its Chief Develop Spy Plan," *New York Times,* 8 August 1954, 23.

8. Snider, *The Agency and the Hill,* 14.

9. Peter Grose, *Gentleman Spy: The Life of Allen Dulles* (Boston: Houghton Mifflin, 1994), 12; James Srodes, *Allen Dulles: Master of Spies* (Washington, DC: Regnery, 1999), 82–83.

10. Grose, *Gentleman Spy,* 16.

11. Allen Dulles to Hamilton Fish Armstrong, 2 March 1954; Dulles to Armstrong, 1 June 1958; and Armstrong to Dulles, 4 June 1958, all in Dulles Papers, series 1, box 4, folder 13.

12. Hamilton Fish Armstrong to Allen Dulles, 29 January 1954; Armstrong to Abbott Smith, 10 March 1961; Armstrong to Smith, 13 March 1961; Robert Amory to Armstrong, 17 May 1955, all in Armstrong Papers, series I, box 15, folder II.

13. Herkin, *The Georgetown Set,* 144.

14. Immerman, *The Hidden Hand,* 42–43.

15. Ibid., 45–47; Christopher Andrew, *For the President's Eyes Only,* 199–201.

16. Robert McCormick to Joseph Ator, 26 March 1953, in McCormick Papers, series I-61, box 8, folder 8. Even noneditorial reporting in the *Tribune* clearly favored McCarthy. See "The Alliance against McCarthy," *Chicago Tribune,* 23 July 1953, 12; "Washington Scrapbook," *Chicago Tribune,* 1 August 1953, 4; Walter Trohan,

"General Tells of CIA Plot to Ruin MacArthur," *Chicago Tribune,* 31 July 1953, 3; "The Sacred CIA," *Chicago Tribune,* 4 August 1953, 14; Willard Edwards, "Sen. McCarthy Vows Probe of CIA Operations," *Chicago Tribune,* 5 August 1953, 5.

17. Herkin, *The Georgetown Set,* 144.

18. Arthur Krock, "Allen W. Dulles Describes 'Warfare for the Brain,'" *New York Times,* 16 April 1953, 28.

19. Hanson Baldwin to Allen Dulles, 16 January 1953, and Baldwin to Dulles, 4 February 1953, both in Dulles Papers, series 1, box 7, folder 4; Henry Luce to Allen Dulles, 5 March 1953, Dulles Papers, series 1, box 38, folder 33; Arthur Hays Sulzberger to Allen Dulles, 4 June 1953, Dulles Papers, series 1, box 54, folder 2; Walter Lippmann to Allen Dulles, 7 April 1953, Dulles Papers, series 1, box 38, folder 21.

20. Allen Dulles to Marquis Childs, 13 October 1953, Dulles Papers, series 1, box 12, folder 18.

21. Allen Dulles to Benjamin M. McKelway, 6 August 1953, Dulles Papers, series 5, box 98, folder 15.

22. Walter Waggoner to Arthur Krock and Whitney (no first name), 3 April 1953, 2 Dulles Papers, series 5, box 98, folder 15.

23. Wilford, *Mighty Wurlitzer,* 65.

24. Cord Meyer Jr., *Peace or Anarchy* (Boston: Little, Brown, 1947); Cord Meyer, Jr., "Which Road to Peace," *Atlantic,* 13 November 1948, 7, 45–46; Cord Meyer to Charles Merz, 24 March 1948; Morris H. Rubin to Cord Meyer, 9 May 1950; McGeorge Bundy to Cord Meyer, 4 April 1950, all in Cord Meyer Jr. Papers (hereafter cited as Meyer Papers), box 1, folder 1934–1957, Library of Congress, Manuscript Division, Washington, DC.

25. Allen Dulles to Cord Meyer, 23 February 1951, Meyer Papers, box 1, folder 1934–1957.

26. John Fischer to Cord Meyer, 11 January 1961, folder 1961, and Cord Meyer to Elizabeth Brown, 14 October 1968, folder 1968, both in Meyer Papers, box 1.

27. John Fischer to Cord Meyer, 11 January 1961; Meyer to Fischer, 11 January 1961; Fischer to Meyer, 14 February 1961, all in Meyer Papers, box 1, folder 1961.

28. Joseph and Stewart Alsop, "Matter of Fact . . . Dynamite from Middle East," *Washington Post,* 4 March 1953, 13; see also Joseph and Stewart Alsop, "Must We Surrender the Middle East to Stalin?" *U.S. News and World Report,* 12 April 1952, 30. This article warned of a potential chain reaction should Iran become a communist state. For other reporting, see John M. Hightower, "Middle East Studied for Clue to Malenkov's Future Plans," *Washington Post,* 8 March 1953, M3; the *Post* followed up in April with William L. Ryan, "Reds Watch Iran Like Cat after Mouse," *Washington Post,* 4 April 1953, 21. See also "Iranian Newspapers Hint Peace Pact with Soviets," *Washington Post,* 10 July 1953, 11; "O Shah," *Chicago Tribune,* 4 March 1953, 24.

29. Johnson, *America's Secret Power,* 157; Kermit Roosevelt, *Countercoup: The Struggle for the Control of Iran* (New York: McGraw-Hill, 1979), 23.

30. For chronology of the crisis in August, see Karabell, *Architects of Intervention,* 88–89.

31. Allen Dulles to Hanson Baldwin, 1 August 1953; "A. W. Dulles Flies to Zurich," *New York Times,* 10 August 1953, 8.

32. "Shah's Coup Gives U.S. Hope, Eases London," *Washington Post,* 20 August 1953, 2; "Turnover in Iran," *Chicago Tribune,* 22 August 1953, 8; Quentin Pope, "U.S. Has Three Major Stakes on Iran Front," *Chicago Tribune,* 24 December 1953, 7; Quentin Pope, "Find Iran Bites American Hand That Feeds it," *Chicago Tribune,* 22 December 1953, 16.

33. "The Royal Comeback,*" Life,* 31 August 1953, 14.

34. House Subcommittee on Oversight, *The CIA and the Media,* 99.

35. See, for example, Dan Kurzman, "Kashani of Iran: Master of Intrigue," *Nation,* 3 April 1954, 275.

36. Robert Repas, "The Curious Capers of the CIA," *Progressive,* September 1953, 26; see also Harlan Cleveland, "Oil, Blood, and Politics: Our Next Move in Iran," *Reporter,* 10 November 1953, 18.

37. A. Kessel, "Iran's Fabulous Oil: And Some Popular Fables," *Nation,* 11 September 1954, 212.

38. Foran, "Discursive Subversions," 163.

39. Merry, *Taking on the World,* 300.

40. Joseph Alsop to Martin Sommers, 25 April 1954, Alsop Papers, part I, box 28, folder 2. While the letter does not specify which Alsop was writing, his references to the First American Volunteer Group (AVG), better known as the Flying Tigers, and China clearly identify the writer as Joseph Alsop.

41. Kip Finch to Henry Luce, 29 September 1953, Henry R. Luce Papers (hereafter cited as Luce Papers), box 22, folder 5—American Friends of the Middle East, Library of Congress, Manuscript Division, Washington, DC.

42. Wilford, *America's Great Game: The CIA's Secret Arabists and the Shaping of the Modern Middle East* (New York: Basic Books, 2013), 130–31.

43. Russell Bourne to C. D. Jackson, memorandum, 25 July 1956, and Marie McCrum to Russell Bourne and C. D. Jackson, 7 August 1956, both in Luce Papers, box 22, folder 5.

44. Roosevelt, *Countercoup,* 209–10.

45. Piero Gleijeses, *Shattered Hope: The Guatemalan Revolution and the United States, 1944–1954* (Princeton: Princeton University Press, 1991), 85, 145.

46. Richard Immerman, *The CIA in Guatemala: The Foreign Policy of Intervention* (Austin: University of Texas Press, 1982), 111–23; Gleijeses, *Shattered Hope,* 232; Stephen Schlesinger and Stephen Kinzer, *Bitter Fruit: The Story of the American Coup in Guatemala,* rev. ed. (Cambridge: David Rockefeller Center for Latin American Studies, Harvard University, 2005), 86; José M. Aybar de Soto, *Dependency and Intervention: The Case of Guatemala in 1954* (Boulder, CO: Westview Press, 1978), 237; Christian G. Appy, "Eisenhower's Guatemalan Doodle, or: How to Draw, Deny, and Take Credit for a Third World Coup," in Appy, *Cold War Constructions,* 183–213.

47. Appy, "Eisenhower's Guatemalan Doodle," 184–85.

48. Schlesinger and Kinzer, *Bitter Fruit,* 94–95, 122–23.

49. Ibid., 179–86.

50. Nick Cullather, *Secret History: The CIA's Classified Account of Its Operations in Guatemala, 1952–1954* (Stanford: Stanford University Press, 1999), 59; Karabell, *Architects of Intervention,* 133–34.

51. Cullather, *Secret History,* 93.

52. See, for example, "A Guatemalan Revolution That Everybody Expected," *Life,* 28 June 1954, 13; "Guatemala Problem Seems to Be Solving," *Los Angeles Times,* 29 June 1954, A4; "Worldgram," *U.S. News and World Report,* 9 July 1954, 37.

53. George Sokolsky, "These Days: Coffee and Communism," *Washington Post,* 10 April 1954, 22. See also Russell Fitzgibbons, "Fear of Guatemala's Reds Varies among Her Neighbors," *Washington Post,* 9 February 1954, 11; "Parlay at Caracas Closes with Signing of 'Final Act,'" *Washington Post,* 29 March 1954, 4; Edwin Lahey, "Guatemala's Red Regime Has Chinks," *Washington Post,* 28 May 1954, 46; Jules Dubois, "How Arbenz Encouraged the Reds," *Chicago Tribune,* 20 June 1954, 2.

54. Jules Dubois, "U.S. Weapons in Red Shipment to Guatemala," *Chicago Tribune,* 27 May 1954, C12. See also "The Atlantic Report on the World Today: Guatemala," *Atlantic,* April 1954, 9.

55. "Reds' Priority: Pin War on US," *Life,* 5 July 1954, 8; see also Milton Bracker, "Lessons of the Guatemalan Struggle," *New York Times,* 11 July 1954, SM11. The *Washington Post* would continue on this theme until the next year, noting that the United States gave a "benediction" to Castillo Armas's forces. See, for example, Edwin Lahey, "U.S. Being 'Sold' to Guatemala," *Washington Post,* 17 July 1955, E3.

56. Quoted in Barrett, *The CIA and Congress,* 167; James Reston to Robert E. Garst, Arthur Hays Sulzberger, Orvil Dryfoos, Nathanial Gerstenzang, Raymond O'Neil, Emanuel Freedman, Jack Desmond, and Harry Schwarz, 10 August 1954, 1, Sulzberger Papers, series II, box 125, folder 125.6.

57. Russell H. Fitzgibbon, "Anti-Red Victory Is Model for U.S. Policy," *Los Angeles Times,* 9 July 1954, A5; Holmes Alexander, "Guatemala Heave Ho," *Los Angeles Times,* 12 July 1954, A5.

58. "Dead Reveal Terror Wave of Pro-Red Forces," *Los Angeles Times,* 3 July 1954, 4; Jules Dubois, "Guatemalans Celebrate as War Is Ended," *Chicago Tribune,* 3 July 1954, 2; Keith Monroe, "Guatemala: What the Reds Left Behind," *Harper's Magazine,* July 1955, 60–65.

59. Jules Dubois, "Guatemala and Its Consequences," *Chicago Tribune,* 30 June 1954, 8.

60. Monroe, "Guatemala: What the Reds Left Behind," 60.

61. Schlesinger and Kinzer, *Bitter Fruit,* 187; Appy, "Eisenhower's Guatemalan Doodle," 206.

62. Jules Dubois, "Peurifoy Hated by Communists—with Cause," *Chicago Tribune,* 5 July 1954, 14; Peurifoy had apparently leaked security files on Alger Hiss, on his own initiative, to Senator Karl Mundt of the House Un-American Activities Committee. See Schlesinger and Kinzer, *Bitter Fruit,* 134.

63. "The Press: Freedom Fighter," *Time,* 15 April 1957.

64. Unknown correspondent to Francis Corrigan, 24 August 1954, Francis P. Corrigan Papers, box 17, folder: Latin America (General), Franklin Delano Roosevelt Presidential Library and Museum, Hyde Park, N.Y. While the writer is unidentified, context clues suggest that he worked with *Time*. This quotation is courtesy of Dr. Aaron Coy Moulton, to whom I would like to extend my thanks.

65. Ibid.

66. Jules Dubois to Robert McCormick, 6 March 1953, McCormick Papers, series I-62, box 4, folder 7.

67. Jules Dubois to Robert McCormick, 22 June 1954, McCormick Papers, series I-62, box 4, folder 7.

68. Robert McCormick to Joseph Ator, 21 May 1952, and McCormick to Ator, 25 August 1952, McCormick Papers, series I-61, box 8, folder 8.

69. Schlesinger and Kinzer, *Bitter Fruit,* 153–54.

70. Joseph Alsop to Martin Sommers, 25 April 1954, Alsop Papers, part I, box 28, folder 2.

71. Stewart Alsop to Martin Sommers, 1 June 1954, Alsop Papers, part I, box 28, folder 2.

72. The story had been related by Gruson himself and Harrison Salisbury, and later confirmed by an examination of *New York Times* records by Tim Weiner. See Tim Weiner, "Role of C.I.A. in Guatemala Told in Files of Publisher," *New York Times,* 7 June 1997, in Sulzberger Papers, series I, box 30, folder 30.1. Weiner reflected, "Contacts of this sort between the C.I.A. and the American news media— as well as far deeper relationships—were common in the 1950's and 1960's, and were thoroughly reported 20 years ago."

73. Sydney Gruson to Emanuel Freedman, 22 March 1954, 2, NYTCR: Foreign Desk Records (hereafter cited as Foreign Desk Records), box 41, folder 7—Gruson, Sydney—1954 (3).

74. Sydney Gruson to Emanuel Freedman, 26 March 1954, Foreign Desk Records, box 41, folder 7.

75. Frank Wisner to Senior CIA Representative in Guatemala City, 21 May 1954, CIA Freedom of Information Act Reading Room (hereafter cited as CIA FOIA), www.foia.cia.gov/sites/default/files/document_conversions/89801/DOC _0000136917.pdf, accessed 30 April 2015. Wisner sent a follow-up message hoping that the *New York Times* would be sympathetic to CIA concerns. See Frank Wisner to Senior CIA Representative in Guatemala City, 29 May 1954, CIA FOIA, www .foia.cia.gov/sites/default/files/document_conversions/89801/DOC_0000136939 .pdf, accessed 30 April 2015.

76. Allen W. Dulles to Julius Ochs Adler, 4 June 1954, Sulzberger Papers, box 30, folder 30.1; for information on Adler's connection to Dulles, see Eric Pace, "Sydney Gruson, 81, Correspondent, Editor and Executive for the New York Times, Dies," *New York Times,* 9 March 1998, www.nytimes.com/1998/03/09/nyregion /sydney-gruson-81-correspondent-editor-and-executive-for-the-new-york-times -dies.html?pagewanted=all&src=pm, accessed 25 August 2013.

77. Sydney Gruson to Emanuel Freedman, 4 June 1954, Foreign Desk Records, box 41, folder 7.

78. Art Gelb to the Foreign Desk, 23 June 1954, Foreign Desk Records, box 41, folder 7.

79. Appy, "Eisenhower's Guatemalan Doodle," 211.

80. Arthur Hays Sulzberger to Robert Garst, 20 July 1954, Sulzberger Papers, series I, box 30, folder 30.1.

81. Allen Dulles to Arthur Hays Sulzberger, 3 July 1954, Sulzberger Papers, series I, box 30, folder 30.1; Sulzberger would write to Dulles again, and in a letter dated 6 July 1954 he inquired whether Dulles could "permit me to come to some judgment in the matter." Dulles, in 10 July 1954 reply, offered to send a "trusted messenger" to brief Sulzberger on specifics but observed that nothing would be appropriate for filing. Both letters are in Sulzberger Papers, series I, box 30, folder 30.1.

82. Jones, "Journalism, Intelligence and the *New York Times*," 234–35.

83. For Sulzberger's status as a contact, see the beginning of chap. 4 of this work; see also Jones, "Journalism, Intelligence and the *New York Times*," 240–42.

84. Arthur Hays Sulzberger, memorandum for the file, 20 July 1954, in Sulzberger Papers, series I, box 30, folder 30.1.

85. Bernstein, "The CIA and the Media"; John M. Crewsdon, "CIA Tried in 50's to Recruit Times Man," *New York Times,* 31 January 1976, 23.

86. Crewsdon, "CIA Tried in 50's to Recruit Times Man"; Abraham M. Rosenthal to Arthur Ochs Sulzberger and James Goodale, 3 March 1976, series II, box 63, folder 63.7, and Sydney Gruson to Stansfield Turner and Gene F. Wilson, 12 September 1977, series II, box 63, folder 63.6, both in NYTCR: Abraham M. Rosenthal Papers (hereafter cited as Rosenthal Papers), New York Public Library.

87. Frank G. Wisner to Henry F. Holland (assistant secretary of state), 9 August 1954, CREST, www.foia.cia.gov/sites/default/files/document_conversions/89801/DOC_0000920167.pdf, accessed 30 April 2015.

88. See, for example, "Secrets Congressmen Can't Get," *U.S. News and World Report,* 16 July 1954, 39.

89. Donald Grant, "Last Chance in Guatemala," *Progressive,* September 1954, 26.

90. J. Alvarez del Vayo, "Aggression Is the Word: The Guatemala Crisis," *Nation,* 26 June 1954, 537–38; J. Alvarez del Vayo, "War against the U.N.: The Guatemalan Chapter," *Nation,* 3 July 1954, 4; J. Alvarez del Vayo, "Guatemala's Strong Man," *Nation,* 14 August 1954.

91. Freda Kirchwey, "Guatemala Guinea Pig," *Nation,* 10 July 1954, 2. For another example of acknowledgment, see "Washington Wire," *New Republic,* 19 July 1954, 3. See also Edwin Lahey, "Perspectives on Guatemala: We Won't Turn Back the Clock—Maybe," *New Republic,* 19 July 1954, 10; Morris Siegel, "Perspectives on Guatemala: What Will the New Regime Offer Its Own?" *New Republic,* 19 July 1954, 11. A year later, the *Progressive* would publish a similar argument. Written by Carleton Beals, it condemned Castillo Armas as a tyrant and asserted

that the United States had a moral role to play in securing civil rights and prosperity in Guatemala because of its "encouragement" of the overthrow of Arbenz, though what kind of encouragement was meant was left unsaid. See Carleton Beals, "Tragic Guatemala," *Progressive,* May 1955, 16.

92. Tad Szulc, "Bonn Aide's Defection Deliberate, U.S. Officials Who Knew Him Say," *New York Times,* 25 July 1954, 1.

93. Aldrich, "American Journalism and the Landscape of Secrecy," 200.

94. Harrison Salisbury, *Without Fear or Favor: The New York Times and Its Times* (New York: Times Books, 1980), 148; M. S. Handler, "Bonn Offers Data on Luring of Aide," *New York Times,* 27 July 1954, 7; M. S. Handler, "Bonn Aide Seen by Border Guard," *New York Times,* 25 July 1954, 30.

95. Turner Catledge to Arthur Hays Sulzberger, 26 July 1954, 1–2, Sulzberger Papers, series I, box 11, folder 3.

96. M. S. Handler, "U.S. Agents Seized, German Reds Say," *New York Times,* 4 August 1954, 3; M. S. Handler, "John Said to Hail East for Asylum," *New York Times,* 5 August 1954, 3; M. S. Handler, "John Says U.S.-Bonn Policy Will Restore Nazi Control," *New York Times,* 12 August 1954, 1; "John Asserts U.S. Gave Him War Aim," *New York Times,* 22 August 1954, 10.

97. James Reston to Robert E. Garst, Arthur Hays Sulzberger, Orvil Dryfoos, Nathanial Gerstenzang, Raymond O'Neil, Emanuel Freedman, Jack Desmond, and Harry Schwarz, 10 August 1954, 1.

98. Ibid.

99. Ibid., 2.

100. Arthur Hays Sulzberger to James Reston, 11 August 1954, Sulzberger Papers, series II, box 125, folder 125.6.

101. Enclosure in Arthur Hays Sulzberger to Orvil Dryfoos, 24 September 1954, Sulzberger Papers, series II, box 125, folder 6.

102. Ibid.

103. Richard Harkness and Gladys Harkness, "The Mysterious Doings of the CIA, Part 1," *Saturday Evening Post,* 30 October 1954, 21.

104. See Richard Harkness and Gladys Harkness, "Private Life of a Steel Boss," *Saturday Evening Post,* 6 December 1953, 32–33, 154–58, which was a glowing portrait of the businessman Clarence Randall, who had served as a spokesman for the steel industry; Richard Harkness and Gladys Harkness, "The Woes of Washington Wives," *Saturday Evening Post,* 1 August 1953, 25, 65–67, on the difficulty of acclimating to Washington's social scene.

105. Allen Dulles to Richard Harkness, 17 December 1953; Dulles to Harkness, 20 April 1956; Dulles to Harkness, 15 February 1958, all in Dulles Papers, series 1, box 31, folder 2. Grose, *Gentleman Spy,* 416. Transcript of broadcast of *Ask Washington,* 17 February 1954, NBC Television, passed along by Dulles's aide Col. Stanley Grogan, Dulles Papers, series 1, box 31, folder 2.

106. Martin Sommers to Stewart Alsop, 2 April 1958, Alsop Papers, part I, box 29, folder 3.

107. Richard L. Borgstedt to Stanley Grogan, 6 August 1954; Robert Fuss to Grogan, 9 August 1954; Grogan to Allen Dulles, 10 August 1954; Richard Harkness to Dulles, 13 August 1954, all in Dulles Papers, series 1, box 31, folder 2.

108. Richard Harkness and Gladys Harkness, "The Mysterious Doings of the CIA, Part 2," *Saturday Evening Post,* 6 November 1954; Harkness and Harkness, "The Mysterious Doings of the CIA, Part 3," *Saturday Evening Post,* 13 November 1954, 131, 134.

109. Allen Dulles to Nulford Colebrook, 19 November 1954, Dulles Papers, series 5, box 98, folder 15.

110. Schlesinger and Kinzer, *Bitter Fruit,* 228.

111. Stanley Grogan to David Lawrence, 17 January 1955, and enclosed letter, Allen Dulles to Joseph McCarthy, 7 July 1954, in David Lawrence Papers (hereafter cited as Lawrence Papers), series Ia, box 38, folder: Allen Dulles, Seeley Mudd Manuscript Library, Princeton, NJ. McCarthy eventually turned his information over to the Hoover commission, then studying the CIA as part of a broader program of government reform. See "CIA 'Red' File Given Clark by McCarthy," *Washington Post,* 15 January 1955, 2. The disclosure of the file produced no apparent results.

112. David L. Graham, "Has Intervention Paid Off?" *New Republic,* 16 September 1957, 9; Carleton Beals, the author of the *Progressive* article "Tragic Guatemala," wrote to the *New Republic* to congratulate its management on making the "revelation." See *New Republic,* 28 October 1957, 23; John Gillin and K. H. Silvert, "Ambiguities in Guatemala," *Foreign Affairs,* 1 April 1955, 469; "Strict Neutrality Takes Shape," *Nation,* 22 March 1958, 245; "The Week," *National Review,* 9 November 1957, 411; James Burnham, "The Third World War," *National Review,* 24 August 1957, 154; Warren Unna, "CIA: Who Watches the Watchman?" *Harper's Magazine,* April 1958; "Guatemala—Back to '54," *The New Republic,* 22 June 1959, 4–5; "The Candidates on Cuba," *New Republic,* 31 October 1960, 6.

113. Russell Baker, "The Other Mr. Dulles—of C.I.A.," *New York Times,* 16 March 1958, 96.

114. Holmes Alexander, "A Plan to Keep Tabs on CIA," *Los Angeles Times,* 26 May 1958, B5.

115. Allen Dulles to Dr. James E. Mooney, 14 November 1955, Dulles Papers, series 1, box 57, folder 14.

3. The Increasing Public Profile of the CIA

1. This chapter is derived in part from an article published in *Intelligence and National Security* on 13 January 2015, www.tandfonline.com/10.1080/02684527 .2014.989685. Used by permission.

2. Herkin, *The Georgetown Set,* 67–68.

3. "Maryland Urges Unit to Eye CIA," *Washington Post,* 11 March 1955, 26; Wes Barthelmes, "Area Planners Hear CIA Urge Langley Office Site," *Washington Post,* 12 March 1955, 21; "Fairfax Woos CIA on Site for Offices," *Washington Post,*

17 March 1955, 17; Robert E. Baker, "Site for CIA 'Wide Open,'" *Washington Post,* 20 April 1955, 15; "Langley Leading as Site for CIA," *Washington Post,* 1 July 1955, 25; Wendell P. Bradley, "Proposed CIA Site Is Last Wild-Life Spot in Area," *Washington Post,* 9 August 1955, 18; this is a sampling of articles on the CIA's location.

4. "Big If Not Good," *Chicago Tribune,* 23 December 1955, 12; "Capital in Flurry over C.I.A. Site," *New York Times,* 12 December 1955, 23.

5. Felix Belair, "President Hails Heroes of C.I.A," *New York Times,* 4 November 1959, 30; see also "Ike Lays Cornerstone for New C.I.A. Building," *Washington Post,* 4 November 1959, B1; Walter Trohan, "Washington Scrapbook," *Chicago Tribune,* 8 November 1959, 48; "Eisenhower Lays CIA Building Cornerstone," *Los Angeles Times,* 4 November 1959, B2.

6. Marquis Childs, "CIA 'Steps Out,' Gets into Policy," *Washington Post,* 3 November 1959, A14.

7. Stewart Alsop to Martin Sommers, 26 May 1959, Alsop Papers, part I, box 29, folder 6. For Alsop's positive evaluation of Dulles, see Stewart Alsop to Martin Sommers, 31 March 1958, Alsop Papers, part 1, box 29, folder 3. Alsop did not specify who had informed him of discontent with Dulles's decision, but he was friendly with two possible candidates, Richard Helms and Richard Bissell, senior members of the CIA.

8. Smith, *The Colonel,* 516–19.

9. Ibid., 514, 521.

10. See, for example, different coverage of a September 1956 speech by Dulles: Paul Southwick (UP), "CIA Head Warns of Reds' New Infiltration Tactics," *Washington Post,* 2 September 1956, A6; C. P. Trussell, "C.I.A. Head Warns of Soviet's Aims," *New York Times,* 2 September 1956, 23; Robert Young, "List 3 Nations Russia Seeks to Gobble Up," *Chicago Tribune,* 2 September 1956, C29.

11. "A Secret Slips thru Hush-Hush Program of CIA," *Chicago Tribune,* 19 July 1956, B6; this revelation came, the *Tribune* explained, because in his report Dulles noted that the plans for the CIA's new headquarters provided 98 square feet per employee. With 1,135,000 total square feet in the new headquarters, the *Tribune* concluded, the CIA must employ approximately 11,000 people.

12. Hanson W. Baldwin, oral history interview by John T. Mason, 25 August 1975, 545, in Baldwin Papers, box 15.

13. Turner Catledge, *My Life and The Times* (New York: Harper & Row, 1971), 255. Baldwin and Catledge did not care for one another; in addition to their divergent political views, Baldwin's antipathy to Catledge might have had something to do with clashes they had had over the content of his articles. See Turner Catledge to Orvil Dryfoos, 2 June 1953, Sulzberger Papers, series I, box 4, folder 30.

14. "Orvil E. Dryfoos Dies at 50," *New York Times,* 26 May 1963, 1.

15. Felix Belair to Emanuel Freedman, 3 June 1955, and Tad Szulc to Freedman, 21 October 1955, both in Foreign Desk Records, box 89, folder 4. While not a communist, Szulc was left-leaning, and he was more explicitly political than other *Times* reporters. He requested at one point that he be allowed to do freelance work for the

Nation, a request denied by his editor for fear of violating the *Times*'s standards of objectivity. See Nathanial Gerstenzang to Turner Catledge, 10 August 1959, Foreign Desk Records, box 90, folder 1.

16. Hanson W. Baldwin, oral history interview by John T. Mason, 6 October 1975, 644, 646, in Baldwin Papers, box 15. When *Time* magazine reported that Baldwin had known about nuclear tests but refrained from reporting, some *New York Times* readers were upset; one wrote to Arthur Hays Sulzberger to complain, but Sulzberger defended Baldwin. When the head of the Atomic Energy Commission, Paul Foster, wrote to thank the *Times* for its forbearance, Sulzberger passed the message along to Baldwin and expressed his great pride in Baldwin's decision. Arthur Hays Sulzberger to Robert R. Schultz, 8 April 1959, Sulzberger Papers, series II, box 125, folder 3; Arthur Hays Sulzberger to Hanson Baldwin, 24 March 1959, Sulzberger Papers, series II, box 125, folder 29.

17. While the *Washington Post* was technically the *Washington Post and Times-Herald* during the 1954–1973 period, I have continued to refer to it only as the *Washington Post* to avoid confusion and because all related articles are found in the *Washington Post* archives, rather than a separate *Washington Post and Times-Herald* archive. The *Times-Herald* portion of the title became increasingly smaller over the years until it was finally removed entirely.

18. Chalmers Roberts, *The Washington Post: The First 100 Years* (Boston: Houghton Mifflin, 1977), 315, 318, 348.

19. Ibid., 263.

20. Herkin, *The Georgetown Set,* 212–13.

21. It was during a trip to the Soviet Union that Joseph Alsop, a closeted homosexual, fell victim to a honeytrap prepared by the KGB. After the KGB attempted to blackmail him with photographic evidence of his tryst, Alsop instead reported the incident to Charles Bohlen, ambassador to Moscow, and, on Bohlen's advice, wrote a detailed report of the incident; this report was passed on to Allen Dulles and from him to J. Edgar Hoover. Herkin, *The Georgetown Set,* 207–9.

22. Herkin, *The Georgetown Set,* 239.

23. Freda Kirchwey to Carey McWilliams, 18 August 1955, 2, Kirchwey Papers, series IIA, box 6, folder 107.

24. Freda Kirchwey to Dorothy Bernhard, 7 September 1955, Kirchwey Papers, series IIA, box 6, folder 107; Kirchwey to Doris Wolson-Tanz, 15 November 1955, Kirchwey Papers, series I, carton 1: folder #1–46, folder 33.

25. William F. Buckley, "Publisher's Statement," *National Review,* 19 November 1955, 55.

26. William F. Buckley Jr., "My Friend, E. Howard Hunt," Los Angeles Times, 4 March 2007, http://articles.latimes.com/2007/mar/04/opinion/op-buckley4, accessed 22 October 2014.

27. Wilford, The Mighty Wurlitzer, 73–79.

28. C. D. Jackson to Cord Meyer, 14 January 1961, Meyer Papers, box 1, folder 1961.

29. Stanley Grogan to Allen Dulles, 28 June 1955, CREST, www.foia.cia.gov /sites/default/files/document_conversions/5829/CIA-RDP86B00269R000100130094 -3.pdf, accessed 30 April 2015.

30. "C.I.A. Spending Questioned," *New York Times,* 28 May 1957, 23; George Dixon, "Rep. Whitten and the Hush-Shushers," *Washington Post,* 6 June 1957, A19; "Mansfield Urged Unit to Eye CIA," *Washington Post,* 7 February 1955, 9; "Check on CIA Press," *New York Times,* 7 February 1955, 15; Herbert Foster, "CIA Watchdog Unit Backed," *Washington Post,* 25 February 1956, 2; "Secrecy Curtain Covers CIA Flaws, Senator Hints," *Washington Post,* 10 April 1956, 27; "Mansfield Urges Watchdog Unit to Check CIA," *Washington Post,* 4 August 1958, A2.

31. "CIA Watchdog," *New York Times,* 26 January 1955, 24; "Intelligence Quotient," *Washington Post,* 31 January 1955, 14; "Report on CIA," *New York Times,* 30 June 1955, 24; "Judging Our Intelligence," *Washington Post,* 14 July 1955, 12; "Controls for C.I.A.," *New York Times,* 19 October 1955, 32; "Watchdog for CIA," *Washington Post,* 21 January 1956, 18; "'Watchdog' for C.I.A," *New York Times,* 26 January 1956, 28; "Scrutiny for CIA," *Washington Post,* 11 April 1956, 14.

32. "Mansfield Calls Intelligence Lax," *New York Times,* 18 November 1956, 23; Marquis Childs, "The Middle East Crisis: Failure in Policy," *Washington Post,* 2 November 1956, A12.

33. Barrett, *The CIA and Congress,* 283.

34. Arthur Krock, "Law and Intervention," *New York Times,* 16 July 1958, 8; "Senators Quiz Allen Dulles on Iraq Today," *Washington Post,* 24 July 1958, A15; "C.I.A. Overhauling Demanded by Morse," *New York Times,* 21 July 1958, A2; "For the Record," *National Review,* 2 August 1958, 98; for information on the survey, see Barrett, *The CIA and Congress,* 295.

35. For examples, see Joseph and Stewart Alsop, "We Underestimate the Russians," *Washington Post,* 8 January 1956, E5; Joseph and Stewart Alsop, "The Race We Are Losing to Russia," *Saturday Evening Post,* 28 April 1956, 25, 80–87; Drew Pearson, "U.S. behind Reds in Many Weapons," *Washington Post,* 31 May 1956, 55; "Soviet Lead in Missiles Discounted," *Washington Post,* 18 June 1956, 4.

36. Stewart Alsop, "Sputnik May be ICBM's Eyes," *Washington Post,* 13 October 1957, E5; Stewart Alsop, "The Meaning of Sputnik II," *Washington Post,* 6 November 1957, A15; Matthew Brzezinski, *Red Moon Rising: Sputnik and the Hidden Rivalries That Ignited the Space Age* (New York: Times Books, 2007), 246. Brzezinski explains that the dog, Laika, "suffered a horrific fate akin to being slow-roasted alive in a convection oven."

37. Stewart Alsop, "Molding Intelligence to Policy," *Washington Post,* 19 March 1957, E5; see also Stewart Alsop, "CIA's Work Interred in a Vacuum," 5 January 1958, E5.

38. See, for examples, Allen Dulles, "Remarks," 29 January 1954, Dulles Papers, series 5, box 98, folder 15; Allen Dulles, "C.I.A. and Its Role in Maintaining the National Security," address to the Ladies Auxiliary V.F.W. National Bulletin, Dulles Papers, series 2a, box 61, folder 11; Allen Dulles, "The Challenge of Soviet Power,"

speech, 4 December 1959, in Dulles Papers, series 2a, box 61, folder 18; Allen Dulles, "The Challenge of Soviet Power," speech to National Association of Manufacturers, 64th Congress of American Industry, Waldorf Astoria Hotel, New York, 4 December 1959; "Soviets Closing Output Gap, Allen Dulles Warns U.S.," *New York Times,* 14 November 1959, 1; "Dulles Brands Nikita Boasts Mostly Myths," *Chicago Tribune,* 14 November 1959, 4; Jay Livingstone, "The Soviet Challenge and What We Can Do," *Washington Post,* 20 November 1959, D15.

39. Robert Young, "CIA Chief Sees 'Weakness' in Soviet Rule," *Chicago Tribune,* 15 November 1956, 12; "U.S. Intelligence Chief Fearful of Return by Soviet to Stalinism," *New York Times,* 15 November 1956, 24.

40. L. Britt Snider, *The Agency and the Hill,* 18.

41. See, for example, "Stalinism Dead, C.I.A. Head Says," *New York Times,* 28 November 1956, 6.

42. "Agency Defended by Allen Dulles," *New York Times,* 16 October 1958, 7.

43. Chalmers M. Roberts, "Role of Intelligence," *Washington Post,* 5 February 1958, A6.

44. Russell Baker, "The Other Mr. Dulles—of C.I.A.," *New York Times,* 16 March 1958, 96.

45. John Scali, "The $350 Million-Year CIA Writes Its Own Tight-Mouthed Ticket," *Washington Post,* 29 June 1958, E3.

46. Lyman Kirkpatrick to Stanley Grogan, 15 November 1957, 1, CREST, www .foia.cia.gov/sites/default/files/document_conversions/5829/CIA-RDP80B01676 R003200160011-0.pdf, accessed 30 April 2015.

47. Stanley Grogan to Allen Dulles, 28 June 1955, CREST, www.foia.cia.gov/sites /default/files/document_conversions/5829/CIA-RDP86B00269R000100130094-3 .pdf, accessed 30 April 2015; Daily Staff Meeting, 11 September 1951, CREST, www .foia.cia.gov/sites/default/files/document_conversions/5829/CIA-RDP80B01676 R002300060038-2.pdf, accessed 30 April 2015; [classified] to L. W. White, 17 September 1965, CREST, www.foia.cia.gov/sites/default/files/document_conversions /5829/CIA-RDP80B01676R001700030003-0.pdf, accessed 30 April 2015; Chalmers Roberts to Allen Dulles, 16 April 1963, Dulles Papers, series 5, box 99, folder 6.

48. James Reston to Arthur Hays Sulzberger, memorandum, 19 November 1958, Sulzberger Papers, series I, box 20, folder 15.

49. For details on the CIA's Indonesia activities, see Audrey Kahin and George McT. Kahin, *Subversion as Foreign Policy: The Secret Eisenhower and Dulles Debacle in Indonesia* (1995; repr., Seattle: University of Washington Press, 1997). Kenneth Conboy and James Morrison, *Feet to the Fire: CIA Covert Operations in Indonesia, 1957–1958* (Annapolis: Naval Institute Press, 1999), present a great deal of on-the-ground history. Robert McMahon, "'The Point of No Return': The Eisenhower Administration and Indonesia, 1953–1960," in *The Eisenhower Administration, the Third World, and the Globalization of the Cold War,* ed. Kathryn C. Statler and Andrew L. Johns (Lanham, MD: Rowman and Littlefield, 2006), 75–100, offers a cogent analysis of the delusions under which the Eisenhower administration labored

in Indonesia. Also covering Indonesia in some detail are Robert J. McMahon, *The Limits of Empire: The United States and Southeast Asia since World War II* (New York: Columbia University Press, 1999); Paul F. Gardner, *Shared Hopes, Separate Fears: Fifty Years of U.S.-Indonesia Relations* (Boulder, CO: Westview Press, 1997); Andrew Roadnight, *United States Policy towards Indonesia in the Truman and Eisenhower Years* (New York: Palgrave Macmillan, 2002).

50. McMahon, *Limits of Empire*, 84.

51. For examples, see "Army Officer Takes Over in Sumatra Area," *Chicago Tribune*, 23 December 1956, 9; Percy Wood, "New Sukarno Press Gag Is Sign of Red Aim," *Chicago Tribune*, 11 November 1957, 19; Raymond Cartier, "Why Does the World Hate America," *National Review*, 2 May 1956, 12–13; Francis Burke, "Sukarno: Pro-Soviet Neutral," *National Review*, 22 December 1956, 9; "The Week," *National Review*, 5 January 1957, 4.

52. James Reston to Arthur Hays Sulzberger, 19 November 1958, Sulzberger Papers, series I, box 20, folder 15.

53. "Bad Gamble in Indonesia," *New Republic*, 31 March 1958, 5; "Strict Neutrality Takes Shape," *Nation*, 22 March 1958, 245.

54. Memorandum of Deputies Meeting, 2 August 1957, CREST, www.foia.cia .gov/sites/default/files/document_conversions/5829/CIA-RDP80B01676 R002300220022-1.pdf, accessed 30 April 2015.

55. See, for examples, "The Week," *National Review*, 5 January 1957, 4; "C.I.A. Spending Questioned," *New York Times*, 28 May 1957, 23; George Dixon, "Rep. Whitten and the Hush-Shushers," *Washington Post*, 6 June 1957, A19.

56. "The Week," *National Review*, 14 December 1957, 531.

57. "A Chance to Make Sense," *National Review*, 1 March 1958, 196.

58. "Indonesia: The Mystery Pilots," *Time*, 12 May 1958; "Odds in Indonesia," *New Republic*, 12 May 1958, 4; Harold H. Martin, "The Troubled Islands of Southeast Asia," *Saturday Evening Post*, 3 January 1959, 64.

59. Andrew, *For the President's Eyes Only*, 244. John Eisenhower later reported that his father was quite annoyed at the CIA over Powers's survival. He commented, "The CIA promised that the Russians would never get a U-2 pilot alive. And then they gave the S.O.B. a parachute!" John Eisenhower as quoted in Andrew, *For the President's Eyes Only*, 246.

60. Brzezinski, *Red Moon Rising*, 270.

61. Andrew, *For the President's Eyes Only*, 247.

62. Brzezinski, *Red Moon Rising*, 117–18.

63. Immerman, *The Hidden Hand*, 124.

64. Hanson Baldwin, "Notes on the Problem of Freedom vs. Security," 6 September 1962, NYTCR: Clifton Daniel Papers (hereafter cited as Daniel Papers), box 1, folder 16, New York Public Library; Anthony Lewis, address to the Institute of Journalists, 21 November 1967, Daniel Papers, box 5, folder 35—Lewis, Anthony.

65. "Intelligence Lag Often Laid to U.S.," *New York Times*, 9 May 1960, 9.

66. Russell Baker, "Congress Leaders Question Herter," *New York Times,* 10 May 1960, 1; "Text of Queries on U-2 Incident and Khrushchev's Replies," *New York Times,* 12 May 1960, 4; "Doubts Russ Story," *Chicago Tribune,* 10 May 1960, 3.

67. Henry Howe Ransom, "How Intelligent Is Intelligence," *New York Times,* 22 May 1960, SM26.

68. Hanson Baldwin, "US Timed Flight of U2 to Weather, Not Summit," *New York Times,* 30 May 1960, 1; George Sokolsky, "Espionage Is a Normal Activity," *Washington Post,* 12 May 1960, A27; "Distasteful but Necessary," *Washington Post,* 12 May 1960, A26.

69. Willard Edwards, "Spy Admission Spills a Secret: CIA Has Grown Up," *Chicago Tribune,* 12 May 1960, 6.

70. "Dulles Bares Secret Story of U-2 Spying," *Chicago Tribune,* 1 June 1960, 3; William Moore, "Blame Agency Snarl for U-2 'Weather' Tale," *Chicago Tribune,* 3 June 1960, 3.

71. David Lawrence, "The Right to Fly U-2s," *U.S. News and World Report,* 11 July 1960, 108; George Sokolsky, "The Central Intelligence Agency," *Washington Post,* 14 June 1960, A11; "The Truth about the U-2 and What It Did," *U.S. News and World Report,* 6 June 1960, 54–55; K. S. Giniger, "Chief Spy: The Story of Allen Dulles," *Washington Post,* 3 July 1960, AW4; "Master Spy of the U.S.," *New York Times,* 1 June 1960, 10; Marquis Childs, "How Allen Dulles Tried to Spare Ike," *Washington Post,* 27 May 1960, A16; "Allen Dulles Made U.S. Spying Professional," *Washington Post,* 6 June 1960, B17.

72. Martin Sommers to Stewart Alsop, 20 June 1960, and Stewart Alsop to Sommers, 26 June 1960, both in Alsop Papers, part I, box 30, folder 3; Stewart Alsop to Ben Hibbs, 23 August 1960, and Hibbs to Alsop, 29 August 1960, both in Alsop Papers, part I, box 3, folder 4; Minutes of CIA Deputies' Meeting, 31 March 1960, CREST, www.foia.cia.gov/sites/default/files/document_conversions/5829/CIA-RDP80B01676R002400060076-9.pdf, accessed 30 April 2015.

73. Brzezinski, *Red Moon Rising,* 270.

74. "Setback," New York Times, 23 April 1961, 81; for a rebuttal to Kennedy's call for greater discretion in reporting, see "Secrecy and Security," *Washington Post,* 29 April 1961, A10.

75. "Are We Training Cuban Guerrillas?" *Nation,* 19 November 1960, 378–79.

76. Carleton Beals, "Cuba: Victim or Aggressor?" *Nation,* 23 July 1960, 45–49; Carleton Beals, "Cuba's Invasion Jitters," *Nation,* 12 November 1960, 360–62; Don Dwiggins, "Guatemala's Secret Airstrip," *Nation,* 30 January 1961, 7–9.

77. See, for example, "U.S. Pro-Castro Unit Asks Inquiry on CIA," *New York Times,* 6 January 1961, 3.

78. Herbert L. Matthews to Clifton Daniel, 21 March 1972, Daniel Papers, box 13, folder 7.

79. Paul Kennedy, "U.S. Helps Train an Anti-Castro Force at Secret Guatemalan Air-Ground Base," *New York Times,* 10 January 1961, 1.

80. Karl E. Meyer, "Exiles Unite in Drive to Oust Castro," *Washington Post,* 22 March 1961, A15; Meyer had previously reported from Cuba, and he had secured an interview in 1959 with Che Guevara. In a subsequent story on Guevara, Meyer portrayed Guevara as a Marxist, if not a Communist, and "less malevolent than misinformed" about Stalinism. Meyer explained that Guevara had been in Guatemala when Arbenz was overthrown "in an invasion covertly supported by the United States." This event, Meyer explained, had a definitive influence on Guevara's worldview. See Karl Meyer, "An Interview with El Che," *Washington Post,* 14 November 1959, A6.

81. Harold Martin, "Angry Exiles," *Saturday Evening Post,* 8 April 1961, 19; see also "The Fight against Castro," *New Republic,* 17 April 1961, 3–4. Ben Hibbs to Stewart Alsop, 29 August 1960, Alsop Papers, part I, box 30, folder 4.

82. Nathaniel Gerstenzang to Tad Szulc, 10 August 1959; Szulc to Emanuel Freedman, 28 October 1959; Herbert L. Matthews to Szulc, 17 December 1959, all in Foreign Desk Records, box 90, folder 1; Matthews to Lester Markel, 20 June 1960; Freedman to Turner Catledge, 12 May 1960, both in Foreign Desk Records, box 90, folder 2.

83. Tad Szulc, "*The New York Times* and the Bay of Pigs," *How I Got That Story,* no. 2374, 121–22, Daniel Papers, box 13, folder 7.

84. Ibid.

85. Tad Szulc, "Anti-Castro Units Trained to Fight at Florida Bases," *New York Times,* 7 April 1961, 1.

86. James Reston, *Deadline: A Memoir* (New York: Random House, 1991), 325; Clifton Daniel, "A Footnote to History: The Press and National Security," speech delivered at the World Press Institute, Macalester College, St. Paul, MN, 1 June 1966, 4–5, Daniel Papers, box 13, folder 7.

87. Catledge, *My Life at The Times,* 262.

88. Ibid., 261.

89. Clifton Daniel, "A Footnote to History," 2–5; Daniel to Paul Cowan, 28 February 1970; Daniel to Horace Sutton, 1 February 1972; and Daniel to Herbert L. Matthews, 17 March 1972, all in Daniel Papers, box 13, folder 7.

90. Clifton Daniel, "A Footnote to History," 6–7.

91. Clifton Daniel to Larry Allyn Grissom, 24 November 1969, Daniel Papers, box 13, folder 7.

92. Roberts, *The Washington Post,* 349; Herkin, *The Georgetown Set,* 264.

93. "Operation Cuba," *Nation,* 29 April 1961, 361; "The Fight against Castro," *New Republic,* 17 April 1961, 3–4; "Shooting War in Cuba," *New Republic,* 24 April 1961, 4; "What Went Wrong," *New Republic,* 1 May 1961, 1–4; "Cuba, RIP," *National Review,* 6 May 1961, 269; "Inquest," *National Review,* 3 June 1961, 338.

94. David Lawrence, "The Campaign against the CIA," *Washington Evening Star,* 14 July 1961, Lawrence Papers, series Ia, box 22, folder: CIA; for Cater, see Douglass Cater and Charles Bartlett, "Is All the News Fit to Print?" *Reporter,* 11 May 1961, 23–24; see also Douglass Cater, "News and the Nation's Security," *Reporter,* 6 July 1961, 26–29.

95. For coverage, see John G. Norris, "CIA Expected to Lose Some Top Functions," *Washington Post,* 26 April 1961, A12; Raymond Morley, "Inept Bureaucracy Is Responsible for Cuba," *Los Angeles Times,* 30 April 1961, B5; "Leashing Up the CIA," *New Republic,* 8 May 1961, 3–5; "Washington Whispers," *U.S. News and World Report,* 8 May 1961, 36; "Inside Story of Cuban Fiasco," *U.S. News and World Report,* 8 May 1961, 44–46; "The U.S.A. Can't Afford Another Fiasco in Cuba," *Saturday Evening Post,* 20 May 1961, 10; Warren Rogers, "JFK Expected to Cut Back CIA to Purely Intelligence Op," *Washington Post,* 1 June 1961, A21; "Breaking Up CIA," *New Republic,* 19 June 1961, 1–3; Harry S. Truman, "Limit CIA Role to Intelligence," *Washington Post,* 22 December 1963, A11.

96. Thomas Brady, "Paris Rumors on CIA," *New York Times,* 2 May 1961, 19; Marquis Childs, "Did a CIA Agent See General Challe?" *Washington Post,* 5 May 1961, A16.

4. The Fracture of the 1960s

1. Richard Helms to Burges Green, 18 December 1962, in Richard Helms Papers 1 (hereafter cited as Helms Papers), box 4, folder 23, Georgetown University Special Collections Research Center, Georgetown University Manuscripts, Washington, DC.

2. When exactly the consensus of the Cold War began to break down is a question of some dispute. Tity de Vries places the fissure toward the end of the 1960s, with the 1967 National Student Association scandal, a subject addressed at the end of this chapter. See Tity de Vries, "The 1967 Central Intelligence Agency Scandal: Catalyst in a Transforming Relationship between State and People," *Journal of American History* 98.4 (2012): 1075–92. Though Vries is correct in noting that the Bay of Pigs was still justified by many within the context of the Cold War consensus, the 1967 scandal is better viewed as a culmination of trends that had begun earlier, even before the Bay of Pigs, than as a catalyst. A more accurate picture is provided by Simon Willmetts. Though Willmetts overstates the degree to which previous media coverage was defined by a "complaisant media who acquiesced in the CIA's polite requests for anonymity," he is undoubtedly correct that the post–Bay of Pigs environment was significantly changed. See Simon Willmetts, "The Burgeoning Fissures of Dissent: Allen Dulles and the Selling of the CIA in the Aftermath of the Bay of Pigs," *History* 100.340 (2015): 173.

3. [Classified] to L. K. White, 17 September 1965, 1, CREST, www.foia.cia.gov /sites/default/files/document_conversions/5829/CIA-RDP80B01676R001700030003 -0.pdf, accessed 30 April 2015.

4. The complete list is as follows: Joseph C. Hersch (*Christian Science Monitor,* NBC); Walter Lippmann (*LA Times*); John Scott (*Time*); Joseph Alsop; Wallace Carroll (*NYT* Washington Bureau); Cyrus Sulzberger (*NYT*); Henry Gemill, Philip Geyelin, Louis Kramer (*Wall Street Journal*); Charles Bartlett (Publishers' Newspaper Syndicate); Max S. Johnson (*U.S. News and World Report*); Harry Schwartz

(*NYT*); Bill Shannon (*NYT*); Jess Cook (*Time*); Stewart Alsop (*Saturday Evening Post*); William S. White (United Feature); Chalmers Roberts (*Washington Post*); Murrey Marder (*Washington Post*); Charles J. V. Murphy (*Fortune*); Russell Wiggins and Alfred Friendly (*Washington Post*); Tad Szulc (*NYT*); Katharine Graham (publisher, *Washington Post*). Cline also reported that he had a meeting with *New York Times* editorial chief John Oakes, though he was not listed. See ibid.

5. Ibid., 3–4.

6. Ibid., 4–5.

7. L. K. White to Ray Cline and Sherman Kent, 2 September 1965, CREST, www .foia.cia.gov/sites/default/files/document_conversions/5829/CIA-RDP80B01676 R001700030004-9.pdf, accessed 30 April 2015.

8. "Black Humor . . . New CIA Chief?" *Washington Post,* 6 March 1961, A2; Associated Press, "Intention of Dulles to Retire Confirmed," *Washington Post,* 1 August 1961, A2.

9. Immerman, *The Hidden Hand,* 55.

10. Allen Dulles, notes for second address to students at UCLA, "The Conduct and Control of Secret Intelligence Operations," 7 December 1965, Dulles Papers, series 5, box 110, folder 2.

11. Willmetts, "The Burgeoning Fissures of Dissent," 173.

12. Lawrence Spivak, presenter, *Meet the Press,* 31 December 1961, NBC, transcript in Dulles Papers, series 5, box 99, folder 1; Hanson Baldwin, commentator, "The Hidden Art of Intelligence," *Under Discussion,* 29 March 1964, network unavailable, Dulles Papers, series 5, box 100, folder 1.

13. Willmetts, "The Burgeoning Fissures of Dissent," 180.

14. John Chancellor, host, "The Science of Spying," 4 May 1965, NBC, transcript, 17, Dulles Papers, series 5, box 104, folder 12.

15. Ibid.

16. Allen Dulles to Stewart Alsop, 12 May 1965, Dulles Papers, series 1; box 1, folder 15; in 1967 Dulles attempted to use television again. He proposed a series involving the activities of the CIA to a former subordinate who had gone on to ascend the CBS corporate ladder. Dulles compared the effort to a similar show the FBI had succeeded in getting on air. Dulles did not want the CIA to be an official sponsor, but he hoped to discreetly urge CBS to this position. His effort was not successful. See Allen Dulles to Michael Burke, 28 December 1966, Dulles Papers, series 1, box 10, folder 10.

17. Stewart Alsop to Martin Sommers, 25 September 1961; Alsop to Sommers, 27 September 1961; Alsop to Sommers, 30 September 1961; all in Alsop Papers, part I, box 30, folder 7.

18. The tortuous path to the production of the article is attested by the voluminous correspondence surrounding it. Stewart Alsop to Martin Sommers, 4 December 1961; Robert Sherrod to Stewart Alsop, 6 December 1961, both in Alsop Papers, part I, box 30, folder 7; Alsop to Sommers, 8 January 1962; Sommers to Alsop, 11 January 1962; Alsop to Sommers, 26 January 1962; Alsop to Sommers, 14 March

1962, all in Alsop Papers, part I, box 31, folder 1; Alsop to Sommers 1 May 1962, Alsop Papers, part I, box 31, folder 2; Allen Dulles to Alsop, 28 September 1962, Dulles Papers, series 1, box 1, folder 15; Alsop to William J. Emerson, 5 April 1963, Alsop Papers, part I, box 31, folder 5; Alsop to Dulles, 19 April 1963, Dulles Papers, series 1, box 1, folder 15. A revision by Dulles was also rejected; see Alsop to Allen Dulles, 4 April 1964, Dulles Papers, series 1, box 1, folder 15.

19. Willmetts, "The Burgeoning Fissures of Dissent," 176–78.

20. Allen Dulles, *The Craft of Intelligence* (New York: Harper and Row, 1963), 194.

21. Chalmers M. Roberts, "Dulles Tells of CIA Craft but Buttons Lip on Secrets," *Washington Post,* 9 October 1963, 4; Chalmers Roberts to Allen Dulles, 16 April 1963, Dulles Papers, series 5, box 99, folder 6. For other reviews, see Thomas A. Lane, "The Craft of Objectivity," *National Review,* 24 March 1964, 244–46; Percy B. Mills, "Mr. Dulles Spills the Beans," *New Republic,* 15 February 1964, 21–22.

22. Willmetts, "The Burgeoning Fissures of Dissent," 186.

23. Stewart Alsop expected the Kennedy administration to choose Fowler Hamilton. He learned he was mistaken only when officials in the government began approaching the press to see if reporters knew anything about McCone. Stewart Alsop to Martin Sommers, 11 September 1961, Alsop Papers, part I, box 30, folder 7. Alsop was not the only one to make the mistake. Hamilton's anticipated nomination was reported in several outlets. For example, see "Successor to Dulles," *New Republic,* 7 August 1961, 6–7; Stewart Alsop to Martin Sommers, 27 September 1961, Alsop Papers, part I, box 30, folder 7.

24. "A Top Man for a Top Job," *Los Angeles Times,* 29 September 1961, B4; Robert S. Allen and Paul Scott, "McCone Set to Curb Free Spending by CIA," *Los Angeles Times,* 4 December 1961, B5; "John McCone: Public Servant," *Los Angeles Times,* 17 January 1961, B4; "McCone Given Informal OK as Boss of CIA," *Chicago Tribune,* 19 January 1962, 8; Chalmers Roberts, "McCone Pictures His CIA Job as All-Intelligence Coordinator," *Washington Post,* 19 January 1962, A2; "New CIA Head Vows to Shun Policy Making," *Chicago Tribune,* 22 January 1962, B5; "The CIA's Role," *Washington Post,* 23 January 1962, A16; "The New Chief of Intelligence," *Chicago Tribune,* 27 January 1962, 10.

25. David M. Barrett, "Explaining the First Contested Senate Confirmation of a Director of Central Intelligence: John McCone, the Kennedy White House, the CIA and the Senate, 1962," *Intelligence and National Security* 31.1 (2016): 74–87.

26. For the *New Republic* coverage, see "The Miscasting of McCone," *New Republic,* 9 October 1961, 3–4; "McCone Miscast," *New Republic,* 16 October 1961, 6; "Why John McCone?" *New Republic,* 23 October 1961, 7–8; "McCone on Fallout," *New Republic,* 6 November 1961, 6; "McCone's Confirmation," *New Republic,* 29 January 1962, 7–8; "They Said 'No' to McCone," *New Republic,* 12 February 1962, 15; "McCone's Successor," *New Republic,* 12 December 1966, 4.

27. Barrett, "Explaining the First Contested Senate Confirmation of a Director of Central Intelligence," 85–86.

28. Ibid., 84.

29. Andrew, *For the President's Eyes Only,* 271; Immerman, *The Hidden Hand,* 71.

30. John A. McCone, Memorandum for the Record, 22 November 1961, in Mark J. White, ed., *The Kennedys and Cuba: The Declassified Documentary History* (Chicago: Ivan Dee, 1999), 77; Immerman, *The Hidden Hand,* 72.

31. David Halberstam to Clifton Daniel, 21 October 1963, Daniel Papers, box 4, folder 16.

32. Stewart Alsop, "CIA: The Battle for Secret Power," *Saturday Evening Post,* 27 July 1963, 17; see also Stewart Alsop, "Telegraphing Khrushchev," *Saturday Evening Post,* 7 March 1964, 14.

33. Stewart Alsop to William J. Emerson, 28 April 1963, Alsop Papers, part I, box 31, folder 5. The only other recorded contact between Stewart Alsop and McCone was in October 1963, when Stewart Alsop reported that McCone had angrily denounced Henry Cabot Lodge to him as "very gung ho" to remove Diem. Alsop took this as potentially biased, however, because of a well-known animus McCone harbored against Lodge. See Stewart Alsop to Otto Friedrich, 15 October 1963, Alsop Papers, part I, box 31, folder 6.

34. Lyman B. Kirkpatrick to Executive Secretary, President's Foreign Intelligence Advisory Board, memorandum, 6 August 1963, CREST, www.foia.cia.gov/sites/default/files/document_conversions/5829/CIA-RDP80B01676R003000120037-8.pdf, accessed 30 April 2015.

35. Stanley J. Grogan, Memorandum for the Record, 20 August 1963, 2–3, CREST, www.foia.cia.gov/sites/default/files/document_conversions/5829/CIA-RDP80B01676R001300140020-3.pdf, accessed 30 April 2015.

36. For accounts of U.S. activities in Laos, see Timothy N. Castle, *At War in the Shadow of Vietnam: U.S. Military Aid to the Royal Lao Government, 1955–1975* (New York: Columbia University Press, 1993); Jane Hamilton-Merritt, *Tragic Mountains: The Hmong, the Americans, and the Secret Wars for Laos, 1942–1992* (Bloomington: Indiana University Press, 1993); Roger Warner, *Backfire: The CIA's Secret War in Laos and Its Link to the War in Vietnam* (New York: Simon and Schuster, 1995); Kenneth Conboy and Dale Andrade, *Spies and Commandos: How America Lost the Secret War in North Vietnam* (Lawrence: University Press of Kansas, 2000).

37. Conboy and Andrade, *Spies and Commandos,* viii; Castle, *At War in the Shadow of Vietnam,* 17–19.

38. "The Sword of Damocles," *Nation,* 17 October 1959, 221–22; "Gamble in Laos," *New Republic,* 3 April 1961, 3–4.

39. Keyes Beech, "How Uncle Sam Fumbled in Laos," *Saturday Evening Post,* 22 April 1961, 28.

40. "Fulbright Opposes U.S. Troops for Laos," *New York Times,* 1 May 1961, 4; Arthur Krock, "Practicing Candor as Well as Preaching It," *New York Times,* 2 May 1961, 36; Walter Lippmann, "The Reappraisal," *Washington Post,* 4 May 1961, A15; Lippmann could be contrarian for its own sake, but he was still greatly respected.

See Ronald Steel, *Walter Lippmann and the American Century* (Boston: Little, Brown, 1980), 447; Marquis Childs, "Bungles in Laos Also Laid to CIA," *Washington Post*, 17 May 1961, A16.

41. Castle, *At War in the Shadow of Vietnam*, 43, 76; Warner, *Backfire*, 17.

42. Warner, *Backfire*, 17; Hamilton-Merritt, *Tragic Mountains*, xi.

43. Stanley Karnow, "Laos: The Settlement That Settled Nothing," *Reporter*, 25 April 1963, 6; "The World: Spies Everywhere," *New York Times*, 7 July 1963, E2; "Over the Boarder," *Nation*, 27 April 1964, 405; Denis Warner, "The Catastrophic Non-War in Laos," *Reporter*, 18 June 1964, 21–24; "U.S. Bombing of Red Batteries Puts Souvanna in Middle," *Washington Post*, 15 June 1964, A8; Dennis Warner, "Our Secret War in Laos," *Reporter*, 22 April 1965, 25; Peter Grose, "U.S. Special Forces Pose a Quandary," *New York Times*, 5 October 1964, 5; see also, for example, Peter Braestrup, "Laotian Hill Tribesmen, with American Help, Harass Pro-Reds," *New York Times*, 7 January 1967, 6.

44. "CIA Allegedly Pays Nhu's Troops Despite Leader's Disfavor Here," *Washington Post*, 9 September 1963, A11; "Brother Nhu and the CIA," *Chicago Tribune*, 11 September 1963, 14; "Folly in Vietnam," *New Republic*, 21 September 1963, 6–7; "Our Man in Saigon," *Progressive*, October 1963, 6–7; Donald J. May, "Secrecy Cloaks CIA's Role in Viet Nam," *Chicago Tribune*, 27 October 1963, A2.

45. Ruth Leacock, *Requiem for Revolution: The United States and Brazil, 1961–1969* (Kent, OH: Kent State University Press, 1990). The CIA knew the coup was coming; see cable, 30 March 1964, National Security archive, www2.gwu .edu/~nsarchiv/NSAEBB/NSAEBB118/bz04.pdf; National Security Archive, "Brazil Marks 40th Anniversary of Military Coup," www2.gwu.edu/~nsarchiv/NSAEBB /NSAEBB118/index.htm#2; see also Ambassador Gordon to Dean Rusk et al., cable, 29 March 1964, www2.gwu.edu/~nsarchiv/NSAEBB/NSAEBB118/bz03 .pdf; Arthur Krock, "A Familiar Lesson Is Disregarded Again," *New York Times*, 7 April 1964, 34; "Wide Open Diplomacy," *New York Times*, 7 April 1964, 34; "Seven Days in April," *National Review*, 21 April 1964, 309.

46. For an extensive but not exhaustive list of examples from the end of the Bay of Pigs until a flurry of coverage surrounding a book released in 1964 on the CIA, see "CIA Watchdog," *New Republic*, 10 July 1961, 7; Irving L. Horowitz, "Nonwar and the Constitution," *Nation*, 9 June 1962, 513–15; "Charge CIA Has a 'Monopoly' on Vital Information," *Washington Post*, 7 September 1962, B5; "CIA Needs Uncovering, Justice Douglas Says," *Washington Post*, 14 December 1962, A7; Richard L. Lyons, "Congressmen Asks Watchdog Group on CIA," *Washington Post*, 28 February 1963, A11; "Slain Yanks Hired by CIA, Says Reporter," *Chicago Tribune*, 6 March 1963, 3; "CIA and Congressional 'Watchdogs,'" *Los Angeles Times*, 8 November 1963, A4; Jack Raymond, "Espionage: It Plays an Important Role in the Cold War," *New York Times*, 2 June 1963, 160; "Who's Spying for Whom," *U.S. News and World Report*, 29 July 1963, 54–55; Hanson Baldwin, "The Growing Risks of Bureaucratic Intelligence," *Reporter*, 15 August 1963, 48–50; "U.S. Intelligence: Is It Good Enough?" *U.S. News and World Report*, 9 September 1963, 66–67; "A Watchdog for the CIA," *Progressive*,

October 1963, 7–9; Joseph Hearst, "Special Retirement Plan Voted for CIA Employees," *Chicago Tribune,* 31 October 1963, A4; "CIA Is Misunderstood, Says Dulles," *Washington Post,* 10 November 1963, A7; Stephen S. Rosenfield, "Soviet Economic Growth Down Sharply, CIA Says," *Washington Post,* 10 January 1964, A8; Henry J. Taylor, "CIA 'Completely Off Its Rocker' in 'Guessing' on Soviet Economy," *Los Angeles Times,* 15 January 1964, A5; Henry J. Taylor, "Trouble in Panama Again Finds CIA Taken by Complete Surprise," *Los Angeles Times,* 17 January 1964, A5; Jules Dubois, "Report from Latin America; Canal Crisis Underscores Failure of U.S. Intelligence," *Chicago Tribune,* 9 February 1964, 12; "CIA-Baiting," *National Review,* 10 March 1964, 185–86; Norman C. Cornish, "Bolton Says People Do Not Trust CIA," *Washington Post,* 22 March 1964, A9; Murrey Marder, "Release of CIA Report Has Political Overtones," *Washington Post,* 23 August 1964, A27.

47. Fred Cook, *Maverick: Fifty Years of Investigative Reporting* (New York: G. P. Putnam's Sons, 1984), 256. Cook was a former writer of the *World Telegram Sun.* He had previously exposed corruption in New York City public services, but he left the paper after his writing partner falsely claimed to have been offered a bribe to stop reporting and Cook did not tell his editor that his partner's claim was a lie.

48. For the two-edged sword comment, see Fred Cook, "The CIA," *Nation,* 24 June 1961, 529–72; for criticism of the Dulles brothers, see Cook, "The CIA," 530; for Guatemalan leaks, see Cook, "The CIA," 532; emphasis added.

49. Ibid., 570.

50. Saunders, *The Cultural Cold War,* 81–84, 129, 259, 293.

51. Hughes Rudd, "My Escape from the CIA," *Harper's Magazine,* October 1961, 45. That December, other references to the CIA's culture operations appeared, such as a reported that John McCone demanded a report from Cord Meyer, who ran the CIA's International Organizations division at the time, on the use of unvouchered funds to support socialists abroad. See Robert S. Allen and Paul Scott, "McCone Set to Curb Free Spending by CIA."

52. Eugene McCarthy, "The CIA Is Getting Out of Hand," *Saturday Evening Post,* 4 January 1964, 6, 10.

53. Harry Howe Ransom, *Can American Democracy Survive the Cold War?* (Garden City, NY: Anchor Books, 1964), 168.

54. David Wise and Thomas B. Ross, *The Invisible Government* (New York: Random House, 1964).

55. Stewart Alsop, "Hogwash about the CIA," *Saturday Evening Post,* 15 February 1964, 15; Alsop sent his rebuttal to Helms because of their friendship. Stewart Alsop to Richard Helms, 6 February 1964, Helms Papers, part I, box 4, folder 30. Allen Dulles appreciated Alsop's later rebuttal to Ross and Wise, thanking him for his contribution to "the cause of decency and sanity with regard to the CIA." Allen Dulles to Alsop, Dulles Papers, 12 May 1965, series 1, box 1, folder 15; William F. Buckley, "Hate CIA Enterprise," *National Review,* 30 June 1964, 541.

56. Harry Howe Ransom, "'Top of the Iceberg' View of CIA No News in Kremlin," *Washington Post,* 24 June 1964, A4.

57. Marquis Childs, "Issue of Secrecy: Books on the CIA," *Washington Post*, 20 May 1964, A18; Gilbert A. Harrison, "The Secret News That's Fit to Print: I. That Massive, Hidden Apparatus," and T. R. Fehrenbach, "The Secret News That's Fit to Print: II. CIA and the Cuban Invasion," both in *New Republic*, 27 June 1964, 19–22.

58. John McCone to Robert D. Loomis, 5 May 1964, CREST, www.foia.cia.gov/document/cia-rdp80b01676r001300140020-3, accessed 30 April 2015; the CIA compiled a time line of events to document CIA interactions with Ross and Wise and defend themselves from charges of cooperation. See Paul M. Chrétien, Memorandum for the Director, 4 May 1964, CREST, www.foia.cia.gov/sites/default/files/document_conversions/5829/CIA-RDP80B01676R001300140026-7.pdf, accessed 30 April 2015; "CIA Attempt to Censor Spy Book Charged," *Chicago Tribune*, 10 June 1964, 4; "CIA Chiefs Reported Trying to Stifle Book," *Los Angeles Times*, 10 June 1964, 3.

59. Morton Mintz, "Hearing Looks into CIA Role in Tax Probe Charity," *Washington Post*, 1 September 1964, A13. Within the nonprofit community, many suspected CIA involvement. Victor Reuther of the AFL-CIO, Walter Reuther's brother, also hinted at CIA involvement in an interview with the *Los Angeles Times*. See Wilford, *Mighty Wurlitzer*, 236, 238.

60. Dan Kurzman, "Lovestone's Foreign Aid Program Bolsters US Foreign Policy," *Washington Post*, 2 February 1966, A6. See also Harry Bernstein, "AFL-CIO Unit Accused of 'Snooping' Abroad," *Los Angeles Times*, 22 May 1966, G20.

61. "MSU Says It Ousted CIA Aides," *Washington Post*, 14 April 1966, 7; "University Aides Explain CIA Tie," *New York Times*, 15 April 1966, 11; "Project 'Cover' Use by CIA is Attacked," *Washington Post*, 17 April 1966, A6; "Inquiry to Study CIA Link to College's Vietnam Work," *New York Times*, 16 April 1966, 7; "Senator Asks Ban on Schools as Cover for CIA Operations," *New York Times*, 17 April 1966, 29; "MIT Center Gets Aid from the CIA," *New York Times*, 18 April 1966, 4; "Sen. Harris to Check CIA Activity in University Research Abroad," *New York Times*, 19 April 1966, A3; "Saltonstall Denies Clandestine Links of CIA and School," *New York Times*, 19 April 1966, 3; Walter Rugaber, "Michigan State Defends Project," *New York Times*, 23 April 1966, 4; "Unaware of CIA, MSU Says," *Washington Post*, 23 April 1966, A8; Fred A. Hechinger, "Lessons of the MSU Affairs," *New York Times*, 24 April 1966, E9.

62. James Reston to Clifton Daniel, 8 July 1964, Daniel Papers, box 12, folder 7.

63. Ibid.

64. Clifton Daniel to James Reston, 9 July 1964, Daniel Papers, box 12, folder 7.

65. Aldrich, "American Journalism and the Landscape of Secrecy," 201–5.

66. To distinguish between the two Arthur Sulzbergers, I will refer to the younger Sulzberger as Punch Sulzberger.

67. In World War II, Punch served as a staff officer for MacArthur; according to Hanson Baldwin, this posting was a result of strings pulled by Arthur Sulzberger.

See Hanson Baldwin to Robert Sherrod, 23 September 1975, Baldwin Papers, box 8, folder 18. In the Korean War, Punch served as a public relations officer for the Marine Corps.

68. Tom Wicker, *On Press* (New York: Viking Press, 1978), 43, 69–70.

69. Ibid., 5.

70. Ibid., 212.

71. Tom Wicker to Harrison Salisbury, 11 January 1965, NYTCR: Tom Wicker Papers (hereafter cited as Wicker Papers), series I, box 7, folder 4, New York Public Library, Manuscripts and Archives Division.

72. Vries, "The 1967 Central Intelligence Agency Scandal," 1080.

73. Wicker, *On Press,* 17.

74. Catledge, *My Life and The Times,* 288.

75. Harrison Salisbury to Henry Tanner, 15 September 1965, Daniel Papers, box 12, folder 7; Salisbury's letter contained a request from Wicker. The letter noted that other, similar notes were sent to Peter Braestrup, W. G. Blair, Hedrick Smith, David Halberstam, Peter Grose, Seymour Topping, Tad Szulc, Paul Kennedy, Juan de Onis, and Paul Hofmann, among others. Daniel also reported his impressions on the CIA despite not being included as a recipient of Wicker's request. Daniel told Wicker that, according to his sources in the State Department, the CIA was almost as big as State, and it had no check on its activities and expenditures. In at least twenty capitals, the CIA representatives were more important than the State Department. See Clifton Daniel to Tom Wicker, 18 October 1965, Daniel Papers, box 12, folder 7.

76. Tom Wicker to Harrison Salisbury, 15 December 1965, Wicker Papers, series I, box 7, folder 4.

77. Catledge, *My Life and The Times,* 289; Clifton Daniel, oral history interview by Susan Dryfoos, 13 June 1983, 3, NYTCR: Oral History Files (hereafter cited as Oral History Files), box 3, folder 4; Wicker assured McCone that the inaccuracies McCone noticed would be corrected, and he thanked him for his aid; see Tom Wicker to John McCone, 24 March 1966, Helms Papers, part I, box 5, folder 14; McCone later reiterated his belief that the series should not have been run, and he refused a request that his participation in the series be acknowledged; see Clifton Daniel to John McCone, 23 January 1967; McCone to Daniel, 27 January 1967, both in Daniel Papers, box 12, folder 7.

78. Catledge, *My Life and The Times,* 290.

79. Tom Wicker, John Finney, Max Frankel, and E. W. Kenworthy, "C.I.A.: Maker of Policy, or Tool?" 25 April 1966, 1. The article notes that, in addition to Wicker, Finney, Frankel, and Kenworthy, a number of other, unnamed reporters were involved in the production of the series.

80. Ibid., 20.

81. Ibid.

82. Tom Wicker et al., "How C.I.A. Put 'Instant Air Force' into Congo," *New York Times,* 26 April 1966, 1.

83. Tom Wicker et al., "Electronic Prying Grows," *New York Times,* 27 April 1966, 1.

84. Tom Wicker et al., "C.I.A. Operations: A Plot Scuttled," *New York Times,* 28 April 1966, 1; Tom Wicker et al., "The C.I.A.: Qualities of Director Viewed as Chief Rein," *New York Times,* 29 April 1966, 1.

85. Nicholas Nabokov to Editor, *New York Times,* 30 April 1966, Daniel Papers, box 12, folder 7; Saunders, *The Cultural Cold War,* 108.

86. Anthony Lewis to Clifton Daniel, 1 May 1966; Harrison Salisbury to Daniel, 2 May 1966; Salisbury to Daniel, 3 May 1966, all in Daniel Papers, box 12, folder 7.

87. Harrison Salisbury to Clifton Daniel, 20 June 1966, Daniel Papers, box 7, folder 5.

88. Richard Helms to Arthur Ochs Sulzberger, 26 May 1966, Helms Papers, part I, box 5, folder 15.

89. Harrison Salisbury to Clifton Daniel, 20 June 1966, 1.

90. Robert Sherrill, "The Beneficent CIA," *Nation,* 9 May 1966, 542–44; James Burnham, "The Not So Secret Service," *National Review,* 12 July 1966, 4; David Lawrence, "The CIA and American Interests," *Washington Evening Star,* 3 May 1966, Lawrence Papers, series Ia, box 22, folder: CIA.

91. Wilford, *The Mighty Wurlitzer,* 239; For information on Eugene Groves and the decision to announce before the *Ramparts* article came out, see Wilford, *Mighty Wurlitzer,* 240; Wilford provides the best account of the *Ramparts* flap to date. For one of the earlier articles, see Andrew Glass, "Foundation Cited as Conduit of CIA finance," *Washington Post,* 16 February 1967, A5.

92. William S. White, "Unfair to CIA," *Washington Post,* 18 February 1967, A13; James Reston, "The Intellectual War," *New York Times,* 17 February 1967, 33; David Lawrence, "The CIA-Students Controversy," *Washington Evening Star,* 16 February 1967, Lawrence Papers, series Ia, box 24, folder: CIA; Gloria Steinem, who worked with the NSA as a student, would not write an article, but her defense of the CIA was covered in Robert G. Kaiser, "Work of CIA with Youths at Festivals Is Defended," *Washington Post,* 18 February 1967, A4; "March of the News: Why the CIA Gave Money to U.S. College Students," *U.S. News and World Report,* 27 February 1967, 10; "Watching the CIA at Work around the Globe," *U.S .News and World Report,* 6 March 1967, 28–29; "CIA: Other Side of the Story—What Reds Are Doing," *U.S. News and World Report,* 13 March 1967, 96–98; "CIA Chickens Come Home to Roost," *National Review,* 3 March 1967, 230–32; Cato, "Focus on Washington," *National Review,* 7 March 1967, 231; James Burnham, "Notes on the CIA in Shambles," *National Review,* 21 March 1967, 294; "The Ramparts Need Watching," *National Review,* 18 April 1967, 393–95.

93. For examples, see "Clumsy Cupidity," *Washington Post,* 15 February 1967, A18; "Kiss of Death," *New York Times,* 16 February 1967, A24; "The Eager Victim," *Washington Post,* 19 February 1967, E6; "Subversion by the CIA," *New York Times,* 20 February 1967, 36; Ernest Conine, "The CIA's Fingers Should Shun the Student

Pie," *Los Angeles Times,* 22 February 1967, A5; "CIA Stooges," *New Republic,* 25 February 1967, 6. For other articles, see "Playing It Straight," *New Republic,* 4 March 1967, 5–9; "Gilt-Edged Sword," *New Republic,* 11 March 1967, 5–6.

94. Stephen S. Rosenfield, "Is the CIA a Culprit or Fall Guy?" *Washington Post,* 19 February 1967, E1; Drew Pearson and Jack Anderson, "Why Public Is in the Dark about CIA," *Washington Post,* 22 February 1967, F11; Joseph Kraft, "The CIA Fuss," *Washington Post,* 24 February 1967, A19; John Chamberlain, "The End of the CIA Era," *Washington Post,* 27 February 1967, A18; Lewis S. Feuer, "Elite of the Alienated," *New York Times,* 26 March 1967, 202. On labor, see Drew Pearson and Jack Anderson, "CIA Figures in Reuther-Meany Rift," *Washington Post,* 24 February 1967, D15.

95. E. W. Kenworthy, "Hobby Foundations of Houston Affirms C.I.A. Tie," *New York Times,* 21 February 1967, 32; Richard Harwood, "O What a Tangled Web the CIA Wove," *Washington Post,* 26 February 1967, E1; Andrew J. Glass, "Foundations Fail to File Reports," *Washington Post,* 21 February 1967, A4; Don Irwin, "Web of CIA Subsidies Linked to Foundations," *Los Angeles Times,* 18 February 1967, 9. See also Ben A. Franklin, "US Eyes Tax Data of Student Group," *New York Times,* 22 February 1967, 17; Don Irwin and Vincent J. Burke, "21 Foundations, Union Got Money from CIA," *Los Angeles Times,* 26 February 1967, G3.

96. "A Hidden Liberal: Cord Meyer, Jr." *New York Times,* 30 March 1967, 30; Wilford, *Mighty Wurlitzer,* 242; "Berlin Students Ask CIA Inquiry," *New York Times,* 22 February 1967, 17; Warren Unna, "Uproar over CIA Imperils Fund's Work in India," *Washington Post,* 3 March 1967, A3; Richard A. Lester to Graduate Program of the Woodrow Wilson School, 2 May 1967, Helms Papers, part I, box 7, folder 5/1967. Helms wrote to a Princeton trustee to object to the policy. See Richard Helms to John N. Irwin, 15 May 1967, Helms Papers, part I, box 7, folder 5/1967.

97. Thomas Braden, "I'm Glad the CIA Is 'Immoral,'" *Saturday Evening Post,* 20 May 1967, 10, 12–14.

98. Alexander Werth, "Literary Bay of Pigs," *Nation,* 5 June 1967, 7–10.

99. Harold Keen, "Braden Reveals He Set Up CIA Aid to Students, Union," *Los Angeles Times,* 7 May 1967, D12A; Henry Bernstein, "Reuther Admits Using CIA Aid, Calls Braden Claim Misleading," *Los Angeles Times,* 8 May 1967, 3.

100. Cord Meyer to Allen W. Dulles, 1 May 1967; Joan Braden to Dulles, June 1967 (no day given); Dulles to Joan Braden, 20 June 1967; Isaac Don Levin to Dulles, 13 July 1967; Dulles to Levin, 28 July 1967, all in Dulles Papers, section 1, box 8, folder 27. Braden would, however, speak in very complimentary terms about Dulles after his death, in January 1969. See transcript of *Newsnight,* same folder.

101. Saunders, *The Cultural Cold War,* 399–403.

102. Richard Helms to Tom Braden, 22 February 1967, Helms Papers, part I, box 6, folder 2/1967.

103. Richard Helms to Katharine Graham, 29 April 1967, Helms Papers, part I, box 7, folder 4/1967; Graham to Helms, 17 May 1967, Helms Papers, part I, box 7, folder 5/1967.

104. Richard Helms to Katharine Graham, 29 April 1967.

105. Herkin, *The Georgetown Set,* 347–48.

106. Christopher Moran, "Turning against the CIA: Whistleblowers during the Time of Troubles," *History* 100.340 (2015), 253–54.

107. Edward L. Katzenbach, "Ideas—A New Defense Industry," *Reporter,* 2 March 1961, 17; Saunders, *The Cultural Cold War,* 406.

108. Ransom, *The Intelligence Establishment,* 179.

109. Seymour Topping to all foreign correspondents, 18 February 1967, Daniel Papers, box 12, folder 7.

110. Henry Tanner to Seymour Topping, 18 February 1967, Foreign Desk Records, box 118, folder 14.

111. Richard Johnson to Seymour Topping, 20 February 1967; Paul Hofmann to Topping, 21 February 1967; Al Friends to Foreign Desk, 21 February 1967; Barnard Collier to Seymour Topping, 28 February 1967; Walter Sullivan to Topping, 21 February 1967; Peter Grose to Topping, 20 February 1967, all in Foreign Desk Records, box 118, folder 14.

112. Paul Montgomery to Seymour Topping, 19 February 1967; Richard Mooney to Topping, 19 February 1967; Malcolm Browne to Seymour Topping, 17 February 1967; Collier to Seymour Topping, 28 February 1967; Tillman Durdin to Topping, 18 February 1967, all in Foreign Desk Records, box 118, folder 14.

113. Edward Morrow to Seymour Topping, 19 February 1967, Foreign Desk Records, box 118, folder 14.

114. Wilford, *Mighty Wurlitzer,* 244, 248.

115. Paget, *Patriotic Betrayal,* 388.

5. The Clash of Intelligence Advocates and Critics

1. Taylor Branch, "The Censors of Bumbledom," *Harper's,* January 1974, 56.

2. Ibid., 63.

3. Hanson Baldwin, "Wanted: An American Military Policy," *Harper's Magazine,* May 1946.

4. Richard Helms to Hugh Sidey, 9 November 1976, Helms Papers, part 3, box 1, folder 48. Helms was especially glad that some of his interview notes had proven useful to John Toland in Toland's biography of Hitler.

5. Richard Helms and William Hood, *A Look over My Shoulder: A Life in the Central Intelligence Agency* (New York: Random House, 2003).

6. Helms quoted in Andrew, *For the President's Eyes Only,* 275.

7. Peter H. Fenn, "Church Committee Oral History, 1975–1976," Oral History Interviews, Senate Historical Office, Washington, DC, 130.

8. Bryce Nelson, "Helms Soothes Irate Senators in 'Salutary' 2-Hour Session," *Washington Post,* 30 July 1966, A2.

9. Richard Helms to Robert Van Roijen, 16 February 1966, Helms Papers, part I, folder 14; Van Roijen had written to the *New Republic* to protest an article by Henry Howe Ransom that criticized the CIA. For another example, Helms thanked

McCone after McCone cooperated with the *New York Times* to mitigate damage to the CIA from the *Times* April 1966 series on the agency. Helms assured McCone that "the cause could not have had a more effective advocate." Richard Helms to John McCone, 14 March 1966, Helms Papers, part I, box 5, folder 14.

10. Cyrus L. Sulzberger to Richard Helms, 3 July 1965, and Helms to Sulzberger, 14 February 1966, both in Helms Papers, part I, box 5, folder 4. Cyrus L. Sulzberger to Richard Helms, 3 March 1966, and Sulzberger to Helms, 3 March 1966, both in Helms Papers, part I, box 5, folder 14; Richard Helms to Cyrus L. Sulzberger, 2 June 1969, Helms Papers, part I, box 7, folder 6/1969.

11. "Jim" (last name unknown) to Cord Meyer, Meyer Papers, box 1 folder 1969; Cord Meyer to Elizabeth Brown, 24 November 1972, Meyer Papers, box 2, folder 1972.

12. Benjamin Welles to Richard Helms, 9 October 1969, and Helms to Welles, 13 October 1969, both in Helms Papers, part I, box 7, folder 10/1969.

13. John McCone to Richard Helms, 20 November 1969, Helms Papers, part I, box 7, folder 11/1969.

14. Benjamin Welles, "H-L-S of the C.I.A.," *New York Times,* 18 April 1971.

15. Benjamin Welles to Abraham Rosenthal, 3 December 1970, Rosenthal Papers, box 46, folder 2.

16. Benjamin Welles to Abraham Rosenthal, 7 December 1970, Rosenthal Papers, box 46, folder 2.

17. Hanson W. Baldwin, oral history interview by John T. Mason, 6 October 1975, 649, in Baldwin Papers, box 15.

18. Arthur Ochs Sulzberger to Richard Helms, 21 October 1969, Helms Papers, part I, box 7, folder 10/1969.

19. Joseph Treaster interviewed in "Censorship," 1970, 18–19, Oral History Files, box 12, folder 2.

20. Tom Wicker, "The Greening of the Press," *Columbia Journalism Review,* May/June 1971, 12, Rosenthal Papers, box 46, folder 23.

21. Robert Miraldi, *Seymour Hersh: Scoop Artist* (Lincoln: University of Nebraska Press, 2013), 132.

22. Clifton Daniel to Turner Catledge, 15 June 1966, Daniel Papers, box 2, folder 21.

23. Daniel, Turner, and Rosenthal proposed that Wicker shift to being a columnist, and James Greenfield would take over the Washington Bureau. Punch Sulzberger initially agreed to make the change, but he reversed himself following the threats of Reston, Wicker, and much of the Washington Bureau to resign. The story is detailed in Paul H. Weaver, "The New Fact of the New York Times," *New York Magazine,* n.d., Rosenthal Papers, box 51, folder 17.

24. Abraham Rosenthal to Arthur Ochs Sulzberger, 26 May 1971, Rosenthal Papers, box 46, folder 23.

25. Henry Kissinger to H. R. Haldeman, 26 May 1970, telecon, in the Digital National Security Archive, George Washington University (hereafter cited as

DNSA); Memorandum for the Record, 15 October 1969, of meeting with members of the *Washington Post,* DNSA.

26. "The 'Forgotten' Conflict in Laos Goes into a New Offensive Phase," *New York Times,* 31 January 1969, 3; "Laos Denies U.S. Has Combat Role," *New York Times,* 23 September 1969, 9; Murray Sayle, "Low Profile Laos War Murky for Both Sides," *Los Angeles Times,* 28 September 1969, E4; "The War: Smoke Screen over U.S. Involvement in Laos," *New York Times,* 19 October 1969, E2; Jack Foisie, "U.S.-Financed War in Laos a Game of Numbers and Graft," *Los Angeles Times,* 30 October 1969, 1.

27. T. D. Allman, "For Americans in War Zone, Training Laotians Is Key Duty," *New York Times,* 19 October 1969, 24; Henry Kamm, "Meo Generals Lead Tribesmen in War with Communists in Laos," *New York Times,* 27 October 1969, 3; Henry Kamm, "Clandestine Laotian Army Turned Tide in Vital Region," *New York Times,* 28 October 1969, 14.

28. T. D. Allman, "'Secret' U.S.-Run Base Deep in Laos Seems Placid," *New York Times,* 6 June 1970, 3.

29. "U.S. Aids Rate Laos above Viet, Fulbright Says," *Chicago Tribune,* 4 March 1970, A3; see also "CIA Role in Laos Is Cited," *Washington Post,* 9 March 1970, A2; Richard Halloran, "Fulbright Reports CIA Confirms Use of Laos Aid Cover," *New York Times,* 14 March 1970, 11; James Reston, "Washington: The Hidden War in Laos," *New York Times,* 35; Max Frankel, "The High Stakes in Laos," *New York Times,* 4 March 1970, 5; James Yuenger and Fred Farrar, "Cost of 'Secret' War in Laos Is Secret Well-Kept by Nixon," *Chicago Tribune,* 7 March 1970, 2; "Laos: Battle for the Plain," *Time,* 2 March 1970.

30. "CIA's Testimony of Laos: (Deleted)," *Washington Post,* 20 April 1970, A7.

31. Don Irwin, "U.S. Aims in Laos Outlined by Nixon," *Los Angeles Times,* 7 March 1970, 1; Jack Foisie, "Laos AID Mission Used as CIA Cover," *Los Angeles Times,* 10 March 1970, 1; Robert Shaplen, "Our Involvement in Laos," *Foreign Affairs,* April 1970, 482. See also an article published the next year, Roland A. Paul, "Laos: Anatomy of an American Involvement," *Foreign Affairs,* April 1971. "CIA Admits Training Irregulars in Laos," *Washington Post,* 14 September 1971, A16; "CIA-Trained Cambodia Troops Killed in Laos," *Los Angeles Times,* 29 July 1971, 11; "TRB from Washington," *New Republic,* 20 March 1972; Fred Branfman, "America's Secret War," *Progressive,* June 1972.

32. Alfred W. McCoy, "Flowers of Evil: The CIA and the Heroin Trade," *Harper's,* July 1972, 47–53; "Commentary: CIA vs. Harper's," *Harper's,* October 1972, 116–21.

33. "CIA Remains Silent," *New York Times,* 16 August 1969, 10; see also "CIA Removal of Beret Case Witness Told," *Los Angeles Times,* 18 August 1969, 22.

34. "Nation: Green Berets on Trial," *Time,* 22 August 1969.

35. Frank McCulloch, "Colonel Robert Rheault, Ex-Green Beret," *Life,* 14 November 1969.

36. L. Fletcher Prouty, "Green Berets and the CIA," *New Republic,* 23 August 1969, 9. Prouty would eventually prove himself unreliable and badly embarrass

himself. Prouty reported to Daniel Schorr during the Church and Pike Committees that Alexander Butterfield, the White House aide who revealed the existence of Nixon's tapes to federal investigators, was in fact a CIA officer spying on the White House for the CIA. The implication of the story was, of course, that the CIA had deliberately set about causing Nixon's downfall. Prouty's story, however, fell apart quickly under closer examination. See Kathryn S. Olmsted, *Challenging the Secret Government: The Post-Watergate Investigations of the CIA and FBI* (Chapel Hill: University of North Carolina Press, 1996), 77–79; William Beecher, "Green Berets: Harsh Light in Dark Places," *New York Times,* 28 September 1969, E2.

37. Matt Schudel, "Robert B. Rheault, Green Beret Commander in Vietnam Scandal, Dies at 87," *Washington Post,* 26 October 2013, www.washingtonpost .com/national/robert-b-rheault-green-beret-commander-in-vietnam-scandal-dies -at-87/2013/10/26/f2b47cb6-3dad-11e3-b7ba-503fb5822c3e_story.html, accessed 4 November 2014.

38. Joseph B. Treaster, "Behind the Intelligence Curtain," *New York Times,* 1 October 1969, 2.

39. "The Special Forces Eight," *Washington Post,* 3 October 1969, A18.

40. Robert Boddington to Ray Cline, 28 June 1974, Ray S. Cline Papers, Library of Congress, Manuscript Division, Washington, DC (hereafter cited as Cline Papers), part 1: Office File, box 1, folder 7—Interviews, June 25, 1974, to Sept. 16, 1975.

41. George Lardner notes re: 1972 Helms Anti-Assassination Directive, Lardner Papers, box 15, folder 2—CIA—Assassination Plots: Notes—undated.

42. Treaster, "Behind the Intelligence Curtain." See also Terence Smith, "The C.I.A.-Planned Drive on Officials of Vietcong Is Said to Be Failing," *New York Times,* 19 August 1969, 12.

43. See, for example, "All Honorable Men," *Progressive,* July 1971, 9.

44. Felix Belair, "US Aide Defends Pacification Program in Vietnam Despite Killings of Civilians," *New York Times,* 20 July 1971, 2; Iver Peterson, "The World: This 'Phoenix' Is a Bird of Death," *New York Times,* 25 July 1971, E2.

45. Don Irwin, "U.S. Pacification Chief Defends Viet Program," *Los Angeles Times,* 18 February 1970, 6.

46. James Greenfield, Gerald Gold, and Allen Siegel, oral history interview by Clifton Daniel, 28 July 1971, in Oral History Files, box 13, folder 11.

47. Salisbury, *Without Fear or Favor,* 315–18.

48. "CIA Warning on Vietnam," *Progressive,* December 1970.

49. David E. Rosenbaum, "Cooper Acts to Force CIA to Report to Congress," *New York Times,* 8 July 1971, 14; "Congress Turns to the CIA," *Washington Post,* 21 July 1971, A20; "Controlling the CIA," *New York Times,* 19 July 1971, 24.

50. Frank Starr, "Back to the Real Goals of the CIA," *Chicago Tribune,* 10 January 1975, A2.

51. Abraham Rosenthal to John Oakes, 8 November 1971, Rosenthal Papers, box 66, folder 23.

52. Abraham Rosenthal, "The Growing Crisis of Press Confidentiality and Its Impact of Foreign Policy," address to the CFR, 27 December 1972, CFR Records, series 4, box 478, folder 3.

53. Arthur Ochs Sulzberger to Abraham Rosenthal, 12 December 1971, Rosenthal Papers, box 42, folder 9.

54. Quoted in Immerman, *The Hidden Hand,* 90.

55. Ibid., 90–91.

56. See, for example, Joseph Novitski, "Military Leader Dies in Santiago," *New York Times,* 26 October 1970, 17.

57. William F. Buckley, "Closing the Curtain," *National Review,* 9 March 1971, 276, 278.

58. Graham Greene, "Chile: The Dangerous Edge," *Harper's,* March 1972, 32.

59. Anderson and Nixon possessed a long-standing, mutual hatred of one another. According to G. Gordon Liddy and E. Howard Hunt, admittedly not the most reliable of sources, Anderson was such a thorn in Nixon's side that plans were prepared to kill him. See Mark A. Felt, *Poisoning the Press: Richard Nixon, Jack Anderson, and the Rise of Washington's Scandal Culture* (New York: Farrar, Straus and Giroux, 2010), 282–87.

60. Jack Anderson, "Memos Bare ITT Try for Chile Coup," *Washington Post,* 22 March 1972, B13; Jack Anderson, "ITT Pledged Millions to Stop Allende," *Washington Post,* 22 March 1972, C23.

61. "ITT: And Now Chile," *Washington Post,* 22 March 1972, A22; Philip Warden, "ITT Denies Trying to Defeat Allende in Chilean Election," *Chicago Tribune,* 22 March 1972, A12; Tad Szulc, "A Private Little Foreign Policy," *New York Times,* 26 March 1972, E4; "The Nation: The Worse Things Get, the Better," *Time,* 9 April 1972. See also "ITT: The Real Scandal," *Progressive,* May 1972, and Dale L. Johnson, John Pollock, and Jane Sweeney, "ITT and the CIA: The Making of a Foreign Policy," *Progressive,* May 1972.

62. "Chilean Notes," *National Review,* 28 April 1972; "ITT and Chile," *Chicago Tribune,* 29 March 1973, 12.

63. Victor Marchetti, "CIA: The President's Loyal Tool," *Nation,* 3 April 1972, 430.

64. Tad Szulc, "US and ITT in Chile," *New Republic,* 30 June 1973, 21.

65. Stephen Kinzer, *Overthrow: America's Century of Regime Change from Hawaii to Iraq* (New York: Times Books, 2006), 190–91.

66. Israel Shenker, "Power Eluded Allende, Then Slipped from His Grasp," *New York Times,* 12 September 1973, 16; "US Had Warning of Coup, Aides Say," *New York Times,* 13 September 1973, 218.

67. "The Chilean Tragedy," *New York Times,* 16 September 1973, 18.

68. John Maclean, "Could U.S. Have Bailed Out Chile's Allende?" *Chicago Tribune,* 16 September 1973, A1; "Chilean Economics in One Lesson," *National Review,* 26 October 1973.

69. "New Challenge for Chile after a Marxist Binge," *U.S. News and World Report*, 24 September 1973; "Chile—the Bloody End to a Marxist Dream," *Time*, 24 September 1973; "Exit Allende," *New Republic*, 22 September 1973.

70. Laurence Stern, "Chile: The Lesson," *Progressive*, November 1973.

71. Chalmers Roberts, "The Credibility Gap," *Washington Post*, 19 September 1973, A26. Tad Szulc made a similar comment in "The View from Langley: The U.S. and Chile," *Washington Post*, 21 October 1973, C1. "Was the U.S. Involved?" *Time*, 1 October 1973.

72. Most notably, Gabriel García Márquez, "The Death of Salvador Allende," *Harper's*, March 1974.

73. Andrew, *For the President's Eyes Only*, 350.

74. Ibid., 388.

75. Transcript of a recording of a meeting between President Richard Nixon and H. R. Haldeman in the Oval Office, 23 June 1972, from 10:04 to 11:39 AM, p. 6, available at the Nixon Presidential Library and Museum, www.nixonlibrary.gov/forresearchers/find/tapes/watergate/trial/exhibit_01.pdf, accessed 11 November 2014.

76. Tad Szulc, "From the Folks Who Brought You the Bay of Pigs: The Watergate Caper," *New York Times*, 25 July 1972, E2.

77. Tom Braden, "Removing Helms from the CIA Had to Be a 'Personal' Decision," *Washington Post*, 16 December 1972, A19; Chalmers Roberts, "Helms, the Shah, and the CIA," *Washington Post*, 29 December 1972, A18.

78. John M. Crewsdon, "CIA and Congress Investigate Ellsberg Burglary Authorization," *New York Times*, 8 May 1973, 26; "Unintelligence," *New York Times*, 10 May 1973, 44; Clayton Fritchey, "CIA Needs a Real Watchdog," *Chicago Tribune*, 15 May 1973, 14.

79. George Lardner, notes of phone conversation with James Angleton, 24 June 1983, Lardner Papers, box 14, folder 5—CIA—Angleton, James, 1977–1981.

80. Lyman Kirkpatrick, "Accent on Intelligence," *New York Times*, 17 May 1973, 43.

81. "Watergate and the CIA," *Washington Post*, 18 May 1973, A30.

82. Bill Anderson, "How Cushman Told Ehrlichman No," *Chicago Tribune*, 29 May 1973, 12; see also "The CIA," *New York Times*, 7 June 1973, 44.

83. "Proxmire Seeks Curbs on CIA," *Washington Post*, 5 June 1973, A7.

84. Jim Squires, "Masterspy Helms Gives Senators Look at a Pro," *Chicago Tribune*, 3 August 1973, 4.

85. Tad Szulc, "E. Howard Hunt," *Chicago Tribune*, 3 June 1973, A2. See also Aldrich, "American Journalism and the Landscape of Secrecy," 205–6.

86. John M. Maury to Richard Helms, 28 September 1973, Helms Papers, part I, box 2, folder 59.

87. Jack Anderson, "Baker Eyes CIA over Watergate," *Washington Post*, 19 March 1974, B15; Rowland Evans and Robert C. Novak, "Sen. Baker and the CIA," *Washington*

Post, 30 March 1974, A19; Harry Kelly, "Sen. Baker Puts His Political Future on Line in Probe of CIA's Bug Role," *Chicago Tribune,* 31 March 1974, 18; "The Nation: Colson's Weird Scenario," *Time,* 8 July 1974; "Some Foolish Mistakes," *Time,* 15 July 1974.

88. "Colson Sage: CIA" *National Review,* 19 July 1974.

89. "1984: Here and Now," *Progressive,* July 1973, 3–5; "Tube Dreams in the Sheikdom," *New Republic,* 11 August 1973, 30; Tad Szulc, "There's More to the Story: CIA and the Plumbers," *New Republic,* 29 December 1973, 19–21; Andrew St. George, "The Cold War Comes Home," *Harper's,* November 1973, 68–82.

90. Hugh Sidey to Richard Helms, 12 August 1974, Helms Papers, part I, box 9, folder 1974.

91. Seymour Hersh, "Hearings Urged on CIA's Role in Chile," *New York Times,* 9 September 1974, 3; Seymour Hersh, "Censored Matter in Book about CIA Said to Have Related Chile Activities," *New York Times,* 12 September 1974, A10.

92. Tom Wicker, "Secret War on Chile," *New York Times,* 13 September 1974, 37; "The CIA in Chile" *New York Times,* 16 September 1974, 34; David Binder, "CIA's Covert Role: Should Agents Come Home?" *New York Times,* 23 October 1974, 2; Russell Baker, "Our Uncle Is Now Dorian Sam," *New York Times,* 1 October 1974, 41; Laurence R. Birns, "Allende's Fall, Washington's Push," *New York Times,* 15 September 1974, 215; Tom Wicker, "Was Ford Conned on Chile?" *New York Times,* 20 September 1974, A2. For non–*New York Times* coverage, see "Meddling in Chile by the CIA," *Los Angeles Times,* 16 September 1974, B6; Laurence Stern, "Panel to Probe CIA Role in Chile," *Washington Post,* 19 September 1974, A6; William Gildea, "A Twin Chilean Celebration," *Washington Post,* 19 September 1974, B11; Joseph Kraft, "Chile, the CIA and National Security," *Washington Post,* 19 September 1974, A31; Laurence Stern, "CIA: Silent Partner of Foreign Policy," *Washington Post,* 29 September 1974, C1; Tad Szulc, "Exporting Revolution," *New Republic,* 21 September 1974; Frank Merrick, "Intelligence: The CIA: Time to Come in from the Cold," *Time,* 30 September 1974; John P. Roche, "Forked Tongues Lash the CIA Again," *Chicago Tribune,* 24 September 1974, A3. For other examples, see Walter Pincus, "Helms, the CIA and Public Trust," *New Republic,* 28 September 1974; Robert Conquest, "The KGB Plays Dirty Tricks, Too" *New York Times,* 29 September 1974, 188; Ray Cline, "The Value of the CIA," *New York Times,* 1 November 1974, 39.

93. Henry Kissinger to William Colby, telecon, 20 September 1974, DNSA.

94. Henry Howe Ransom, "Much Policy, Little Intelligence," *New York Times,* 26 December 1970, 17.

95. "Dossier Dictatorship," *New York Times,* 4 March 1971, 34; "The Threat to Privacy," *New York Times,* 8 March 1971, 32; Gaylord Nelson, "How to Stop Snooping," *Progressive,* August 1973.

96. For example, see James Mann, "Ex-CIA 'Spook' Enjoined," *Washington Post,* 19 April 1972, A2; David E. Rosenbaum, "Judge Bars Book by Ex-C.I.A. Agent," *New York Times,* 19 April 1972, 9; "U.S. Court Bars Ex-Agent from Publishing Article on CIA," *Chicago Tribune,* 19 April 1972, A6; "CIA Oath on Secrecy Is

Upheld," *Washington Post,* 12 September 1972, A3; "Author to Defy Court on Book Ban," *Chicago Tribune,* 12 December 1972, A7.

97. Joseph Alsop, "The CIA Analysts: Changes at the Top," *Washington Post,* 23 February 1973, A23.

98. John Maclean and Jim Squires, "Central Intelligence Agency: It Keeps Its Own Directors in the Dark on Some Secrets," *Chicago Tribune,* 20 May 1973, A12; Louis Fisher, "Dark Corners in the Budget," *Nation,* 19 January 1974.

99. James Reston, "Millions for Defense behind Iron Curtain," *New York Times,* 9 December 1951, 169.

100. For examples, see Stephen S. Rosenfield, "It's Time to Look at the CIA," *Washington Post,* 24 November 1972, A28; Tom Braden, "CIA Housecleaning: The Cold War Is Over," *Washington Post,* 6 January 1973, A15; Clifton Daniel, "CIA Apparently Plans Cut in Some Covert Roles," *New York Times,* 2 April 1973, 73; John Maclean and Jim Squires, "Central Intelligence Agency: It Keeps Its Own Directors in the Dark on Some Secrets"; David Wise, "Colby of the CIA: Dark Side Up," *New York Times,* 1 July 1973, 186; "A 'Supersleuth' Takes Over a Troubled CIA," *U.S. News and World Report,* 13 August 1973; Seymour Hersh, "Should the CIA Abandon Dirty Tricks?" *New York Times,* 22 September 1974, 201.

101. Jeremy Stone, "Institutional Dirty Tricks," *New York Times,* 16 February 1973, 37; see also Andrew Hamilton, "The CIA's Dirty Tricks under Fire—at Last," *Progressive,* September 1973, 14.

102. William Anderson, "One Can't Trust Spies Anymore," *Chicago Tribune,* 7 November 1971, A4; the title, it should be noted, is facetious.

103. Miles Copeland, "The Unmentionable Uses of the CIA," *National Review,* 14 September 1973; Miles Copeland, "There's a CIA in Your Future," *National Review,* 26 October 1973. Also writing in the *National Review,* James Burnham, himself formerly associated with the CIA, criticized Copeland for insisting that the United States could rest its security on unquestionable guardians with no oversight. See James Burnham, "Brief for the Offense," *National Review,* 25 October 1974.

104. "Three Dozen American Journalists Are Said to Do Work for CIA," *New York Times,* 1 December 1973, 69.

105. "CIAntics," *New Republic,* 15 December 1973, 7.

106. Stuart Loory, "Press Credibility and Journalists as Spies," *Washington Post,* 13 January 1974, B6; Stuart Loory, "CIA Must Stop Using Newsmen as Spies Abroad," *Los Angeles Times,* 1 January 1974, A7. For similar reporting, see "Integrity and Safety Are at Stake," *Los Angeles Times,* 3 December 1973, B6.

107. Loory, "The CIA's Use of the Press: A 'Mighty Wurlitzer,'" 9.

108. Murray Seeger, "CIA Tells a Few Secrets in Bid to Polish Its Image," *Los Angeles Times,* 18 November 1974, A1.

109. Seymour Hersh, "Huge CIA Operation Reported in U.S. against Antiwar Forces, Other Dissidents in Nixon Years," *New York Times,* 22 December 1974, 1.

110. William Colby, interview by George Lardner, 17 June 1983, Lardner Papers, box 18, folder 3: CIA—Chile, undated.

6. The Year of Intelligence Begins

1. Laurence Stern and Susan Dooley, "Spook," *Washington Post*, 23 March 1975, 14.

2. The committees also investigated the FBI and National Security Agency; however, those elements of the investigation will be included only to the extent that they affected the investigation of the CIA.

3. To date, the most complete account of the Year of Intelligence is Olmsted, *Challenging the Secret Government*.

4. Olmsted has argued that the *Post* was likelier than other major publications to remain silent on the CIA, focusing instead on concurrent investigations of the FBI. While the *Washington Post* was not as active as the *New York Times* in covering the CIA, that does not mean it was silent on the issue. See Olmsted, *Challenging the Secret Government*, 36.

5. Seymour Hersh, interview by George Lardner, 14 March 1983, Lardner Papers, box 18, folder 3: CIA—Chile, undated.

6. Miraldi, *Seymour Hersh*, 186–87.

7. Hersh, "Huge C.I.A. Operation Reported in U.S. against Antiwar Forces, Other Dissidents in Nixon Years," *New York Times*, 22 December 1974, 26.

8. George Lardner notes on phone conversation with James Angleton, 24 June 1983, Lardner Papers, box 14, folder 5: CIA—Angleton, James, 1977–1981.

9. Hersh interview by Lardner, 14 March 1983.

10. Ibid.

11. See, for example, a documentary made by Colby's son, *The Man Nobody Knew: In Search of My Father, CIA Spymaster William Colby*, directed by Carl Colby (2011), Netflix.

12. Andrew, *For the President's Eyes Only*, 399.

13. Miraldi, *Seymour Hersh*, 201–2.

14. Telephone conversation between DCI Colby and [redacted], 23 January 1974, Lardner Papers, box 23, folder 1: CIA—Hughes, Howard; Glomar Explorer and Project Jennifer Research Material, CIA Documents, 1974–1977.

15. Miraldi, *Seymour Hersh*, 203–4. Miraldi examined a transcript of a conversation between Colby and an unnamed official from the *New York Times*. Miraldi, taking cues from context, reasonably argues that the unidentified figure was probably Daniel.

16. Telephone conversation between DCI Colby and Seymour Hersh, 30 January 1974; telephone conversation between DCI Colby and General Scowcroft, 2 February 1974; telephone conversation between DCI Colby and [redacted], 4 February 1974, Lardner Papers, box 23, folder 1.

17. Hersh interview by Lardner, 14 March 1983.

18. Colby interview by Lardner, 17 June 1983, Lardner Papers, box 18, folder 3.

19. Hersh, "Huge C.I.A. Operation Reported in U.S.," 1.

20. Ibid., 26.

21. Ibid.

22. National Security Act of 1947, Sec. 102 (d)3, reproduced in CIA, *CIA Cold War Records: The CIA under Harry Truman.*

23. William Colby and Peter Forbath, *Honorable Men: My Life in the CIA* (New York: Simon and Schuster, 1978), 244–45.

24. Ibid., 334.

25. Ibid., 364–65.

26. Hersh interview by Lardner, 14 March 1983.

27. See, for example, "Angleton—a Troubled CIA Veteran," *Chicago Tribune,* 26 December 1974, 5. Tom Braden, who knew Angleton from his days in the CIA, provided a detailed portrait of Angleton that supported this narrative. See Tom Braden, "CIA: 'A Service, Not a Weapon,'" *Washington Post,* 31 December 1974, A9.

28. Tom Wicker, "The Truth Is Needed," *New York Times,* 24 December 1974, 19; see also Tom Wicker, "Spying for Liberty," *New York Times,* 31 December 1974, 21, which reviewed previous stories about the CIA.

29. David Rosenbaum, "Intelligence Oversight Is Done with a Blindfold," *New York Times,* 29 December 1974, 121; Anthony Lewis, "The Crisis of Law," *New York Times,* 23 December 1974, 27; William Safire, "Who Else Is Guilty?" *New York Times,* 2 January 1975, 33; David Wise, "In the Beginning, the CIA Seemed Harmless Enough," *New York Times,* 12 January 1975, 176.

30. "The CIA Crisis," *Washington Post,* 24 December 1974, A10; "The CIA's Private War," *Chicago Tribune,* 27 December 1974, A2; "McCone Urges Probe of Charge against CIA," *Los Angeles Times,* 23 December 1974, 8; "Investigation the CIA," *Los Angeles Times,* 27 December 1974, B6; "Playing Games with the CIA," *Nation,* 11 January 1975, 2; "Spying Is Contagious," *Nation,* 25 January 1975, 68.

31. Seymour Hersh, "Colby Said to Confirm C.I.A. Role in U.S.," *New York Times,* 1 January 1975, 37.

32. Seymour Hersh, "CIA Had File on Eartha Kitt," *New York Times,* 3 January 1975, 25.

33. John D. Marks, "How to Unmask CIA Spies Hidden in Our Embassies," *Chicago Tribune,* 19 January 1975, A1.

34. Jack Anderson and Les Whitten, "CIA Love Traps Lured Diplomats," *Washington Post,* 5 February 1975, B15.

35. "The CIA's 'Illegal Domestic Spying,'" *Washington Post,* 5 January 1975, 26; Rod MacLeish, "The CIA—Up Front," *Washington Post,* 4 January 1975, A14.

36. Frank Starr, "Do We Require an Effective CIA?" *Chicago Tribune,* 8 January 1975, A2; Frank Starr, "Back to the Real Goals of the CIA," *Chicago Tribune,* 10 January 1975, A2.

37. "CIA in Wonderland," *National Review,* 31 January 1975, 89; "A CIA Scandal—and the Backlash," *U.S. News and World Report,* 6 January 1975, 52. For additional examples of backlash against calls for investigation, see: ". . . And a P.S. to Pravda," *Chicago Tribune,* 8 January 1975, A2; Rowland Evans and Robert C. Novak,

"Congressional Straitjacket for the CIA," *Washington Post,* 22 January 1975, A21; Jack Anderson and Les Whitten, "Secret Heroes in CIA Go Unsung," *Washington Post,* 22 January 1975, B15; "What's Ahead: Winner Lose All," *National Review,* 24 January 1975, 4.

38. Rowland Evans and Robert Novak, "The Tragedy of the CIA," *Washington Post,* 6 January 1975, A19.

39. Rowland Evans and Robert Novak, "Colby and CIA Morale," *Washington Post,* 12 January 1975, B7.

40. Hugh Sidey, "Intelligence: Rattling Skeletons in the CIA Closet," *Time,* 6 January 1975.

41. Hugh Sidey, "The Presidency: Another Look at the CIA," *Time,* 20 January 1975, 40.

42. Olmsted, *Challenging the Secret Government,* 38.

43. Miraldi, *Seymour Hersh,* 194.

44. John B. Oakes to Abraham Rosenthal, 27 December 1974, Rosenthal Papers, box 63, folder 7.

45. Abraham Rosenthal to John Oakes, 3 January 1975, Rosenthal Papers, box 63, folder 7.

46. Memorandum of a meeting between Alexander Greenfield and Clifton Daniel, 7 January 1975, and Angus MacLean Thuermer to Seymour Hersh, 14 January 1975, both in NYTCR: General Files, New York Public Library (hereafter cited as General Files), box 92, folder 11.

47. Colby, *Honorable Men,* 400–402.

48. Walter Pincus, "Covering Intelligence," *New Republic,* 1 February 1975, 12.

49. Pincus, "Covering Intelligence," 11.

50. John Herbers, one of the *Times* reporters mentioned by name in Pincus's article, wrote to protest. See Herbers to Walter Pincus, 30 January 1975, Rosenthal Papers, box 63, folder 7.

51. Abraham Rosenthal to Max Frankel, 10 February 1975, Rosenthal Papers, box 63, folder 7.

52. Hersh interview by Lardner, 14 March 1983.

53. Lardner notes re: 1972 Helms Anti-Assassination Directive, Lardner Papers, box 15, folder 2.

54. Leslie H. Gelb, "Bearing Out Seymour Hersh: The CIA and the Press," *New Republic,* 23 March 1975, 14–15.

55. See, for example, Jo Pomerance, "Some Questions to Be Answered," *Nation,* 22 February 1975, 204.

56. See, for example, Tom Braden, "Imperial Presidents and the CIA," *Washington Post,* 3 February 1975, A21; Walter Pincus, "Using the CIA for Political Advantage," *Washington Post,* 10 February 1975, A20.

57. Franklin Lindsay, "The Dangers of Damaging the CIA," *Washington Post,* 28 January 1975, A18; see also "The Senate Select Committee on Intelligence,"

Washington Post, 29 January 1975, A20; Marquis Childs, "Helms and the Hoover Empire," *Washington Post,* 11 February 1975, A15.

58. James Reston, "Clean Sweep at CIA?" *New York Times,* 16 March 1975, E19; see also C. L. Sulzberger, "Spooks in an Open Society," *New York Times,* 10 May 1975, 29; "Washington Whispers," *U.S. News and World Report,* 3 February 1973, 5; "CIA under Pressure While KGB Is Thriving," *U.S. News and World Report,* 24 February 1975, 44–46.

59. William F. Buckley, "On Leveling with the Reader," *National Review,* 11 April 1975, 415.

60. "Not Much Dirt in Them Diggings," *National Review,* 14 February 1975, 147; for a similar charge in a different publication, see Carolyn Lewis, "The Scandal Habit," *Washington Post,* 31 March 1975, A18.

61. George Lardner Jr., phone interviewed by David Hadley, 27 July 2017.

62. Andrew, *For the President's Eyes Only,* 404.

63. Seymour Hersh, "Ford Names Rockefeller to Head Inquiry into C.I.A.; Wants Report in 90 Days," *New York Times,* 6 January 1975, 55; "Keeping the CIA under Control," *Los Angeles Times,* 7 January 1975, C6.

64. Anthony Ripley, "Views and Background of Ford Commission Investigating C.I.A.," *New York Times,* 14 January 1975, 16.

65. Seymour Hersh, "Griswold, CIA Panel Member Called a Target of '74 ITT Inquiry," *New York Times,* 8 January 1975, 25.

66. Frank van Riper, "Panel Is Unbiased Despite CIA Ties, White House Says," *Chicago Tribune,* 7 January 1975, 8.

67. Joseph Kraft, "'A Sad Commission,'" *Washington Post,* 7 January 1975, A23. Kraft, unlike more regular critics of the CIA, ascribed the problems of the commission to ineptitude rather that conspiracy. See Joseph Kraft, "The Rockefeller Role," *Washington Post,* 9 January 1975, A23.

68. "Editorials," *Nation,* 18 January 1975, 35–36.

69. Colby, *Honorable Men,* 400. Though Colby clearly had reason to portray himself as a cooperating witness and the Rockefeller commissioners as the perpetrators of obfuscation, Colby's record of open testimony and the negative reactions of many establishment figures, such as Helms, to that policy lend some credence to his account. Fenn, "Church Oral History," 122.

70. Seymour Hersh, "Senators Vote on C.I.A. Inquiry," *New York Times,* 20 January 1975, 16.

71. Nicholas M. Horrock, "Senator Church Decries Furor over CIA Inquiry," *New York Times,* 22 February 1975, 14; "Investigations: Church: 'Entering the 1984 Decade,'" *Time,* 24 March 1975.

72. Rowland Evans and Robert Novak, "Alarm Bells over the CIA Investigator," *Washington Post,* 9 February 1975, 39.

73. Frederick D. Baron, "Church Committee Oral History, 1975–1976," Oral History Interviews, Senate Historical Office, Washington, DC, 37.

74. Fenn, "Church Oral History," 121.

75. See Mark H. Gitenstein, 155–56; Karl Frederick "Rick" Inderfurth, 17; Loch K. Johnson, 232, all in "Church Committee Oral History, 1975–1976," Oral History Interviews, Senate Historical Office, Washington, DC.

76. Snider, *The Agency and the Hill,* 28–29, 31.

77. Elliot E. Maxwell, "Church Committee Oral History, 1975–1976," Oral History Interviews, Senate Historical Office, Washington, DC, 311.

78. Memorandum of a conversation among Henry A. Kissinger, James R. Schlesinger, William Colby, Philip Areeda, Laurence Silberman, Martin R. Hoffman, and Brent Scowcroft, 20 February 1975, DNSA.

79. Ibid.

80. Joe Alsop, "Why Hoover Made a KGB Safe House," *Chicago Tribune,* 23 February 1975, A6.

81. A letter from Alsop to Nancy Kissinger speaks to friendly, fairly regular socializing and correspondence. See Joseph Alsop to Nancy Kissinger, 13 October 1975, Alsop Papers, part IV, box 229, folder 1975-I-J; see also Alsop to Viscountess Head, 9 January 1978, Alsop Papers, part IV, box 234, folder 8-1978, H, reflecting the continued interaction. Quote is from Joseph Alsop to James Akins, 23 January 1974, Alsop Papers, part III, box 140, folder 1974, A; see also Joseph Alsop to Donald L. Miller, 26 February 1975, Alsop Papers, part IV, box 22, folder 1975, M.

82. Herkin, *The Georgetown Set,* 66–67, 154–55.

83. Ibid., 208. Herkin notes that there may have been some effort by Hoover and other members of the government, including Allen Dulles, to use the incident to pressure Alsop to desist from his unfriendly reporting of the Eisenhower White House, though there is no definitive evidence.

84. Olmsted, *Challenging the Secret Government,* 61.

85. Ibid., 62.

86. Memorandum of luncheon at the White House with President Ford by Clifton Daniel, 1 February 1975, Rosenthal Papers, box 13, folder 51.

87. Hersh interview by Lardner, 14 March 1983.

88. Quoted in Olmsted, *Challenging the Secret Government,* 65.

89. "Ford Said to Fear Baring CIA Role in Assassinations Abroad," *New York Times,* 1 March 1975, 49. The *Times,* while not confirming what was said at the luncheon, was still free to report on Schorr's statements.

90. "The Problem of the CIA," *Nation,* 15 March 1975, 290; Art Buchwald, "Stand Up for America and Help Us Play God, Godfather," *Washington Post,* 16 March 1975, 81; Jim Squires, "The Oswald-CIA Link Won't Connect," *Chicago Tribune,* 16 March 1975, A1; George Lardner, "CIA Reportedly Compiled 700 Pages on Questionable Agency Activities," *Washington Post,* 8 March 1975, A9; "CIA Involvement Is Alleged in Plots to Kill 3 Dictators," *New York Times,* 10 March 1975, 49; Jack Anderson and Les Whitten, "CIA Plots against Castro Recounted," *Washington Post,* 10 March 1975. Russell Baker provided a very droll take on a conversation between CIA agents plotting assassinations; see Russell Baker, "Social Distinctions," *New York Times,* 11 March 1975, 35. "The CIA: Prying into Murder,"

Time, 17 March 1975; "Scope of CIA Mail Spying Told," *Chicago Tribune,* 22 March 1975, N6.

91. Tom Braden, "CIA: Power and Arrogance," *Washington Post,* 27 April 1975, C2; William Colby, "CIA: 'Things Have Changed,'" *Washington Post,* 4 May 1975, 34.

92. Tom Wicker, "'Big Brother' at Hand," *New York Times,* 2 March 1975, 185.

93. Arthur Ochs Sulzberger to Tom Wicker, 3 March 1975, Wicker Papers, series I: Correspondence, box 7, folder 11—Sulzberger, Arthur Ochs, 1964–1991.

94. Abraham Rosenthal to Tom Wicker, 1 September 1977, Wicker Papers, box 63, folder 6—Central Intelligence Agency, 1971–1986 (3): 1977–1979.

95. Abraham Rosenthal to Arthur Ochs Sulzberger, 2 February 1976, Rosenthal Papers, box 63, folder 7.

96. Miraldi, *Seymour Hersh,* 206; for the *Los Angeles Times*'s eventual product, see "CIA Reportedly Contracted with Hughes in Effort to Raise Sunken Soviet A-Sub," *Los Angeles Times,* 8 February 1975, 18.

97. Telephone conversation between DCI Colby and General Scowcroft, 10 February 1975; Seymour Hersh to DCI Colby, message, 10 February 1975; both in Lardner Papers, box 23, folder 1.

98. Telephone conversation between DCI Colby and Seymour Hersh, 10 February 1975, Lardner Papers, box 23, folder 1.

99. Telephone conversation between DCI Colby and Carl Duckett, 11 February 1975; telephone conversation between DCI Colby and General Scowcroft, 14 February 1975; [redacted *New York Times* representative] to William Colby, 3 March 1975, all in Lardner Papers, box 23, folder 1.

100. Telephone conversation between DCI Colby and Jack Nelson, 12 March 1975, Lardner Papers, box 23, folder 1.

101. Telephone conversation between DCI Colby and Lloyd Shearer, 13 March 1975, Lardner Papers, box 23, folder 1.

102. Telephone conversation between DCI Colby and Carl Duckett, 13 March 1975, Lardner Papers, box 23, folder 1.

103. Telephone conversation between DCI Colby and Angus Thuermer, 13 March 1975; telephone conversation between DCI Colby and [redacted], 11:19 A.M., 13 March 1975; telephone conversation between DCI Colby and [redacted], 4:55 P.M., 13 March 1975, all in Lardner Papers, box 23, folder 1.

104. Telephone conversation between DCI Colby and Jack Nelson, 13 March 1975, Lardner Papers, box 23, folder 1.

105. Telephone conversation between DCI Colby and Carl Duckett, 13 March 1975.

106. Telephone conversation between DCI Colby and Brent Scowcroft, 14 March 1975.

107. Ibid. (parentheses in original).

108. Telephone conversation between DCI Colby and Carl Duckett, 17 March 1975, Lardner Papers, box 23, folder 1. The document notes that the stenographer

was initially unable to identify which party was speaking in the conversation, but it does not materially affect the information contained in the document.

109. Telephone conversation between DCI Colby and Angus Thuermer, 17 March 1975, Lardner Papers, box 23, folder 1 (parentheses in original).

110. Telephone conversation between DCI Colby and Brent Scowcroft, 17 March 1975, Lardner Papers, box 23, folder 1.

111. Telephone conversation between DCI Colby and Jack Anderson, 18 March 1975, Lardner Papers, box 23, folder 1.

112. Notes of conversation with Les Whitten by George Lardner, 25 October 1983, Lardner Papers, box 22, folder 13: CIA—Hughes, Howard, Glomar Explorer and Project Jennifer, Interviews and Notes, 1974, n.d.

113. Telephone conversation between DCI Colby and Laurence Silberman, 27 February 1975; telephone conversation between DCI Colby and Carl Duckett, 27 February 1975, both in Lardner Papers, box 23, folder1 (parentheses in original).

114. Telephone conversation between Colby and Duckett, 13 March 1975; notes of conversation with Les Whitten by George Lardner, 25 October 1983.

115. Tom Wicker, "The Submarine Story," *New York Times*, 21 March 1975, 37; Seymour Hersh, "CIA Salvage Ship Brought Up Sub Lost in 1968, Failed to Raise Atom Missiles," *New York Times*, 19 March 1975, 97.

116. Olmsted, *Challenging the Secret Government*, 71.

117. Abraham Rosenthal to Tom Wicker, 1 September 1977, 1–2, Rosenthal Papers, box 63, folder 6.

118. Ibid., 3–4.

119. Abraham Rosenthal to James Goodale, 1 November 1977, Rosenthal Papers, box 63, folder 6.

120. Memorandum for the Record, 17 March 1975, CREST, www.foia.cia.gov /sites/default/files/document_conversions/5829/CIA-RDP86B00269R000600030031 -8.pdf, accessed 30 April 2015.

7. The Year of Intelligence's Contentious End

1. Taylor Branch and George Crile III, "The Kennedy Vendetta," *Harper's*, August 1975, 51–61.

2. Joseph Alsop to Arthur Schlesinger, 4 April 1975, Alsop Papers, part IV, box 229, folder 8.

3. Ray Cline to Arthur Schlesinger, 29 August 1975; Schlesinger to Cline, 10 September 1975; and Cline to Schlesinger, 19 September 1975, all in Cline Papers, part 2 Organizations File, box 32, folder 18—Schlesinger, Arthur M., Dr., 1975.

4. Baron, "Church Oral History," 40.

5. For reference to Cline's appearance on *The Dick Cavett Show*, see Cord Meyer Jr. to Ray Cline, 27 June 1974, Cline Papers, part 1, box 1, folder 7: Interview: June 25, 1974, to Sept. 16, 1975.

6. Ray Cline to Stephen Fleischman, 11 June 1975, Cline Papers, part 1, box 1, folder 7.

7. Austin Scott, "CIA Defender Cites Chile Cables: Denies Agency Role in Anti-Allende Coup," *Washington Post,* 11 May 1975, 3; Linda Charlton, "Ex-C.I.A. Official Denies Role in Overthrow of Chile's Leader," *New York Times,* 11 May 1975.

8. David Atlee Phillips, "This Is about (shh)," *New York Times,* 25 May 1975, 181.

9. Andrew, *For the President's Eyes Only,* 410; "Operation Chaos," *New York Times,* 11 June 1975, 42; "'Operation Chaos': Files on 7,200," *Washington Post,* 11 June 1975, A10.

10. For criticism of the decision to release the report, see Tom Wicker, "CIA and Confusion," *New York Times,* 8 June 1975, 199; Joseph Kraft, "Our Intelligence Apparatus," *Washington Post,* 10 June 1975, A19. For reactions to the report, see Tom Wicker, "The Rocky Report: Better Than Expected," *New York Times,* 13 January 1975, 37; Seymour Hersh, "At Its Best, How Good Is CIA in a Democracy," *New York Times,* 15 June 1975, E1; Alan Wolfe, "The Rockefeller CIA Report," *Nation,* 16 August 1975, 109–12.

11. Seymour Hersh, "Family Plans to Sue CIA over Suicide in Drug Test," *New York Times,* 10 July 1975, 61; Boyce Rensberger, "CIA in the Early Nineteen-Fifties Was among Pioneers in Research on LSD's Effects," *New York Times,* 12 July 1975, 11; "CIA: Tantalizing Bits of Evidence," *Time,* 4 August 1975; "Widow Plans to Sue CIA in LSD Case," *Los Angeles Times,* 11 July 1975, A5. Olson's son Eric continues to be skeptical of the official story, however, and believes the LSD story was a fabrication to conceal an even more disturbing possibility: that the CIA purposefully assassinated Olson.

12. J. Michael Harrington, "CIA: Can We Reform It? Can We Afford It at All?" *Nation,* 405–6; Walter Pincus, "Inside the Company," *New York Times,* 3 August 1975, 191.

13. Inderfurth, "Church Oral History," 200–201.

14. "CIA Kept Poisons against Orders, Sen. Church Says," *Los Angeles Times,* 9 September 1975, 1A; Tom Wicker, "Destroy the Monster," *New York Times,* 12 September 1975, 33; Nicholas M. Horrock, "Colby Describes CIA Poison Work," *New York Times,* 17 September 1975, 93; Nicholas van Hoffman, "Dastardly Deeds of an Old US Policy," *Chicago Tribune,* 20 September 1975, N10; "CIA: Toxin Tocsin," *Time,* 22 September 1975.

15. Johnson, "Church Oral History," 233.

16. Rowland Evans and Robert C. Novak, "Rebuilding the CIA," *Washington Post,* 25 September 1975, A19; see also Joan Beck, "So Maybe a Foreign CIA Got into Our Leader's Hair," *Chicago Tribune,* 26 November 1975, A3.

17. Patrick A. Shea, "Church Committee Oral History, 1975–1976," Oral History Interviews, Senate Historical Office, Washington, DC, 508.

18. Oswald Johnston and Ronald J. Ostrow, "CIA Plotted Death or Downfall of 5 Leaders," *Los Angeles Times,* 21 November 1975, A1; Bill Richards, "Summary of

CIA Plots, 1959–1972," *Washington Post,* 21 November 1975, A9; "Texts on Alleged U.S. Assassination Plots," *New York Times,* 21 November 1975, 49.

19. "Plots to Kill Castro Strain Imagination," *Chicago Tribune,* 21 November 1975, 4.

20. John M. Crewsdon, "Castro Plot Study Finds No Role by White House," *New York Times,* 21 November 1975, 52.

21. Nick Thimmesch, ". . . As Church Looks to the Future," *Chicago Tribune,* 26 November 1975, A3; "The CIA: Plots Written in Disappearing Ink," *Time,* 1 December 1975, 14. See also "CIA Murder Plots—Weighing the Damage to U.S." *U.S. News and World Report,* 1 December 1975, 13–16.

22. Seymour Hersh, "CIA's Work Unimpeded by Inquiries and Reports, Officials of Agency Assert," *New York Times,* 10 November 1975, 69. Hersh's writing in this vein would annoy at least one member of the Church Committee, Loch Johnson, as he felt it undermined the committee while it was working with secret material. Johnson, "Church Oral History," 232.

23. Michael J. Madigan, "Church Committee Oral History, 1975–1976," Oral History Interviews, Senate Historical Office, Washington, DC, 289. See also Baron, "Church Oral History," 35.

24. Rowland Evans and Robert Novak, "Covert Operations: A Showdown," *Washington Post,* 25 December 1975, A19.

25. Quoted in Olmsted, *Challenging the Secret Government,* 152.

26. George Crile, "The Fourth Estate: A Good Word for the CIA," *Harper's,* January 1976, 28–32.

27. George Crile to Richard Helms, 25 February 1977, Helms Papers, part I, box 1, folder 66.

28. House Subcommittee on Oversight, *The CIA and the Media,* 53.

29. Anthony Lewis, "The Covert Presidency," *New York Times,* 19 January 1976, 29; see also Ernest Gellhorn, "Controlling the Central Intelligence Agency," *New York Times,* 19 January 1976, 29; Anthony Lewis, "A Test of Seriousness," *New York Times,* 9 February 1976, 27. An increasingly minority voice at the *Tribune,* Jim Squires also wrote along similar lines; see Jim Squires, "Runaway Mules Head for the Cliff," *Chicago Tribune,* 15 February 1976, A6.

30. House Subcommittee on Oversight, *The CIA and the Media,* 189–90.

31. Ibid., 199.

32. Gitenstein, "Church Oral History," 162.

33. House Subcommittee on Oversight, *The CIA and the Media,* 37–41.

34. "Intelligence: Backlash over All Those Leaks," *Time,* 23 February 1976, 13.

35. Tom Wicker, "Defending Dan Schorr," *New York Times,* 24 February 1976, 35.

36. U.S. Senate, *Final Report of the Select Committee to Study Governmental Operations with Respect to Intelligence Activities* (Washington, DC: U.S. Government Printing Office, 1976), 424.

37. Tom Wicker, "Is Oversight Enough?" *New York Times,* 14 May 1976, 21.

38. "Intelligence: New Policemen to Battle Abuses," *Time,* 1 March 1976, 13; "Intelligence: A Watchdog at Last," *Time,* 31 May 1976, 22.

39. Tom Wicker to Seymour Topping, undated letter, though by context sometime after 6 August 1976, Wicker Papers, series I, box 3, folder 10.

40. David R. Jones to Abraham Rosenthal, 1 September 1976, Rosenthal Papers, box 19, folder 18.

41. Walter Pincus, "CIA Funding Journalistic Network Abroad," *Washington Post,* 16 January 1976, A19; "Report 11 CIA Agents Posed as Journalists," *New York Times,* 22 January 1976, C13; John Crewsdon, "CIA Tried in 50's to Recruit Times Man," *New York Times,* 31 January 1976, 23. Phillips himself informed Crewsdon of the CIA's approach; Wayne Phillips to John Crewsdon, 23 January 1976, Rosenthal Papers, box 63, folder 7. For other reporting, see David Halverson, "The CIA's 'Journalists' Are a Cause for Press Concern," *Chicago Tribune,* 1 February 1976, A4; Nicholas Horrock, "C.I.A. Infiltration of Press Overseas Viewed as Influencing News Received by Americans," *New York Times,* 9 February 1976, 32; Nicholas M. Horrock, "C.I.A. to Stop Enlisting Agents from the Press and the Church," *New York Times,* 12 February 1976, 65; "Let's Name Names," *Los Angeles Times,* 13 February 1976, D6; Jack Nelson, "CIA Use of Educators, Media Told in Report," *Los Angeles Times,* 27 April 1975, B1; U.S. Senate, *Final Report,* 192.

42. Abraham Rosenthal to Arthur Ochs Sulzberger, 30 January 1976, Rosenthal Papers, box 63, folder 7.

43. Abraham Rosenthal to Arthur Ochs Sulzberger, 2 February 1976, Rosenthal Papers, box 63, folder 7.

44. Abraham Rosenthal to Richard Halloran, 11 February 1976, Rosenthal Papers, box 63, folder 7.

45. George H. W. Bush to Abraham Rosenthal, 3 February 1976; Bush to Sulzberger, 9 February 1976; and Abraham Rosenthal to Sulzberger, 2 February 1976, all in Rosenthal Papers, box 63, folder 7.

46. Abraham Rosenthal to Arthur Ochs Sulzberger and James Goodale, 3 March 1976, Rosenthal Papers, box 63, folder 7. For example, Rosenthal was informed in January 1978 that another *Times* reporter had actively worked for the CIA while with the *Times.* See Bill Kovach to Rosenthal, 23 January 1978, Rosenthal Papers, box 63, folder 6.

47. Clifton Daniel to Gene Wilson, 11 March 1976, Foreign Desk Records, box 118, folder 12.

48. Arthur Ochs Sulzberger to George Bush, 27 May 1976, Rosenthal Papers, box 63, folder 7.

49. Joseph A. Califano Jr., Memorandum for the Record, 7, Philip L. Geyelin Papers (hereafter cited as Geyelin Papers), Library of Congress, box 1, folder 4—Central Intelligence Agency—Geyelin Involvement, 1976–1977.

50. David Atlee Phillips to Philip Geyelin, 11 July 1975, Geyelin Papers, box 4, folder 2, Correspondence, 1975 Jul–Dec.

51. John Bross to Richard Helms, 14 April 1976, and Helms to Bross, 21 April 1976, both in Geyelin Papers, box 1, folder 4.

52. John Bross to Philip Geyelin, 28 April 1976; Memorandum for the Record, 29 April 1976 and 24 May 1976, both in Geyelin Papers, box 1, folder 4.

53. John Bross to Philip Geyelin, 2 June 1976, Geyelin Papers, box 1, folder 4.

54. Jones, "Journalism, Intelligence, and the *New York Times*," 240–46.

55. Ibid., 240, 246.

56. Ibid., 246–48.

57. Transcript of an interview of Carl Bernstein by Tom Brokaw, 28 September 1977, Rosenthal Papers, box 63, folder 6.

58. Ibid.

59. Sydney Gruson to Stansfield Turner and Gene Wilson, 12 September 1977, Rosenthal Papers, box 63, folder 6.

60. Abraham Rosenthal to Arthur Ochs Sulzberger, 20 December 1977, Rosenthal Papers, box 63, folder 6.

61. Abraham Rosenthal, draft statement, December 1977, 2, enclosed in Rosenthal to Arthur Ochs Sulzberger, 20 December 1977.

62. Abraham Rosenthal to Arthur Ochs Sulzberger, 20 December 1977.

63. House Subcommittee on Oversight, *The CIA and the Media*, 334–35.

64. Ibid., 3.

65. Ibid., 68, 94–95.

66. Ibid., 98.

67. Ibid., 99–100.

68. Ibid., 113.

69. Ibid., 39.

70. Ibid., 221.

Conclusion

1. Remarks by former President Bush at CIA Headquarters (Retirees Day), 17 September 1997, 2, Helms Papers, part I, box 10, folder 10/3/487.

2. Ibid., 3.

3. Wicker, *On Press*, 212.

4. Abraham Rosenthal to Professor George Ridge, 24 October 1975, Rosenthal Papers, box 19, folder 18.

5. Wicker, *On Press*, 62.

6. William Colby, interview by George Lardner, 20 June 1975, 14, Lardner Papers, box 18, folder 3.

7. Michael Muskal, "Ex-Tribune Reporter Said to Have 'Collaborative' Relationship with CIA," *Los Angeles Times*, 4 September 2014, www.latimes.com/nation/nationnow/la-na-nn-tribune-dilanian-20140904-story.html, accessed 10 March 2015.

8. Immerman, *The Hidden Hand*, 3–4.

Bibliography

Primary Sources

Archives

Arthur and Elizabeth Schlesinger Library on the History of Women in America, Cambridge, MA
    Freda Kirchwey Papers
Colonel Robert R. McCormick Research Center, First Division Museum, Cantigny, IL
    Robert R. McCormick Papers
Franklin Delano Roosevelt Presidential Library and Museum, Hyde Park, NY
    Francis P. Corrigan Papers
George C. Marshall Research Foundation, Alexandria, VA
    Hanson W. Baldwin Collection
Georgetown University Special Collections Research Center, Georgetown University Manuscripts, Washington, DC
    Richard M. Helms Papers
Library of Congress, Manuscript Division, Washington, DC
    Joseph Alsop and Stewart Alsop Papers
    Ray S. Cline Papers
    Philip L. Geyelin Papers
    George Lardner Papers
    Henry R. Luce Papers
    Cord Meyer Jr. Papers
New York Public Library, Manuscripts and Archives Division, New York
    New York Times Company Records
        Clifton Daniel Papers
        Foreign Desk Records
        Robert Garst Papers
        General Files
        Oral History Files
        Abraham M. Rosenthal Papers
        Arthur Hays Sulzberger Papers
        Tom Wicker Papers

Seeley Mudd Manuscript Library, Princeton, NJ
   Hamilton Fish Armstrong Papers
   William Colby Papers
   Council on Foreign Relations Records
   Allen Welsh Dulles Papers
   Arthur Krock Papers
   David Lawrence Papers

Electronic Archives

Central Intelligence Agency Records Search Tool Twenty-five-Year Program Archive
Digital National Security Archive, George Washington University
Freedom of Information Act Reading Room, Central Intelligence Agency
Nixon White House Tapes—Online, Nixon Presidential Library and Museum

Government Publications

Central Intelligence Agency. *CIA Cold War Records: The CIA under Harry Truman.*
   Edited by Michael Warner. Washington: Center for the Study of Intelligence, 1994.
Church Committee Oral History, 1975–1976, Oral History Interviews, Senate His-
   torical Office, Washington, DC.
U.S. Department of State. *Foreign Relations of the United States, 1945–1950: Emer-
   gence of an Intelligence Establishment, Retrospective Volume.* Edited by C. Thomas
   Thorne Jr. and David S. Patterson. Washington, DC: U.S. Government Printing
   Office, 1996.
U.S. House of Representatives. Subcommittee on Oversight of the Permanent Select
   Committee on Intelligence. *The CIA and the Media.* 59th Cong., 1st and 2nd
   sess., 27–29 December 1977, 4–5 January and 20 April 1978.
U.S. Senate. *The Final Report of the Select Committee to Study Governmental Opera-
   tions with Respect to Intelligence Activities.* Washington, DC: U.S. Government
   Printing Office, 1976.

Books

Bernays, Edward L. *Biography of an Idea: Memoirs of Public Relations Counsel.* New
   York: Simon and Schuster, 1965.
Bissell, Richard. *Reflections of a Cold Warrior: From Yalta to the Bay of Pigs.* New
   Haven: Yale University Press, 1996.
Braden, Joan. *Just Enough Rope: An Intimate Memoir.* New York: Villard Books, 1989.
Catledge, Turner. *My Life and The Times.* New York: Harper & Row, 1971.
Colby, William, and Peter Forbath. *Honorable Men: My Life in the CIA.* New York:
   Simon and Schuster, 1978.
Cook, Fred. *Maverick: Fifty Years of Investigative Reporting.* New York: G. P. Putnam's
   Sons, 1984.

Cutler, Richard W. *Counterspy: Memoirs of a Counterintelligence Officer in World War II and the Cold War.* Washington, DC: Brassey's, 2004.

Eisenhower, Dwight D. *Mandate for Change, 1953–1956.* Garden City, NY: Doubleday, 1963.

Graham, Katharine. *Personal History.* New York: Alfred A. Knopf, 1997.

Helms, Richard, and William Hood. *A Look over My Shoulder: A Life in the Central Intelligence Agency.* New York: Random House, 2003.

Hunt, E. Howard. *Undercover: Memoirs of an American Secret Agent.* New York: Berkley, 1974.

Meyer, Cord. *Facing Reality: From World Federalism to the CIA.* New York: Harper and Row, 1980.

Reston, James. *Deadline: A Memoir.* New York: Random House, 1991.

Rudd, Hughes. *My Escape from the CIA and Other Improbable Events.* New York: E. P. Dutton, 1966.

Secondary Sources

Aldrich, Richard J. "American Journalism and the Landscape of Secrecy: Tad Szulc, the CIA and Cuba." *History* 100.340 (2015): 189–209.

Alsop, Stewart, and Thomas Braden. *Sub Rosa: The O.S.S. and American Espionage.* New York: Reynal & Hitchcock, 1946.

Ambrose, Stephen. *Ike's Spies: Eisenhower and the Espionage Establishment.* Jackson: University of Mississippi Press, 1981.

Andrew, Christopher. *For the President's Eyes Only: Secret Intelligence and the American Presidency from Washington to Bush.* New York: HarperCollins, 1996.

Andrew, Christopher, and Vasili Mitrokhin. *The Sword and the Shield: The Mitrokhin Archive and the Secret History of the KGB.* New York: Basic Books, 1999.

Appy, Christian G. "Eisenhower's Guatemala Doodle, or: How to Draw, Deny, and Take Credit for a Third World Coup." In *Cold War Constructions: The Political Culture of United States Imperialism, 1945–1966,* edited by Christian G. Appy, 183–216. Amherst: University of Massachusetts Press, 2000.

Aronson, James. *The Press and the Cold War,* 2nd ed. New York: Monthly Review Press, 1990.

Ashby, LeRoy, "The Church Committee's History and Relevance: Reflecting on Senator Church." In *US National Security, Intelligence and Democracy: From the Church Committee to the War on Terror,* edited by Russell A. Miller, 57–75. New York: Routledge, 2008.

Aybar de Soto, José M. *Dependency and Intervention: The Case of Guatemala in 1954.* Boulder, CO: Westview Press, 1978.

Baldwin, Hanson. *The Price of Power.* New York: Harper and Brothers, 1947.

Barrett, David. *The CIA and Congress: The Untold Story from Truman to Kennedy.* Lawrence: University Press of Kansas, 2005.

————. "Explaining the First Contested Senate Confirmation of a Director of Central Intelligence: John McCone, the Kennedy White House, the CIA and the Senate, 1962." *Intelligence and National Security* 31.1 (2016): 74–87.

Baughman, James L. *Henry R. Luce and the Rise of the American News Media*. Baltimore: Johns Hopkins University Press, 1987.

Belmonte, Laura A. *Selling the American Way: U.S. Propaganda and the Cold War*. Philadelphia: University of Pennsylvania Press, 2008.

Bennett, Lance. *News: The Politics of Illusion*, 8th ed. New York: Pearson Longman, 2009.

Bernhard, Nancy E. *U.S. Television News and Cold War Propaganda, 1947–1960*. Cambridge: Cambridge University Press, 1999.

Bernstein, Carl. "The CIA and the Media." *Rolling Stone*, 20 October 1977. www.carlbernstein.com/magazine_cia_and_media.php (accessed 7 May 2011).

Berry, Nicholas O. *Foreign Policy and the Press: An Analysis of the* New York Times' *Coverage of U.S. Foreign Policy*. New York: Greenwood Press, 1990.

Bill, James A. *The Eagle and the Lion: The Tragedy of American-Iranian Relations*. New Haven: Yale University Press, 1988.

Black, Jan Knippers. *United States Penetration of Brazil*. Philadelphia: University of Pennsylvania Press, 1977.

Blaiser, Cole. *The Hovering Giant: U.S. Responses to Revolutionary Change in Latin America, 1910–1985*, rev. ed. Pittsburgh: University of Pittsburgh Press, 1985.

Blanchard, Robert O., ed. *Congress and the News Media*. New York: Hastings House, 1974.

Blight, James, and Peter Kornbluh, eds. *Politics of Illusion: The Bay of Pigs Invasion Reexamined*. Boulder, CO: Lynne Rienner Publishers, 1998.

Bowen, Gordon L. "U.S. Foreign Policy toward Radical Change: Covert Operations in Guatemala, 1950–1954." *Latin American Perspectives* 10.1 (1983): 88–102.

Breckenridge, Scott D. *The CIA and the US Intelligence System*. Boulder, CO: Westview Press, 1986.

Brzezinski, Matthew. *Red Moon Rising: Sputnik and the Hidden Rivalries That Ignited the Space Age*. New York: Time Books, 2007.

Burton, Hersh. *The Old Boys: The American Elite and the Origins of the CIA*. New York: Charles Scribner, 1992.

Casey, Steven. *Selling the Korean War: Propaganda, Politics, and Public Opinion in the United States, 1950–1953*. Oxford: Oxford University Press, 2008.

Cassel, Elke van. "In Search of a Clear and Overarching American Policy: The *Reporter* Magazine (1949–68), the US Government and the Cold War." In *The US Government, Citizen Groups, and the Cold War*, edited by Helen Laville and Hugh Wilford. London: Routledge, 2006, 116–40.

Castle, Timothy N. *At War in the Shadow of Vietnam: U.S. Military Aid to the Royal Lao Government, 1955–1975*. New York: Columbia University Press, 1993.

Cater, Douglass. "The Fourth Branch, Then and Now." In *The Media and Congress*, edited by Stephen Bates, 1–13. Columbus, OH: Publishing Horizons, 1987.

Chester, Eric Thomas. *Covert Network: Progressives, the International Rescue Committee, and the CIA.* London: M. E. Sharpe, 1995.

Cohen, Bernard C. *The Public's Impact on Foreign Policy.* Boston: Little, Brown, 1973.

Colby, Carl, dir. *The Man Nobody Knew: In Search of My Father, CIA Spymaster William Colby.* Netflix, 2011.

Conboy, Kenneth, and Dale Andrade. *Spies and Commandos: How America Lost the Secret War in North Vietnam:* Lawrence: University Press of Kansas, 2000.

Conboy, Kenneth, and James Morrison. *Feet to the Fire: CIA Covert Operations in Indonesia, 1957–1958.* Annapolis: Naval Institute Press, 1999.

Cottam, Richard W. *Iran and the United States: A Cold War Case Study.* Pittsburgh: University of Pittsburgh Press, 1988.

Crosswell, D. K. R. *Beetle: The Life of General Walter Bedell Smith.* Lexington: University Press of Kentucky, 2010.

Cullather, Nick. *Secret History: The CIA's Classified Account of Its Operations in Guatemala, 1952–1954.* Stanford: Stanford University Press, 1999.

Davies, David R. *The Postwar Decline of American Newspapers, 1945–1965.* Westport, CT: Praeger, 2006.

Davis, Deborah. *Katharine the Great: Katharine Graham and the Washington Post.* New York: Harcourt Brace Jovanovich, 1979.

Dean, Robert. *Imperial Brotherhood: Gender and the Making of Cold War Foreign Policy.* Amherst: University of Massachusetts Press, 2001.

Destler, I. M., Leslie H. Gelb, and Anthony Lake. "Breakdown: The Impact of Domestic Politics on American Foreign Policy." In *The Domestic Sources of American Foreign Policy: Insights and Evidence,* edited by Charles W. Kegley and Eugene R. Wittkopf, 20–26. New York: St. Martin's Press, 1988.

Diamond, Sigmund. *Compromised Campus: The Collaboration of Universities with the Intelligence Community, 1945–1955.* Oxford: Oxford University Press, 1992.

Dorman, A. "Playing the Government's Game: The Mass Media and American Foreign Policy." In *The Domestic Sources of American Foreign Policy: Insights and Evidence,* edited by Charles W. Kegley and Eugene R. Wittkopf, 79–84. New York: St. Martin's Press, 1988.

Dulles, Allen. *The Craft of Intelligence.* New York: Harper and Row, 1963.

Dunn, Delmer D. "Symbiosis: Congress and the Press." In *Congress and the News Media,* edited by Robert O. Blanchard, 241–46. New York: Hastings House, 1974.

Entman, Robert M. *Projections of Power: Framing News, Public Opinion, and U.S. Foreign Policy.* Chicago: University of Chicago Press, 2004.

Felt, Mark A. *Poisoning the Press: Richard Nixon, Jack Anderson, and the Rise of Washington's Scandal Culture.* New York: Farrar, Straus and Giroux, 2010.

Fisher, Zachary C. "American Propaganda, Popular Media, and the Fall of Jacobo Arbenz." Master's thesis, University of Nevada, Las Vegas, 2012.

Foran, John. "Discursive Subversions: *Time* Magazine, the CIA Overthrow of Mussadiq, and the Installation of the Shah," in *Cold War Constructions: The Political*

Culture of United States Imperialism, 1945–1966, edited by Christian G. Appy, 157–82. Amherst: University of Massachusetts Press, 2000.

Foyle, Douglas C. *Counting the Public In: Presidents, Public Opinion, and Foreign Policy.* New York: Columbia University Press, 1999.

———. "Public Opinion." In *Routledge Handbook of American Foreign Policy,* edited by Steven W. Hook and Christopher M. Jones, 264–85. New York: Routledge, 2012.

Free, James. *The First 100 Years! A Casual Chronicle of the Gridiron Club.* Washington: Gridiron Club, 1985.

Gardner, Paul F. *Shared Hopes, Separate Fears: Fifty Years of U.S.-Indonesia Relations.* Boulder, CO: Westview Press, 1997.

Gasiorowski, Mark J. "The 1953 Coup d'Etat in Iran." *International Journal of Middle East Studies* 19.3 (1987): 261–86.

Gleijeses, Piero. *Shattered Hope: The Guatemalan Revolution and the United States, 1944–1954.* Princeton: Princeton University Press, 1991.

———. "Ships in the Night: The CIA, the White House and the Bay of Pigs." *Journal of Latin American Studies* 27.1 (1995): 1–42.

Golding, Peter, and Graham Murdock. "Culture, Communications, and Political Economy." In *News: A Reader,* edited by Howard Tumber, 155–65. Oxford: Oxford University Press, 1999.

Griffith, Thomas. *Harry and Teddy: The Turbulent Friendship of Press Lord Henry R. Luce and His Favorite Reporter, Theodore H. White.* New York: Random House, 1995.

Grose, Peter. *Gentleman Spy: The Life of Allen Dulles.* Boston: Houghton Mifflin, 1994.

Hallin, Daniel C. *The "Uncensored War": The Media and Vietnam.* Berkeley: University of California Press, 1986.

Hamilton-Merritt, Jane. *Tragic Mountains: The Hmong, the Americans, and the Secret Wars for Laos, 1942–1992.* Bloomington: Indiana University Press, 1993.

Hart, Gary. "Liberty and Security." In *US National Security, Intelligence and Democracy: From the Church Committee to the War on Terror,* edited by Russell A. Miller, 13–21. New York: Routledge, 2008.

Herkin, Gregg. *The Georgetown Set: Friends and Rivals in Cold War Washington.* New York: Alfred A. Knopf, 2014.

Herman, Edward S. "Returning Guatemala to the Fold." In *Cold-War Propaganda in the 1950s,* edited by Gary D. Rawnsley, 205–24. New York: St. Martin's, 1999.

Herman, Edward S., and Noam Chomsky. *Manufacturing Consent: The Political Economy of the Mass Media.* New York: Pantheon Books, 1988.

Hero, Alfred O. *The Southerner and World Affairs.* Baton Rouge: Louisiana State University Press, 1965.

Higgins, Trumbull. *The Perfect Failure: Kennedy, Eisenhower, and the CIA at the Bay of Pigs.* New York: W. W. Norton, 1987.

Hilsman, Roger. *To Move a Nation: The Politics of Foreign Policy in the Administration of John F. Kennedy.* Garden City, NY: Doubleday, 1967.

Hixson, Walter L. *Parting the Curtain: Propaganda, Culture, and the Cold War, 1945–1961.* New York: St. Martin's, 1996.

Hogan, Michael J. *A Cross of Iron: Harry S. Truman and the Origins of the National Security State, 1945–1954.* Cambridge: Cambridge University Press, 1998.

Immerman, Richard H. *The CIA in Guatemala: The Foreign Policy of Intervention.* Austin: University of Texas Press, 1982.

———. *The Hidden Hand: A Brief History of the CIA* (Malden, MA: Wiley Blackwell, 2014).

Isaacson, Walter, and Evan Thomas. *The Wise Men: Six Friends and the World They Made: Acheson, Bohlen, Harriman, Kennan, Lovett, McCloy.* New York: Simon and Schuster, 1986.

Jeffreys-Jones, Rhodri. *The CIA and American Democracy,* 2nd ed. New Haven: Yale University Press, 1998.

Jensen, Danny, and Rhodri Jeffreys-Jones. "The Missouri Gang and the CIA." In *North American Spies: New Revisionist Essays,* edited by Rhodri Jeffreys-Jones and Andrew Lownie, 123–37. Lawrence: University Press of Kansas, 1991.

Jessup, John K., ed. *The Ideas of Henry Luce.* New York: Atheneum, 1969.

Johnson, Haynes. *The Bay of Pigs: The Leaders of Brigade 2506.* New York: W. W. Norton, 1964.

Johnson, Loch K. *America's Secret Power: The CIA in a Democratic Society.* Oxford: Oxford University Press, 1989.

Jones, Matthew. "Journalism, Intelligence and the *New York Times:* Cyrus L. Sulzberger, Harrison Salisbury and the CIA." *History* 100.340 (2015): 229–50.

Kackman, Michael. *Citizen Spy: Television, Espionage, and Cold War Culture.* Minneapolis: University of Minnesota Press, 2005.

Kahin, Audrey R., and George McT. Kahin. *Subversion as Foreign Policy: The Secret Eisenhower and Dulles Debacle in Indonesia.* 1995. Reprint. Seattle: University of Washington Press, 1997.

Karabell, Zachary. *Architects of Intervention: The United States, the Third World, and the Cold War, 1946–1962.* Baton Rouge: Louisiana State University Press, 1999.

Katz, Barry M. *Foreign Intelligence: Research and Analysis in the Office of Strategic Services, 1942–1945.* Cambridge: Harvard University Press, 1989.

Kegley, Charles W., and Eugene R. Wittkopf, eds. *The Domestic Sources of American Foreign Policy: Insights and Evidence.* New York: St. Martin's Press, 1988.

Kinzer, Stephen. *All the Shah's Men: An American Coup and the Roots of Middle East Terror,* 2nd ed. Hoboken, NJ: John Wiley and Sons, 2008.

———. *The Brothers: John Foster Dulles, Allen Dulles, and Their Secret World War.* New York: Times Books, 2013.

———. *Overthrow: America's Century of Regime Change from Hawaii to Iraq.* New York: Times Books, 2006.

Laqueur, Walter. *A World of Secrets: The Uses and Limits of Intelligence.* New York: Basic Books, 1985.

Leacock, Ruth. *Requiem for Revolution: The United States and Brazil, 1961–1969.* Kent, OH: Kent State University Press, 1990.

Levering, Ralph. *The Public and American Foreign Policy, 1918–1978.* New York: William Morrow, 1978.

Loory, Stuart H. "The CIA's Use of the Press: A 'Mighty Wurlitzer.'" *Columbia Journalism Review* 13.3 (1974): 9–18.

Marchetti, Victor, and Marks, John D. *The CIA and the Cult of Intelligence.* New York: Alfred A. Knopf, 1974.

Markel, Lester. *Public Opinion and Foreign Policy.* New York: Harper and Brothers, 1949.

McMahon, Robert J. *The Limits of Empire: The United States and Southeast Asia since World War II.* New York: Columbia University Press, 1999.

———. "'The Point of No Return': The Eisenhower Administration and Indonesia, 1953–1960." In *The Eisenhower Administration, the Third World, and the Globalization of the Cold War,* edited by Kathryn C. Statler and Andrew L. Johns, 75–100. Lanham, MD: Rowman and Littlefield, 2006.

Medhurst, Martin J., ed. *Eisenhower's War of Words: Rhetoric and Leadership.* East Lansing: Michigan State University, 1994.

Merry, Robert W. *Taking on the World: Joseph and Stewart Alsop—Guardians of the American Century.* New York: Viking, 1996.

Meyer, Cord. *Peace or Anarchy.* Boston: Little, Brown, 1947.

Meyer, Karl, and Tad Szulc. *The Cuban Invasion: The Chronicle of a Disaster.* New York: Praeger, 1962.

Miller, Nathan. *Spying for America.* New York: Paragon House, 1989.

Miraldi, Robert. *Seymour Hersh: Scoop Artist.* Lincoln: University of Nebraska Press, 2013.

Mistry, Kaeten. "Approaches to Understanding the Inaugural CIA Covert Operation in Italy: Exploding Useful Myths." *Intelligence and National Security* 26.2–3 (2011): 246–68.

Montague, Ludwell Lee. *General Walter Bedell Smith as Director of Central Intelligence, October 1950–February 1953.* University Park: Pennsylvania State University Press, 1992.

Moran, Christopher. "Turning against the CIA: Whistleblowers during the 'Time of Troubles.'" *History* 100.340 (2015): 251–74.

Mosley, Leonard. *Dulles: A Biography of Eleanor, Allen, and John Foster Dulles and Their Family Network.* New York: Dial Press, 1978.

Nation, R. Craig. *Black Earth, Red Star: A History of Soviet Security Policy, 1917–1991.* Ithaca, NY: Cornell University Press, 1992.

Neville, John F. *The Press, the Rosenbergs, and the Cold War.* Westport, CT: Praeger, 1995.

Olmsted, Kathryn S. *Challenging the Secret Government: The Post-Watergate Investigations of the CIA and FBI.* Chapel Hill: University of North Carolina Press, 1996.

Osgood, Kenneth. *Total Cold War: Eisenhower's Secret Propaganda Battle at Home and Abroad.* Lawrence: University Press of Kansas, 2006.

O'Toole, George J. A. *Honorable Treachery: A History of U.S. Intelligence, Espionage, and Covert Action from the American Revolution to the CIA*. New York: Atlantic Monthly Press, 1991.

Paget, Karen. *Patriotic Betrayal: The Inside Story of the CIA's Secret Campaign to Enroll American Students in the Crusade against Communism*. New Haven: Yale University Press, 2015.

Parenti, Michael. *Inventing Reality: The Politics of the Mass Media*. New York: St. Martin's Press, 1986.

Park, Phyllis R. *Brazil and the Quiet Intervention, 1964*. Austin: University of Texas Press, 1979.

Parmar, Inderjeet. *Think Tanks and Power in Foreign Policy: A Comparative Study of the Role and Influence of the Council on Foreign Relations and the Royal Institute of International Affairs, 1939–1945*. New York: Palgrave Macmillan, 2004.

Peterson, Theodore. *Magazines in the Twentieth Century*, 2nd ed. 1964. Reprint. Urbana: University of Illinois Press, 1975.

Pettee, George S. *The Future of American Secret Intelligence*. Washington, DC: Infantry Journal Press, 1946.

Powers, Thomas. *The Man Who Kept the Secrets: Richard Helms and the CIA*. New York: Alfred A. Knopf, 1979.

Prados, John. *President's Secret Wars: CIA and Pentagon Covert Operations from World War II through Iranscam*. New York: William Morrow, 1986.

———. *Vietnam: The History of an Unwinnable War, 1945–1975*. Lawrence: University Press of Kansas, 2009.

Rabe, Stephen G. *Eisenhower and Latin America: The Foreign Policy of Anticommunism*. Chapel Hill: University of North Carolina Press, 1988.

Ranleigh, John. *The Agency: The Rise and Decline of the CIA*. New York: Simon and Schuster, 1986.

Ransom, Henry Howe. *Can American Democracy Survive the Cold War?* Garden City, NY: Anchor Books, 1964.

———. *Central Intelligence and National Security*. Cambridge: Harvard University Press, 1958.

———. *The Intelligence Establishment*. Cambridge: Harvard University Press, 1970.

Roadnight, Andrew. *United States Policy towards Indonesia in the Truman and Eisenhower Years*. New York: Palgrave Macmillan, 2002.

Roberts, Chalmers. *The Washington Post: The First 100 Years*. Boston: Houghton Mifflin, 1977.

Roosevelt, Kermit. *Countercoup: The Struggle for the Control of Iran*. New York: McGraw-Hill, 1979.

Ruehsen, Moyara de Moraes. "Operation 'Ajax' Revisited: Iran, 1953." *Middle Eastern Studies* 29.3 (1993): 467–86.

Salisbury, Harrison. *Without Fear or Favor: The New York Times and Its Times*. New York: Times Books, 1980.

Saunders, Frances Stonor. *The Cultural Cold War: The CIA and the World of Arts and Letters.* New York: New Press, 1999. Published in the United Kingdom as *Who Paid the Piper? The CIA and the Cultural Cold War.*

Schiller, Dan. *Objectivity and the News: The Public and the Rise of Commercial Journalism.* Philadelphia: University of Pennsylvania Press, 1981.

Schlesinger, Stephen, and Stephen Kinzer. *Bitter Fruit: The Story of the American Coup in Guatemala.* Rev. ed. Cambridge: David Rockefeller Center for Latin American Studies, Harvard University, 2005.

Schudson, Michael. *Discovering the News: A Social History of American Newspapers.* New York: Basic Books, 1978.

Simpson, Christopher. *Science of Coercion: Communication Research and Psychological Warfare, 1945–1960.* Oxford: Oxford University Press, 1994.

Smith, Bradley F. "An Idiosyncratic View of Where We Stand on the History of American Intelligence in the Early Post-1945 Era." *Intelligence and National Security* 3.4 (1988): 111–23.

———. *The Shadow Warriors: O.S.S. and the Origins of the C.I.A.* New York: Basic Books, 1983.

Smith, R. Harris. *OSS: The Secret History of America's First Central Intelligence Agency.* Berkeley: University of California Press, 1972.

Smith, Richard Norton. *The Colonel: The Life and Legend of Robert R. McCormick, 1880–1955.* Boston: Houghton Mifflin, 1997.

Snider, L. Britt. *The Agency and the Hill: CIA's Relationship with Congress, 1946–2004.* Washington, DC: Center for the Study of Intelligence (Central Intelligence Agency), 2008.

Sobel, Richard. *The Impact of Public Opinion on U.S. Foreign Policy since Vietnam: Constraining the Colossus.* Oxford: Oxford University Press, 2001.

Srodes, James. *Allen Dulles: Master of Spies.* Washington, DC: Regnery, 1999.

Stebenne, David. "The Military and the Media: The Gulf Conflict in Historical Perspective." In *The Media at War: The Press and the Persian Gulf Conflict,* by Craig LaMay, Martha FitzSimon, Jeanne Sahadi, et al., 8–24. New York: Gannett Foundation Media Center, 1991.

———. *Modern Republican: Arthur Larson and the Eisenhower Years.* Bloomington: Indiana University Press, 2006.

Steel, Ronald. *Walter Lippmann and the American Century.* Boston: Little, Brown, 1980.

Stein, Jeff. *A Murder in Wartime: The Untold Spy Story That Changed the Course of the Vietnam War.* New York: St. Martin's Press, 1992.

Streeter, Stephen M. *Managing the Counterrevolution: The United States and Guatemala, 1954–1961.* Athens: Ohio University Center for International Studies, 2000.

Sweeney, Michael S. *Secrets of Victory: The Office of the American Press and Radio in World War II.* Chapel Hill: University of North Carolina Press, 2001.

Valero, Larry. "'We Need Our New OSS, Our New General Donovan, Now . . .': The Public Discourse over American Intelligence, 1944–53." *Intelligence and National Security* 18.1 (2003): 91–118.

Van Belle, Douglas A., Jean-Sébastien Rioux, and David M. Potter. *Media, Bureaucracies and Foreign Aid: A Comparative Analysis of the United States, the United Kingdom, Canada, France and Japan.* New York: Palgrave Macmillan, 2004.

Vries, Tity de. "The 1967 Central Intelligence Agency Scandal: Catalyst in a Transforming Relationship between State and People." *Journal of American History* 98.4 (2012): 1075–92.

Warner, Roger. *Backfire: The CIA's Secret War in Laos and Its Link to the War in Vietnam.* New York: Simon and Schuster, 1995.

Weiner, Timothy. *Legacy of Ashes: The History of the CIA.* New York: Doubleday, 2007.

Weis, W. Michael. *Cold Warriors and Coups d'Etat: Brazilian-American Relations, 1945–1964.* Albuquerque: University of New Mexico, 1993.

Welch, Richard E. *Response to Revolution: The United States and the Cuban Revolution, 1959–1961.* Chapel Hill: University of North Carolina Press, 1985.

White, Mark J., ed. *The Kennedys and Cuba: The Declassified Documentary History.* Chicago: Ivan Dee, 1999.

Wicker, Tom. *On Press.* New York: Viking Press, 1978.

Wilford, Hugh. *America's Great Game: The CIA's Secret Arabists and the Shaping of the Modern Middle East.* New York: Basic Books, 2013.

———. *The CIA, the British Left, and the Cold War: Calling the Tune?* London: Frank Cass, 2003.

———. *The Mighty Wurlitzer: How the CIA Played America.* Cambridge: Harvard University Press, 2008.

Willmetts, Simon. "The Burgeoning Fissures of Dissent: Allen Dulles and the Selling of the CIA in the Aftermath of the Bay of Pigs." *History* 100.340 (2015): 167–88.

Winks, Robin W. *Cloak & Gown: Scholars in the Secret War, 1939–1961.* New York: William Morrow, 1987.

Wise, David, and Thomas Ross. *The Invisible Government.* New York: Random House, 1964.

Yergin, Daniel. *The Prize: The Epic Quest for Oil, Money, and Power.* New York: Free Press, 1991.

Index